Learning Library

Teacher's Strategies

Learning Books
Springhouse Corporation
Springhouse, Pennsylvania

Learning Library

vii, 182p. : ill.

SPRINGHOUSE CORPORATION BOOK DIVISION

Chairman
Eugene W. Jackson

Vice-Chairman
Daniel L. Cheney

President
Warren R. Erhardt

Vice-President, Book Operations
Thomas A. Temple

Vice-President, Production and Purchasing
Bacil Guiley

Program Director, Reference Books
Stanley E. Loeb

TEACHER'S STRATEGIES

Editorial Director
Helen Klusek Hamilton

Art Director
John Hubbard

STAFF FOR THIS VOLUME

Editorial Services Manager: David R. Moreau

Copy Editors: Diane M. Labus, Doris Weinstock, Debra Young

Production Coordinator: Susan Hopkins Rodzewich

Designers: James J. Flanagan, Julie Carleton Barlow

Art Production Manager: Robert Perry III

Typography Manager: David C. Kosten

Typographers: Elizabeth A. DiCicco, Diane Paluba, Nancy Wirs

Senior Production Manager: Deborah C. Meiris

Assistant Production Managers: Pat Dorshaw, T.A. Landis

Indexer: Barbara Hodgson

Researcher: Nancy Lange

Editorial Assistants: Maree E. DeRosa, Denine Lichtfuss

Cover and Chapter Dividers
Illustrated by Ross Culbert Holland & Lavery, NYC

Library of Congress Cataloging-in-Publication Data
Teacher's strategies.
   (Learning Library)
   Includes index.
   1. Teaching.   2. Classroom management.
I. Springhouse Corporation.   II. Series.
LB1025.2.B484 1987   372.11'02   87-10054
ISBN 0-87434-121-3

Contents

Teacher's Strategies

CONTRIBUTORS AND CONSULTANTS

Linda Armstrong
Los Angeles, California

Nancy Aronson, PhD
Bala Cynwyd, Pennsylvania

Sue Baird Blake
Texarkana, Texas

Dave E. Borbe
Central Elementary School
Allentown, Pennsylvania

Dr. Nancy Naumann Boyles
Southern Connecticut State University

Marilyn Burns
Sausalito, California

Barry R. Culhane
National Technical Institute for the
Deaf
Rochester, New York

Richard L. Curwin
National Technical Institute for the
Deaf
Rochester, New York

Monte Davis
Brooklyn, New York

Edward L. Deci, PhD
University of Rochester
Rochester, New York

J.T. Dillon
University of California
Riverside, California

Joan Donnelly
Mamaroneck Public Schools
Mamaroneck, New York

Dr. Kenneth Dunn
Queens College
New York, New York

Dr. Rita Dunn
St. John's University
Jamaica, New York

Mari E. Endreweit
Montclair Cooperative School
Montclair, New Jersey

Sandra Sutherland Fox, PhD
Judge Baker Guidance Center
Boston, Massachusetts

Barbara Schneider Fuhrmann
Virginia Commonwealth University
Richmond, Virginia

Kathleen E. Gann
Torrance, California

Jean Gatch
Rapid City, South Dakota

Bruce F. Godsave
State University College
Genesee, New York

Farnum Gray
Atlanta, Georgia

Janice Hammond-Matthews
Quarton Elementary School
Birmingham, Michigan

Rebecca Harrison
Portland State University
Portland, Oregon

Sandy Heffelfinger
Helena, Montana

Barbara Hendrickson
Berkeley, California

Eric W. Johnson
Philadelphia, Pennsylvania

Kenneth Komoski
Educational Products Information
Exchange Institute
Watermill, New York

Robert B. McCall, PhD
University of Pittsburgh

Maureen Mackey
Beaverton, Oregon

Robert J. Martin
Lafayette, Indiana

Janice J. Mercurio
Central High School
Providence, Rhode Island

Donald Mowrer, PhD
Arizona State University
Tempe, Arizona

Susan Ohanian
Learning Staff
Springhouse, Pennsylvania

Anita Rui Olds, PhD
Tufts University
Cambridge, Massachusetts

Myrna R. Olson
University of North Dakota
Grand Forks, North Dakota

Robert O'Rourke
Fort Collins, Colorado

Craig Pearson (deceased)
Durham, Connecticut

Bill Prindle
Arlington, Virginia

Bonnie Prudden
Institute for Physical Fitness
Stockbridge, Massachusetts

Dr. Steven M. Ross
Memphis State University
Memphis, Tennessee

Masha K. Rudman
University of Massachusetts
Amherst, Massachusetts

Beverly Schreifels
Saint Francis School
Saint Francis, Minnesota

Alice V. Shelby
Yorktown Heights, New York

Deborah Simon Silliman
Dundee, New York

Dr. Sidney Simon
University of Massachusetts
Amherst, Massachusetts

Annette Smith
Syracuse, New York

Elizabeth Strauss
Chicago, Illinois

Jerry Vogel
Palo Alto, California

Dr. M. Mark Wasicsko
Texas Wesleyan College
Fort Worth, Texas

Audrey Weitkamp
Seattle, Washington

Philip Zimbardo
Stanford University
Stanford, California

EDITORIAL ADVISORY BOARD

Foreword

Effective teacher's strategies are classroom behaviors that promote enthusiastic student involvement in classroom activities, minimize disruptive student behavior, and make efficient use of instructional time. In other words, such strategies produce the kind of classroom environment that promotes positive learning for students and professional satisfaction for teachers. How to acquire such strategies? The job of an educator has become increasingly complex. Teachers want changes: they want to see students who are better motivated; they want to spend less time on discipline; and they want more latitude to organize their classrooms in ways that will promote student achievement and feelings of self-worth. To realize these changes, teachers need up-to-date, reality-tested methods they can use to influence their classroom situations. An excellent resource is the teacher-to-teacher exchange of ideas and experiences.

Teacher's Strategies, the second volume in the new LEARNING LIBRARY for teachers, offers just such sharing of classroom expertise. In every chapter, the reader will find teacher-approved methods to evaluate and improve classroom behavior in both ordinary and challenging situations.

The opening chapter, "Review Your Classroom Style," offers suggestions for self-evaluation of your teaching patterns. The next chapter, "Review Classroom Strategies," provides hands-on methods that can make teaching easier and help students learn. In Chapter 3, "Boost Self-Esteem and Motivation," teachers share methods they have found useful to help students strengthen a positive sense of self-worth. Chapter 4, "Tips for Testing and Evaluating," offers some practical ways to deal with classroom and standardized testing. Chapter 5, "Help Students with Special Problems," offers guidelines for coping with the various difficulties that complicate the lives of today's students and so often interfere with learning. In Chapter 6, "Cope with Change," teachers offer suggestions for dealing effectively with new or changing teaching assignments. The final chapter, "Prevent and Overcome Stress," offers practical suggestions for overcoming the stress associated with teaching, for example, by following an easy exercise plan offered by an expert, Bonnie Prudden.

This volume can confirm many of the practices you are currently using and can serve as a reminder of ideas you used successfully in the past. In addition, there is a wealth of new ideas for your professional consideration. The information is meant to be shared. The strategies can provide the basis for rich discussions with colleagues.

Nancy Aronson, PhD
Educational Consultant and
Codeveloper and Codirector of the School Climate
Renewal Project in Pennsylvania

Review Your Classroom Style

1
REVIEW YOUR CLASSROOM STYLE

Whether you're a novice or veteran teacher, your concern for effectiveness in the classroom is real and continuous. How to evaluate your own teaching style and find out if you're the teacher you want to be? Read on for some aspects of teaching style and classroom behaviors that other teachers have identified as important to your effectiveness.

Is your teaching what you think it is?

How can a teacher become more effective? This is a question that deserves more than the reflexive marshmallow retort of "Open up your classroom" or "Redefine your role; become a facilitator of learning." It deserves, in fact, careful consideration of two different sets of information. First, the teacher needs a clear picture of his present classroom performance. This means accurate information about attitudes, behavior, and interaction with students. Second, he needs to know how to process and use it to reach his goals. These two areas of concern are the basis for our work in improving teacher effectiveness. We have developed a method we think can give teachers the information they need about themselves and tell them how to use that information to become the teachers they want to be.

The most helpful types of information you can use in your quest for self-knowledge are those that are nonevaluative and are linked to your purposes as a teacher. External judgments, such as those from your administrators or supervisors, can help in your development, but you will change your behavior as a teacher only if you want to. If the purposes of an external agent do not concur with your own, you will probably not change.

Our plan is to facilitate the accomplishment of three basic tasks: (1) to recognize the factors that comprise your intentions and concept of good teaching; (2) to collect, with the help of a colleague or on your own, specific data that clarifies your actual teaching behaviors; and (3) to try to make your actions congruent with your ideals.

In developing activities for each of the three steps, you can work on your own, with a partner, or with a group. Each of the following activities is designed to help you clarify your ideals, appraise your present position, and help you work toward the goal you have set for yourself.

Review your values

Values exert a powerful influence on behavior. Yet rarely do many of us stop to think about what qualities we value or bother to look at how, or even whether, our behavior reflects our highest value priorities. We teachers are not alone in failing to relate our values to our behavior, but to ignore this relationship is to miss one of the most powerful data sources for effective classroom decision making.

Consider a teacher who says he values creativity more than he values quiet. This same teacher may, in actual practice, ask his students to quiet down during a creative activity. What he says is not congruent with what he does. Of course, he may be afraid of the reaction of the principal or the teacher next door to the noise. In that case, another value-laden factor has entered the situation, for the teacher apparently values the approval of the principal or colleague more highly than he values creativity. While it is difficult to act at all times in ways that are congruent with our beliefs, we can and should work toward a healthy integration of the two. The most effective teacher is the one whose behavior is closest to the values he espouses. Check your own values and their congruence with your classroom behavior with the activity that follows. It's a first step toward identifying the priorities you attach to values in the classroom and seeing how your teaching reflects these priorities. Its objectives are: To rank a list of classroom qualities that could be influenced by your teaching; to examine the priorities in terms of observable classroom behavior; and to note congruence between the qualities you most value and your classroom behavior.

Consider how you would rank the 22 qualities below in your ideal classroom. Place a *1* next to the classroom quality you think deserves the highest value, a *2* next to the second most important, and so on through *22*, which will represent the quality that you value least.

____ Alienation	____ Freedom
____ Chaos	____ Laughter
____ Concentration	____ Love
____ Creativity	____ Orderliness
____ Disorder	____ Passivity
____ Dogmatism	____ Privacy
____ Dominance	____ Purposefulness
____ Equality	____ Quiet
____ Fairness	____ Respect
____ Favoritism	____ Rigidity
____ Fear	____ Self-Direction

Then, on the worksheet on page 4, list the qualities you valued most highly—those ranked in the top three positions. For each, list three classroom indicators that would demonstrate that value in a classroom. Then list the qualities you put in the bottom three value positions, and list for each one three classroom indicators that would reflect their presence in a classroom. For example, if *freedom* is on your list, you might select the following as classroom indicators:

• Students have an open reading list and read books on their own.
• Students interact with one another without stimulus from teacher.
• Teacher does not give tests.

Or if *dogmatism* is on either of your lists, you might list the following as classroom indicators:

• Teacher gives only one choice of course readings.
• Teacher asks for no student input into course curriculum.
• Students do not initiate any classroom activities.

Application to your classroom

What specifically can you do to ensure that the nine classroom indicators that represent your three highest-valued qualities are incorporated into your classroom daily? What can you do to ensure that you've eliminated (or never introduced) the nine classroom indicators of your three least-valued qualities into your classroom? What qualities, other than those listed, are important to you? You might wish to add some of your own items to the list, rank them again, and compare the results with your first ranking. What qualities on the new list are too important for compromise? Which would you try to preserve at the cost of your job?

Follow-up activity

Give an observer your worksheet containing nine positive and nine negative indicators. Have him watch you teach a variety of lessons and record each time he identifies an indicator. Try to act as naturally as possible with the observer present, or the activity will be less helpful. After you have completed the lessons, compare the data collected by your observer with the data on your worksheet. If your actions were not congruent with your stated values, reevaluate your priorities or change your behavior.

Repeat this follow-up activity at various times throughout the year for continual feedback.

VALUES WORKSHEET

QUALITIES VALUED MOST HIGHLY

1 ST QUALITY:

CLASSROOM INDICATORS:
-
-
-

2 ND QUALITY:

CLASSROOM INDICATORS:
-
-
-

3 RD QUALITY:

CLASSROOM INDICATORS:
-
-
-

QUALITIES LEAST VALUED

1 ST QUALITY:

CLASSROOM INDICATORS:
-
-
-

2 ND QUALITY:

CLASSROOM INDICATORS:
-
-
-

3 RD QUALITY:

CLASSROOM INDICATORS:
-
-
-

Practice acceptance

Recognizing and accepting the feelings behind a person's words and behavior is difficult, but it is essential to an effective relationship. Except for parents, teachers need this skill more than anyone else. Often, we evaluate and judge, and the very process of evaluating keeps us from understanding and accepting. When a child is sullen after a lost ball game, we are just as apt to admonish him as to recognize his very real feelings. Instead of scolding, "Stop slouching, Jim; look on the bright side," how much more understanding it would be to say, "Jim, you seem very upset. I guess that game meant a lot to you." In the first instance, Jim will probably respond with hostility—if he responds at all. In the second, he will probably recognize and respond to the understanding that you've shown. Although we cannot change the situation, we have made it clear we understand his feelings. Most of our responses to others' behavior can be classified as:

Judgmental/positive: We judge the behavior to be good and respond in an attempt to reinforce it. We may or may not recognize and understand the feelings that motivated the behavior.

Judgmental/negative: We judge the behavior to be undesirable and respond in an attempt to change it. We probably do not recognize the feelings that motivated the behavior.

Acceptant: We recognize the feelings underlying the behavior and convey that we understand and accept them, but we neither encourage nor discourage them.

Cultural influences have taught us to respond to others in judgmental ways, but psychological insight tells us that acceptant responses are almost always preferable; acceptant responses alone recognize that each individual must ultimately be responsible for himself. When we evaluate another's behavior, *even with a positive evaluation,* we are assuming responsibility for him and exercising control over him. When we say, "That's excellent!" we're implicitly reserving the right to say, "That's terrible!" In both instances we are attempting to control the person to whom we are responding, for we are judging him by some set of standards external to him.

Of course, adults must at times exercise some control over children, but these times are far less frequent than most of our behavior indicates. Acceptant, nonjudgmental responses, in which the other person is granted the responsibility for behavior that is rightfully his, facilitate the growth of responsible behavior.

Note the differences between acceptant and judgmental responses in the following examples:

• A third grader comes in crying, "Johnny won't give me back my mitten."

Judgmental/positive: "You poor thing. I'll take care of it." (The child is likely to repeat the behavior, since he was rewarded for it. The teacher solves the problem.)

Judgmental/negative: "Oh, don't be a crybaby. You'll get it back." (The child's feelings are ignored, and the relationship between teacher and him is not enhanced. The problem remains.)

Acceptant: "You feel angry because you don't have your mitten. How might you get it?" (The child's feelings are recognized, and he is encouraged to seek his own solution to the problem.)

• A junior-high student slams into your room, throws down his books, and tells you how unfair Mr. _____ is for reprimanding him.

Judgmental/positive: "That's OK. When you have problems with him, just come in here."

Judgmental/negative: "Well, if you acted as ugly with him as you are right now, I don't blame him. Sit down."

Acceptant: "You're very upset because Mr. _____ scolded you. Let's talk about it."

• A student hands you a bedraggled-looking assignment, sheepishly explaining that she dropped it in a puddle on the way to school.

Judgmental/positive: "That's OK. I'm sure it wasn't your fault."

Judgmental/negative: "That looks awful. You should know better than to try to turn it in that way."

Acceptant: "I can see that you're embarrassed about it. What would you like to do now?"

Consider your own responses

To distinguish between judgmental and acceptant responses, to identify judgmental and acceptant responses in your verbal classroom behavior, and then to use acceptant responses, try the following practice activity. First, *practice making acceptant responses* to the following situations. If you are working with a partner or a group, use each other to get feedback as to whether your responses are acceptant or judgmental. Consider what you would say when...

• A child of early elementary age refuses to work with another child, saying, "He keeps picking on me."

• A high-school student tells you that he's thinking of dropping out of school.

• A colleague tearfully tells you that she expects to be fired.

• During a student/teacher conference, a young girl stares at the floor when you ask her why she hasn't been participating.

Second, you and a group of your peers can set up role-playing situations for each other to practice making nonjudgmental, acceptant responses. Think of individual situations like those above and role-play the individuals involved.

Third, record responses in your own classroom. Use a tape recorder or have an observer record every response you make to students. On a separate sheet, record each response from the tape or the observer's notes. Then classify each response as judgmental/positive, judgmental/negative, or acceptant.

Evaluate your responses

Into which category did most of your responses fall? Combining the two judgmental categories, did you make more judgmental or more acceptant responses? Is it easier for you to make one kind of response than another? What does that mean to you? Find one response that you are especially pleased to have made. What was the effect (or probable effect) of that response on the student? (You might ask the student for his reaction to it.) Find one response that could have been better. What was the effect (or probable effect) of that response on the student? (Again, you might ask the student for feedback.) How could you have responded differently? Are you satisfied with the data before you? Why or why not?

Follow-up activity

Don't expect overnight change. Remember that significant change takes time. Daily and weekly analyses, with comparisons drawn and trends noted, are essential if you're serious about changing your behavior. Repeat this activity as you feel it necessary.

Monitoring your verbal acceptance of behavior may also be helpful in problem situations with particular students. If you have such a student, an observer might record every response you make to him over a significant period of time (4 hours or more). You can then classify those responses and draw meaningful implications.

Evaluate your movement in the classroom

The way you move about your classroom has a profound effect on the messages you convey to students, on how you relate to them, and ultimately on their learning. Your movement shows something about how you feel *about* students, while at the same time determining your relationships *with* students. For example, a teacher who always sits or stands behind a desk puts a physical barrier between himself and his students. Whether or not he remains behind the desk because he feels uncomfortable relating closely to students, his students will probably see him as emotionally and physically distant. Understandably, the students reciprocate in kind, and the emotional distance widens. Thus the very act of remaining behind a desk—which may not have been a conscious choice—reinforces the feeling that motivated the action. Even if the teacher is aware of an emotional distance between himself and his students, he is unlikely to find a way to bridge that gap until he understands how his physical actions contribute to it.

Let's look at another example, this time of a generally active teacher who unknowingly but consistently avoids one corner of his classroom because a student in that area makes him uncomfortable. By avoiding the corner, the teacher conveniently avoids the student, but the distance between them widens steadily. Until the teacher becomes aware of his pattern of movement, he is unlikely to confront his own discomfort and try to correct the avoidant behavior.

To help you monitor your movement in a classroom, to identify its effects on your students, and to help you make your movement functional to your goals, try this exercise.

Draw a walking map

For a specified period of time (one period, one hour, or whatever time is convenient), have a colleague observer map, on paper, your movement through the classroom. The observer can use the following directions: Draw a map of the classroom, including the furniture arrangement. Note with the number 1 the teacher's location in the room at the beginning of the lesson. Then consecutively number each place where the teacher stops during the agreed-upon time period. Draw concentric circles around places where the teacher remains for a significant time: one circle for each three minutes. A map of a traditional classroom, with a teacher who spends most of his time in front, is illustrated on page 8.

Review the map

In which areas of your classroom did you spend most of your time? Did you neglect any area(s)? Did the students' activities determine your movements in any way? How? What effect did the seating arrangement have on your movement? What effect might your movement have had on students? Do you want to make any changes, based on the information you now have? Why or why not?

Application and follow-up

Because a teacher's classroom movements can influence learning, becoming aware of your

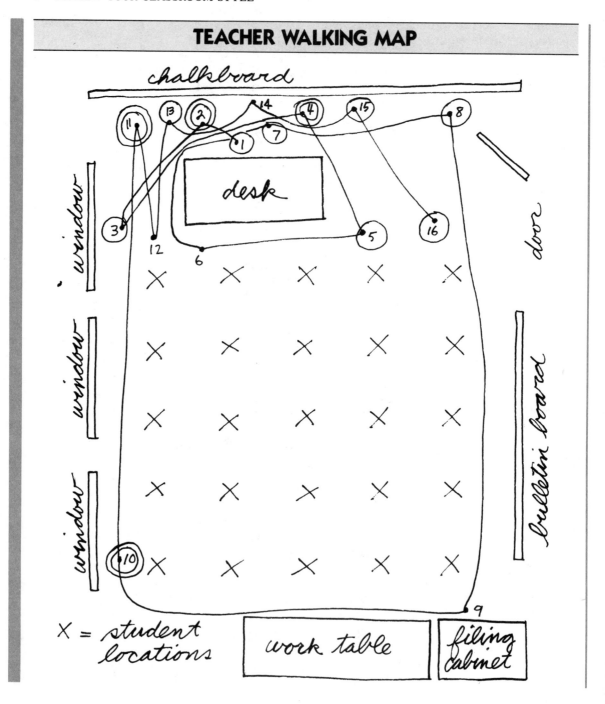

movements, analyzing their possible effects, and planning for movements that will support your teaching goals should become part of your overall teaching plan. Consider that your lessons may determine some or all of your movements in the classroom. If you consistently include references to a map in your plans, or if you consistently use the chalkboard, you are limiting your movements. So, if you wish to spend less time at the map or at the board, distribute dittoed maps or other materials to students, which frees you to move in different ways. Your lesson plans should allow you as many options for movement as possible. Your objective should be to free, rather than to restrict, your movement in the classroom.

Use the information you gained from your walking map to devise a movement plan for a lesson you will use in the next few days. Be as specific in your plan as the lesson will permit. The following questions will help you in your planning.

1. Does the lesson itself restrict your movements? For example, do you have to remain in one place to use audio-visual aids? Specify those elements of your lesson that require you to move in specific ways.

2. What effect might the movements you cited above have on learning?

3. How else can you plan the lesson to allow a greater choice of movement in the classroom?

After giving the lesson for which you planned free movement, evaluate for yourself how your movements might have influenced learning.

Analyze your lessons

Your own analysis of your teaching self is by far the most meaningful, and it's most useful when it can easily be transferred into specific directions. Lesson-analysis continuums like the worksheet on page 10 are useful tools in generating specific ways to improve your teaching. Used regularly, these continuums can generate a continuous input of relevant data about your teaching. You may wish to use an observer to help you check out your perceptions of your teaching, but this is not necessary; lesson-analysis continuums lend themselves nicely to self-evaluation.

To generate specific steps for improving your teaching, use the model shown on page 10 as a guide to preparing your own lesson-analysis worksheet. As soon after teaching a lesson as possible, complete the worksheet as follows:

1. On part 1 of the worksheet, find the spot on the continuum that best describes your feelings of how well the lesson went. A mark of *0* would indicate that the lesson went as badly as possible; you did not accomplish your goals and you are very uncomfortable with the way you handled situations as they came up. A mark of *8* would indicate that the lesson went as perfectly as you thought possible; you accomplished what you set out to and you are completely satisfied with your performance. (You are not allowed to rate the lesson exactly in the middle; therefore, there is no *4* on the continuum.)

2. List all the factors that contributed to your rating the lesson the way you did. Why was it a *5* instead of a *3*, a *2*, or a *1?* Make this list as complete as possible. When you feel you have run out of ideas, try to add two more factors.

3. List all the factors that you think might have made the lesson better. To ensure that the sentences are in a form that can easily be transferred to action, start each item on this list with "I will." Check this list for com-

LESSON ANALYSIS   Date _____

Class: Social Studies - Celebration of Massachusetts being admitted to the Union on this date in 1788.

1.

Worst possible lesson |___|___|___|___| ✓ |___|___| Perfect lesson
0   1   2   3   5   6   7   8

2.

What factors contributed to your rating this lesson as you did?

1. I asked a lot of questions that elicited class discussion. 1
2. I was prepared. 4
3. I called on every member in the class at least once. 2
4. I moved about the room as I had planned, making physical contact with those students I often avoid. 3

3.

What will you do to make it a perfect lesson?

1. I will be more humorous — lesson too dry. 4
2. I will let each student speak longer when one is interested in a topic. 1
3. I will try to find more personal meanings in the material for the students. 3
4. I will listen to the students' responses better without rehearsing my next comment. 2

4.

Self-contracts:

1. I will continue to ask many opinion-generating questions.
2. I will continue to call on every member of the class.
3. I will be sure to let every student speak until he is finished.
4. I will listen to student comments without rehearsing.

pleteness by asking yourself: "Would this lesson now be as perfect as possible?" Keep adding to your list until you can answer that question affirmatively.

4. Rank the items on both your lists according to their potential importance in accomplishing your goals, *1* being the most important, *2* the next most important, and so forth.

5. On part 4 of the worksheet, write four self-contracts, two from your responses to the part 2 question, and two from your responses to part 3. The next time you teach a similar lesson, refer to your self-contracts.

If you wish to use an observer, have him fill out a worksheet simultaneously but independently. Then compare your perceptions and discuss any discrepancies.

Check for change

Repeat this activity at least once a week for 6 to 8 weeks. See what patterns emerge. Check to see if you have items moving from part 3 of the worksheet to part 2 of the next worksheet. This is an indication of progress. If you are having trouble improving, perhaps your items are not specific enough. A common problem is that the items are too vague to note specific improvement.

Richard L. Curwin is chairman of teacher improvement programs at the National Technical Institute for the Deaf in Rochester, N.Y. **Barbara Schneider Fuhrmann** is assistant professor of counselor education at Virginia Commonwealth University in Richmond. The activities from this article were adapted from their book *Discovering Your Teaching Self: Humanistic Approaches to Effective Teaching* with permission of the publisher, Prentice-Hall, Inc., Englewood Cliffs, N.J.

Make the most of classroom discussions

Let's face it: most of the learning that occurs in our classrooms occurs not because of direct oral instruction, but because of conditions we help to create that cause students to learn for themselves and from one another. Now and then, the right utterance at the right moment may cause a sudden surge of understanding or clarify a point, but not often. When a student or a group really wants to know an answer and needs it now, and when there is an answer and the teacher has it, often it is best to say, "OK, I'll explain." But if the main value to the students will come from thinking out the answer or figuring out for themselves what to do, then it is best for the teacher not to instruct or give an answer. Mainly, teaching is posing good questions and providing the means to find answers. And most of the questions should be the sort that can't be answered yes or no.

Of course, teachers shouldn't merely preside over exchanges of ignorance. That's an even greater waste of time than giving too many answers. When misstatements of fact are made, they should be corrected, and when no one knows the facts, they should be found out, preferably by a student. Sometimes a few minutes of organized information-giving are called for, when interest is high and facts are needed in order to continue the discussion.

For example, if someone writes on the board, "Having eaten our lunch, the car wouldn't start," it's usually better to give the class time to examine the sentence, discover the errors, and correct them, rather than for the teacher simply to fix them or call on the first person who shouts out. If in the process some further understanding can be developed about rules (generalizations that are true), so much the better. But if somebody says, "You don't need an apostrophe to understand wouldn't," that's not an error for correction; it's an opinion worth discussing, requiring the class to weigh the values of "correctness" as a social advantage versus the apostrophe as a bother and problem. The class may then discover, on a deeper level, that understanding is not something to be crammed into us, but to be drawn out of us.

The essentials of good discussion

First, be clear about two things that discussion is not. It's not reciting memorized facts (although there is a place for that), and it's not the class trying to guess an answer that is hidden in the teacher's mind. Good discussion occurs when questions that do not have yes or no answers are posed to the class and the teacher steps back to let thinking and an exchange of ideas and opinions take place. A major challenge for any teacher is to formulate good questions worth discussing. Spend a significant amount of your preparation time thinking up such questions that grow naturally out of the subject your class is studying.

When a good question is raised before an attentive class ("Is violence ever the best way to settle a problem?" "How can fiction be truer than nonfiction?" "Is it ever all right to tell a lie? What were the effects of lying in the story we just finished reading?"), then come the moments of intense education, intense thinking—unless the intensity is sprung by a blurt or, worse, by the teacher giving *an* answer that is taken as *the* answer.

Far better to ask the question and wait— 10, even 15, seconds, a long time in most classrooms, but a thin slice of the thick hours of a school day—until several hands are up, with everybody thinking, and then to call on one person to speak. Post-question silences are the best and, too often, the rarest in schools.

To have that kind of discussion, you need to make sure the class understands that no one is to speak without raising a hand and being recognized. Letting people speak as soon as they have a thought interrupts others and allows fast thinkers and confident talkers to dominate the discussion. Those who think more carefully or thoroughly may have some good ideas, too—even the best ideas. Don't confuse a spirited conversation among the teacher and the four quickest students with genuine class discussion.

An important skill for presiding over a discussion is being able to turn a question back to the class instead of giving the answer. For example, if in discussing hand raising a student says, "But I don't see why we can't speak when we have an idea," you can say, "Well, why not?" and let the answers arise from the class.

Techniques and arrangements

Here are several suggestions for conducting a class discussion:

Don't repeat a student's comments. It is all too common for teachers to repeat or paraphrase, in a loud, clear voice, what a student has said so that everyone will be sure to hear and understand it clearly. But that is a harmful practice, for it says to students that they don't need to speak up, but only to the teacher, who will be the source of all truth.

Don't dominate the discussion. Your main function in a discussion is to *preside over an exchange of ideas and opinions.* Whatever questions you ask should be for the purpose of keeping the group on the subject and thinking with greater clarity. The art is in asking questions, or getting students to ask questions, that require clarification of ideas and that move the class toward resolving the issue. One exception to your not making comments about an answer arises when a timid student who needs encouragement finally does say something quite good and everybody passes it by out of habit. Here's a chance to build the student up a bit, not just by saying, "Good, Jamie," but by taking his idea and showing its worth by adding an example or stating another dimension of it, perhaps ending with a question like, "What else can you think of that shows that Jamie has made a really key point?"

Don't always call on the first student whose hand goes up. Allow time for several hands to go up. Perhaps you'll call on the last one up, that of the less bold contributor who needs encouragement, or the one who arrives at the talking point more slowly than the others.

Move desks into a circle or a semi-circle. It is much harder to have an all-class discussion if the students can't see anybody's face but the teacher's without turning around. It's worth taking the time to move the furniture.

When a student is talking, move away from him, not closer. That will make his voice carry across more of the entire group. Avoid private exchanges with and between individual students, which tend to be inaudible to the rest of the class.

Always ask a question before naming a person to answer it. "What are some advantages of having opposable thumbs...(pause), John?" not "John, what are...?" The first way makes everyone think about the question, not just John.

Never call on students in any predictable order, for that will make a low percentage of involvement more likely.

Keep track of who has spoken and who has

not. If some students have not taken part at all during the period, or for several periods, look for ways to involve them, perhaps by calling on them even if they don't raise their hands but you think that they have something to say. You might even think up an "easy" question to ask and then call on the quiet person or ask him or her to report on a familiar and relevant experience.

But never invade a student's privacy. All students have a right to be silent, and we teachers have no right to insist that they relate their experiences. We do, however, have a right, and perhaps a duty, to put some pressure on them to answer questions on material they have been assigned to master. That can be good motivation for future effort.

Allow an occasional outburst of comment or reaction. If some student makes a comment that stimulates almost everyone to talk and you find that the class has become a noisy jumble of excited comments, let it happen for a few moments. Good communication and exchange often go on at such times. After the buzz has died down, say something like, "Well, Mary, that really got a reaction. Now let's discuss it. Mary, repeat what you said."

Small-group discussions are occasionally better than all-class ones. If there are 25 or more students in your class, it may be hard to maintain interest and general participation in a discussion. Breaking the class into small groups of five or six students each can work well and gives everyone a much better chance to participate. Each group needs a discussion leader, and it is a good idea to write the discussion question on the board so that all groups can refer to it. It also helps to write down discussion "tasks" for the group to accomplish: (1) Be ready to report on one or two ideas that the group has agreed on; (2) Be ready to state several interesting facts or ex-periences that relate to the subject; or (3) Try to report on the two or three most interesting opinions that came up. The group leaders, or selected reporters, should be ready to speak for their groups after the small-group discussion. A summary—which is almost always dull and trite—is not called for.

Some benefits of discussion

From good discussions come important benefits. People develop the skill and habit of listening. They learn to express themselves and to stand up for their ideas with greater confidence. Students learn to communicate and to let their minds be opened and changed as they hear new ideas.

Further, discussion trains students to question and seek answers—to think—and not to accept others' statements unthinkingly as truth, a skill especially necessary for citizens in a democracy. Discussion can reveal aspects, dimensions, and possibilities of an assignment that are less likely to emerge if merely explained by the teacher.

Finally, discussion shows you, the teacher, and the class how people are thinking and feeling, what sort of people they are, what sorts of ideas and experience they have, and how people can stimulate each other toward answers and toward even better questions.

Eric W. Johnson, who has taught English and sex education in public and independent schools for over 30 years, is the author or co-author of 37 books, including: *Language for Daily Use; How to Live Through Junior High-School; Love and Sex in Plain Language* (now in 4th edition, Harper and Row, 1985); *How to Live With Parents and Teachers* (Westminster Press, Phila., 1986); and *Teaching School*, 3rd edition, 1987, published by the National Association of Independent Schools, 18 Tremont Street, Boston, MA 02108.

A baker's dozen of teaching sins

Over the years, in different schools in different countries, I have visited a good many classrooms and watched a lot of good and bad teaching. I even spend some useful time visiting my own classroom and watching myself teach—well and poorly. The following paragraphs describe some common teaching sins I have seen and some corresponding virtues.

1
Repeating the answer

We've all heard—and probably participated in—dialogues like this:

TEACHER: What do we mean, then, by *cooperation?*

STUDENT ROBERT: Well, it means people working together to, you know, get something done that they all want to do and maybe can't do by themselves.

TEACHER: Right!—a working together toward a common objective.

This is a sin because when the teacher repeats the answer, the students learn that they don't have to listen to their fellow student, only to the teacher. Further, the answerers learn that they need not speak loudly enough to be audible to the entire class, only to the teacher.

Corresponding virtue: Letting the student's answer or comment stand, unamplified and unrefined, as a stimulus to the next step in the lesson or discussion:

STUDENT ROBERT: Well, it means people working together to, you know, get something done that they all want to do and maybe can't do by themselves.

Teacher says nothing.

VOICE FROM CLASS: What? I didn't hear. I don't get it.

TEACHER: Robert?

STUDENT ROBERT (louder): It's people working...

From this the class learns to listen to Robert. Robert practices speaking loudly and clearly enough to be understood, the teacher dominates less, and the class learns more.

2
Mistaking brilliant conversation for good discussion

Often a teacher experiences an almost euphoric exhilaration from a brilliant exchange of views involving the teacher and the 4 or 5 best students in a class of 25. Teachers allow themselves to forget the 20 who aren't taking part, many of whom are confused by the rapid-fire exchange or have stopped paying attention.

Corresponding virtue: Trying to be constantly aware of the state of mind and attention of every person in the class and—during any period—directing questions or remarks to bring out at least two thirds of the students, especially the quiet ones who need encouraging. At least once or twice during the week everyone participates in classroom discussions. If the teacher does engage in dialogue with a single student, the teacher moves away from the student so that the conversation flows across the class.

3
Talking too much

Most teachers, including me, talk too much. We somehow believe that what we have to say is terribly important and that we must not let any aspect of any subject go uncommented upon.

Corresponding virtue: Listening. Teachers moderate discussions among students by listening, observing, and now and then throwing in a guiding question, but mostly by simply keeping the students talking—one at a time.

4
Giving pat answers

I have heard teachers say something like this when considering whether or not to teach a topic: "I really don't want to go into that because I don't know what to say about it." If a student's question is not neatly answerable, teachers tend to avoid it. They limit discussion in class to those neat packages of truth that they possess and can unwrap and bestow upon their students as comforting gifts.

Corresponding virtue: Considering raising questions more important than giving answers. Good teachers believe that thinking out answers is a more vital skill than remembering answers. We should teach *how* to think, not *what* to think.

5
Using the teacher's mind as a filter

A few years ago an ad hoc student curriculum committee criticized the teaching at a well-known school by observing that too often all the ideas from students were filtered through the mind of the teacher. Because in most schools some students are brighter than some of us teachers (even a kindergartner has insights that we have long since forgotten or rejected), this is a sinful limitation on learning.

Corresponding virtue: Seeing the classroom as a hotbed of new ideas, methods, and approaches to truth. This does not mean that obvious and simple matters are grappled with as philosophical questions (there *is* the multiplication table; there *is* the alphabet; there *are* conventions of punctuation), but the more the teacher can learn *with* the students or even be surpassed by them, the better.

6
Not returning tests and papers promptly

The sinful teacher requires the work to be in on time but allows days, even weeks, to pass before the work is dealt with—edited, "corrected," marked, commented on, and handed back. The teacher forgets that the sooner the paper is returned, the greater the learning will be. Furthermore, a poor example of promptness and caring is set.

Corresponding virtue: Not procrastinating, getting the papers back in a day or two. Experience has taught teachers not to assign so many papers that prompt action on all of them is impossible.

7
Making pupils learn at home using class time for testing

"All right, for tomorrow learn the material on pages 25 to 32 and write a one-page essay on it" is too often the kind of assignment teachers give. Who's left to do the teaching? The parents or the poor, struggling kids themselves. Classroom time is spent on testing whether or not the students learned whatever it was they were supposed to learn—a sterile process called recitation.

Corresponding virtue: Using class time to teach. For the assignment mentioned in the preceding paragraph, teachers would *pre-teach;* that is, they would make sure there were no insurmountable difficulties in the material to be read, and they would teach or review how to go about writing a one-page essay.

8
Not helping students to understand the purpose of their work

When students ask, "Why do we have to do this? I don't see the point," we too often answer, "Because it will help you" or "Because you should do your homework" or "Because I say so." Thus the students, if they're dutiful, go through the academic motions without understanding how the assignment is a part of a larger objective worth accomplishing.

Corresponding virtue: Being constantly alert to opportunities for showing why the work is important and worth doing—even if the reward is in the distant future. We need continually to cultivate in the minds of our students an understanding of the larger context within which the specific pieces of work are done. A sense of context tremendously improves learning, and it's not enough that the grand scheme be in *our* minds. It must be in the minds of our students.

9
Mistaking silence for learning

Many students, unless they are extremely honest or rebellious, discover how to put on the look of learning even though their minds may be buzzing about subjects far from the classroom. It's a sin for a teacher or visiting administrator to fail to detect when a high percentage of the classroom population is not mentally engaged. Many teachers waste months maintaining a quiet, orderly, polite, mindless class.

Corresponding virtue: Learning to recognize the glazed eye, the absent mind, the false face of surface respect. Good teachers keep things open enough so that true lack of interest can be expressed. When that happens, teachers explain the purpose (or get the students to do so), change the pace, or urge tolerance and application for the sake of later academic or aesthetic rewards.

10
Failing to distinguish freedom from chaos

It is a professional sin not to be able to control a class—most of the time and when we really mean it. If a teacher does not get whatever help he or she needs, either from the class itself or from outside authority, the teacher is derelict. I have seen too many teachers accept the noisy, random, purposeless activity of their classes (which is not the same thing as a businesslike buzz) and rationalize it as a constructive use of freedom.

Corresponding virtue: Recognizing that order is the first principle but that order is a many-splendored thing and not necessarily synonymous with silence or motionlessness. A good class, using stimulating materials and discussing stimulating ideas, often departs from a basis of strict order, but it can be called back to strict order if need be.

Even good teachers occasionally have trouble with order. They don't hesitate to require a class to go to a strictly one-at-a-time, raise-hand-and-be-called-on basis; to send for help; to remove a student; to have a talk with a troublemaker after class. During this talk they try to help the student figure out for himself ways to make his behavior more acceptable. A good teacher, of course, never uses sarcasm or public embarrassment to achieve order.

11
Allowing past performance to affect current evaluation

Too many teachers judge their students by what they expect them to do rather than by what pupils actually do. Such teachers don't allow for the possibility that four bad papers may precede one excellent one, that the prankster of last week may not be the prankster today, that the liar of February is telling the truth in March. In short, we are not alert enough to give our students a chance to be reborn.

Corresponding virtue: Never irretrievably categorizing a student as dull or bright, poorly behaved or well behaved, lazy or hard working. If we must err, however, we should err on the side of optimism and high expectation.

12
Failing to study student records

A good school keeps good records that give such information as whether a child has had remedial work, whether he habitually has a midwinter slump, whether he needs extra challenge, whether he loves to act in skits or has starred in painting. Good records tell whether there was a family catastrophe last year or a final triumph over a long-term difficulty. It is a sinful waste to believe that teachers should not use the school records to find out these things about each pupil.

Corresponding virtue: Finding out all one can about the history of each student and using that knowledge to help, support, and encourage. Good teachers are enlightened by the knowledge but never limited by it.

13
Playing psychiatrist

A tempting sin is to believe that we teachers should probe into personal problems. This approach fails to recognize that our knowledge of the student is really rather superficial. Few teachers know enough to pronounce on serious personal problems.

Corresponding virtue: Acting within the bounds of one's information and training. Good teachers recognize that they do know something about their academic subjects, something about how children learn, and perhaps, if they've had some experience, something about how students of given ages and circumstances are likely to act. They can report on observed facts and help students and parents see things in perspective. They concentrate on learning and behavior, not on emotions and deprivations.

Wise teachers recognize when a student's problem is beyond their ability to deal with it; they refer the student to a specialist. Meanwhile, they don't give up on the student but steadily offer help and fair treatment—lovingly and consistently.

Eric W. Johnson is a teacher and the author of numerous books about teaching including *Teaching School,* 3rd edition, 1987, published by the National Association of Independent Schools.

Do your questions prevent thinking?

Few teachers would argue the benefits of classroom discussion. Discussion gives individual students a chance to express themselves—their ideas, opinions, feelings; to hear others' viewpoints and experiences; and, by listening and reacting to others' views, to formulate, clarify, and reevaluate their own ideas and attitudes. Discussion also provides teachers with valuable insight into their students' thinking, information that enables them to understand and evaluate their students, and thus to plan subsequent lessons and discussions.

At least those are the *ideals* of classroom discussion. In reality, discussion as it is practiced in most classrooms rarely achieves such noble and worthwhile results, often because of teachers' overuse and misuse of questioning.

Teachers often ask questions hoping to stimulate students' thinking, to open up dialogue, to draw out responses, and to keep a discussion flowing. But what the teacher actually does is initiate a question-and-answer exchange that has little chance of evolving into true classroom discussion. Far from promoting expressiveness, active participation, and independent thinking, the teacher has established a process that encourages student reactivity, passivity, and dependency. Despite recommendations in education manuals, the use of questioning may not be the best way to bring about interactive, thoughtful classroom discussion and may, in fact, inhibit it.

When not to question

Questioning has become such a traditional and common device for teachers to use for gen-erating discussion that it is difficult to imagine *not* using questions. But let us take a closer look at some of the situations in which questions are frequently used, and try to understand how they actually foil the purposes of classroom discussion.

● *To initiate discussion.* Using questions to initiate discussion can quickly lead *not* to in-depth discussion among students, but to a question-and-answer interchange between teacher and students, an interchange in which the teacher asks the questions and the students answer, directing their answers only at the teacher. This routine is easily established, and once it has been established, it is almost impossible to break away from. Thus, if you hold back from asking questions from the start, you will not only avoid falling into a question-answer pattern, you will also be telling your students that a new situation is being established, one for which they will be asked to take some initiative and responsibility.

● *To make a point.* Often a teacher will pose a question whose answer is either implied or obvious, just to underscore a particular piece of information or idea. This technique is unnecessary and counterproductive because the same information can be put forth more effectively as a declarative statement.

● *To help a student who pauses or falters in his response, or to prompt one who ostensibly has finished speaking.* Most students have been conditioned to speak in staccato bursts of a few seconds' duration, punctuated at each end by a teacher's questions. But if discussion is to occur, time for sustained expression of the students' thoughts must be given. Expressing complex thoughts, personal opinions, and interpretations requires more time, including time for pauses and hesitations, than uttering factual knowledge or recounting straightforward events. It requires experience and practice to fashion views, support and integrate them, puzzle out their implications, and so on. A teacher who rushes in with a question the moment the student pauses interrupts the student (and thus models inappropriate discussion behavior) to substitute the teacher's thoughts for the student's, and thus further confounds the student, who must break off from his struggle to communicate his own thoughts to look for an answer to satisfy the teacher.

• *To elicit a predetermined answer*. Teachers frequently ask a student a question with the aim of getting him to give the answer the teacher has in mind. In some situations, such as recitation, this practice is useful, but it is less useful in discussion. If, during the student's contribution, a thought occurs to the teacher, the appropriate response is to wait until the student is finished speaking, and then to state the thought directly, allowing students to react to it as they will.

• *To reply to a student's question*. A teacher's counter-question, no matter how amiably intended, has the force of rejecting student initiative, of refusing the student the right to ask questions, of withholding cooperation in the exchange, and of wresting control of the interchange away from the student and reassigning it to the teacher. It says, in effect, "Only the teacher gets to ask questions." A more positive response would be to reflect on the question, perhaps attempt an answer (or let a student attempt an answer), and let the discussion proceed.

• *To try to "draw out" nonparticipating students*. At first glance it seems helpful to ask a taciturn student a question in order to get him to join in the discussion. But rather than elicit a thoughtful response or encourage participation, this procedure is more likely to intimidate the student and put others in the class on guard, causing them to prepare a response

in case called upon rather than to listen to and think about the issue under discussion. Given time, the silent student may contribute to the discussion on his own when he is sure enough about his views to state them aloud. Far from drawing him out, however, a question may cause him to withdraw even more.

• *To probe students' personal feelings and experiences*. Exposing feelings, opinions, and other personal information in public is a risky venture for many people. To ask a direct question to get at such feelings is not only indelicate but inept behavior. Far from involving an individual, probing questions can make him fearful, resentful, and resisting. If the teacher wishes to express personal feelings or experiences, and then wait for the more venturesome to tell of theirs in turn, the effect can be positive for all. But only a rueful effect can be counted on when the discussion is filled with probing questions.

When questioning helps

Teachers *should* question when they are personally perplexed and need the information. That is not always easy to do, since in asking such a question the teacher admits ignorance and confusion—something "knowledgeable people in authority" don't ordinarily do. But in asking a true information-seeking question, the teacher models appropriate question-asking behavior during discussion, and encourages students to ask genuine, inquiry-oriented questions themselves. Teachers can also legitimately ask a question to ensure correct hearing of a student's response ("I'm sorry; what did you say?"), for defining or summarizing the issue at the start of or during the discussion ("Today we are going to ask together why..."), or for regaining control of the classroom. But for most purposes, the use of questioning during discussion should be avoided whenever possible.

Nonquestioning techniques

Consider seven techniques designed to stimulate student thinking and response and to teach appropriate discussion behavior.

1. *Make a declarative statement.* Instead of asking a question, use a declarative statement to express the idea you have in mind. Suppose Dennis is talking about poisonous snakes, and rattlesnakes and copperheads occur to you. Instead of asking a question (for example, "What other poisonous snakes are there, Dennis?") that tries to get Dennis to state the thought that is in your mind (and makes him guess the universe of poisonous snakes), you can declare your thought directly: "Rattlesnakes and copperheads are poisonous, too, Dennis." Contrary to what might be supposed, declarative statements receive longer and more complex responses than questions.

2. *Restate the speaker's words.* To indicate your understanding of a student's contribution, summarize what the student has just said. Suppose Barbara has reported, "The Earth is closer to the sun than Venus is." Instead of asking, "What do you mean by that, Barbara?" or, "Why did you reverse them?" restate what Barbara has said: "Then I guess you think, Barbara, that the Earth is closer to the sun than Venus is." The restatement not only signals the importance of careful listening, it also gives the speaker an opportunity to elaborate on her thought.

3. *Declare your perplexity when it occurs.* If you are, in fact, perplexed by what the student has said, say so ("I'm confused about what you are saying").

4. *Invite elaboration.* If you truly wish to hear more of a student's views, say so. "I'd like to hear more of your views on that" or, "I'd be interested to know the reasons behind that."

5. *Encourage class questions.* Permit and invite students to ask questions about their classmates' contributions or about the issue at hand. Studies show that students' responses to student questions are both longer and more complex than responses to a teacher's questions. Encouraging student questions enhances discussion, promotes student interaction, and helps develop inquiry skills.

6. *Let the speaker ask a question.* When a student demonstrates confusion or difficulty in expressing his thought, suggest that he try to formulate a question. This solution is preferable to the teacher starting in on a series of so-called diagnostic questions ("Do you mean this or are you saying that?"), which only serve to further confuse the speaker.

7. *Maintain silence.* When a student stops speaking, try saying nothing at all. Maintain a deliberate, attentive silence for 3 to 5 seconds. This technique is both simple and effective—and the hardest to put into practice. However, once students become accustomed to such odd teacher behavior, they will understand that the speaker is being given an opportunity to continue his thought, or that another student is being given the chance to enter the discussion. The result invariably is greater student participation, thought, and response—the goals of classroom discussion.

J.T. Dillon is associate professor of education at the University of California at Riverside. The ideas in this article were adapted from his two-part series, "To Question and Not To Question During Discussion," in the *Journal of Teacher Education* (Sept.-Oct. and Nov.-Dec., 1981), with permission of the publisher. These ideas are expanded in his book for teachers, *Questioning and Teaching* (London-Croom, 1987).

Do you draw the line on good questions?

A student asks a question.

It's a good question—relevant, pointed—a real one. Whatever they say about teachers, you know that there are a lot of things you'd rather hear than your own voice. And here's one of them: a good question. Fine. It's a credit to you for inspiring it, to the student for asking it.

But it's unexpected, creative; not the kind of question anticipated in the Teachers' Manual, or in your practice teaching, or in any class you took. No preparation can match the range of interests you encounter every day with lively students. When a good teacher and a good student are together, questions are being asked on every level at all times, and some of the best ones are unexpected. Fine. It means there's life in the classroom, something more than a cut-and-dried sequence of ideas.

In any case, you're aware that answering the question might lead you far afield. It's certainly not on the line you plotted, the line you *had* to plot, whether unconsciously or on paper, for today's lesson. You'd be happy if every lesson could be completely spontaneous, but you have to keep in mind that this moment in the classroom is part of the module, the week, the term. Fine, fine! You've given the problem some consideration, then?

Then what do you do? There's that question hanging there in front of you, and here you stand with your thumb...

"Miss Lennart? In this problem it doesn't come out to zero at the bottom. What does that mean?" (You know perfectly well that all the long divisions in today's problem set have no remainders, so either Rick is doing the wrong set or he's made a mistake. And you intend to take up remainders and how to deal with them first thing tomorrow. But a remainder *means* something, and that's what he asked. But it's late in the day and you're tired.) So...

"I think it does come out to zero, Rick. Go over your work again."

"Mr. Johnson, if so few people came over on the *Mayflower,* how come there are so many now?" (There were a lot of other ships, of course; and then there were the slaves; and something you read recently pointed out that the biggest factor was those 15-child families and plenty of room. Sally's a very bright girl, and she could understand all that, but it would be a bit complicated for most of the others and lead to a lot more questions. Better not get into it, at least until the Thanksgiving pageant is over and you have more time.) So...

"It was a long time ago. Let's get into our places and we'll sing the harvest song one more time."

"Why are there two ways of spelling some words?" (They ought to learn about English and American variants. In fact, it probably wouldn't be a bad time to let them see that spelling, and grammar for that matter, aren't as simple and only-one-way-is-right as the book seems to say. But right now you have to get through the list of double-consonant endings for *-ed* and *-ing*.)

"Don't worry about that right now. Now, who knows what happens to *prefer* when you add *-ed*?"

It's a shame to have to do that, because the children's questions are sincere.

But there's so much to cover, and so little time. Maybe education should be a seamless web, or a big ball of string, but we all recognize that one way or another we have to break that continuity. Some things are more important (or urgent, or socially necessary, or valuable) than others. In the very idea of a curriculum we grant the assumption that schools exist to pass along a certain amount of a child's total learning. Certain matters—facts, attitudes, opinions—are important enough that we write them into our plans. From telling time to penmanship to literacy itself, there are areas of learning that can't wait too long. Wherever they may lie in the seamless web, we have to snip them out and present them in what seems to us a logical sequence.

In doing so we gain a good deal. We can test the students, and indirectly ourselves, to see how far we've progressed along the line. We can provide mass education, which would be chaotic or impossible without at least some standardization. We can prepare students for "subject" courses and studies in secondary school and beyond, and there the need for organization is unmistakable.

But along with these advantages goes a price. If you answer a child's question with "We'll be getting to that next week," or "That's not really part of this lesson," it hurts you and it hurts the student. You, because you are justifying means by ends, saying that this question must be passed over for the sake of getting where you're going. The student, because his primary energy in school, his curiosity, is set aside and discouraged.

It's a matter of values, like every matter in education. Some teachers resent the price more than others, but to work in any school system is to pay it.

And when we do pay it, let's make sure we know just what it is we're doing. Remember, there is a radical difference between your point of view and the student's. More simply stated,

you know where the lesson is going and the student does not. You have been through elementary and secondary schools, college and professional training—the student hasn't. You can think of 150 ways that today's lesson ties in with lessons before and those to come. That's your job, or part of it.

But it is not the student's.

For the student, especially the young student, the *ordering* of what is taught is essentially arbitrary. The student doesn't often concern himself with the teacher's reasons for taking up this first, that second, the other one third. And there's a large reservoir of trust, too. You can justify this bit of rote learning by the interesting work it makes possible later on. He'll trust you; he knows that exercises that may have seemed pointless have led him to the mastery of skills he enjoys.

That trust is one of any teacher's most valuable resources. It must not be abused. It is frighteningly easy to do just that. The teacher who ignores or sets aside questions too often may get through the curriculum in record time, but at the cost of permanently blunting the edge of the student's mind, the ability to see connections between apparently unrelated matters. Worse, the teacher may succeed in convincing the student that the curriculum is *it*. That questions are somehow wrong unless they are asked at the right moment. That teachers have the Big Picture and the student ought to sit back and simply follow the dots.

It can't hurt to keep in mind the other side of the Big Picture. If you are any good as a teacher, you are still learning yourself. This year's presentation is not the same as last year's, and by next year you'll have improved it again. And keep in mind that no matter how incomplete or fragmentary the student's knowledge may be to you, *it's all he has*. If he sees a chance to extend it, and you reply that the piece he's seeking will fit in better later on, you may be right—but there's no way for him to know that yet.

In general, then, we might do well to be a bit more humble in our judgments of what is relevant and what isn't, what we'll take time to deal with and what we won't. Everyone knows how maddening a small child's incessant "whys" can be, but that is where learning and the love of learning begin. As we channel those whys into the areas of study, the skills, and the disciplines that we want to transmit, we should not put our ideas of what must be taught, and when, above the student's curiosity.

As the teacher, the guide, you can see where the student is blind. But your sight is probably not quite so clear as you think, and the student just might have a glimpse of something you missed. It's not a disaster if the names of the months don't get learned this week, if penmanship practice doesn't get finished before lunch today, if the general science quiz waits on an explanation of something on television last night.

But when the clock says the line should be drawn now, and a student asks a question, stop and remember that the clock means more to you than it does to the student.

Monte Davis is a high-school teacher and a free-lance writer in New York City.

Is your teaching style frustrating your students?

When a child in your class consistently complains "I don't *get* it," you may have to adjust to his learning style. Here's how a yearlong effort to individualize teaching according to maturation level brought dramatic improvement to a frustrated child.

October—Erik shifts uneasily in his chair as I explain the day's language lesson. I've asked the children to arrange four out-of-order sentences so they make sense. Most of my second graders seem to enjoy the challenge, but I see Erik's expression change quickly from bewilderment to frustration to anger. "Where are we?" he blurts out.

Another child shows him our place in the book as I repeat the explanation. Erik explodes again. "I don't *get* it!"

Keeping calm, I start over. "Look at the directions at the top of the page. What do they say?"

"I *see* the words. I can *see* perfectly. But what are we supposed to *do*?"

The thundercloud look on Erik's face and vivid memories of previous storms warn me that Erik may erupt at any moment into a screaming rage, ripping up papers and throwing books across the room. If he gets to that point, he won't be able to accept help from me or from the other children. I could remove him from the classroom to produce a temporary calm, but I know that wouldn't relieve his frustration or meet his desperate need.

Instead I try another strategy. I draw some pictures on the chalkboard to suggest what is happening in the four-sentence story. My stick figures soon have everyone laughing, and Erik is delighted. "I get it now," he says. Relaxed, he works energetically on the assignment and occasionally asks for help from a classmate.

I quickly switch from the lesson I'd planned to do next to one I think will work for Erik as well as the other students. I draw a "Two Meanings" chart on the chalkboard. To match it, the children fold a blank sheet into eight "boxes." At the top of each they write a common word that has two meanings, such as *foot, yard, stamp, bank, bark,* or *light*. Under each word they draw two pictures to illustrate its different meanings. Erik provides lots of words for the chart and even suggests renaming it "Three Meanings."

A portrait of Erik

By myself after school, I think again about Erik's problems. I've already met with his parents, previous teachers, and the many specialists who've worked with him. Everyone agrees that Erik *is* bright, even though he's had much difficulty learning to read and write.

Now repeating second grade, he spends part of each day in the resource room working to overcome his learning problems. He's had a few successes like today's, but he's virtually a nonreader, and his writing is painfully slow, poorly controlled, and full of reversals.

He has trouble recognizing words without clues provided by pictures or reading context. He fails at tasks requiring fine-motor control. And he can't remember things. He forgets words he knew the day before. His mother says she's learned to tell him to do only one thing at a time, rather than several.

Sequencing gives Erik the most trouble. He writes numbers and letters in the wrong order. In fact, this morning's near blowup was triggered by his difficulty with sequencing.

Despite his language problems, Erik has many strengths. He excels in sports. He runs the fastest, plays the hardest—has a tremendous urge to be first and best. Because of these skills and his lively imagination and dramatic flair, he's well liked and even admired by his classmates. He's also good at reading maps and understanding charts. Recently, he scored highest in the class on a test involving patterns and spatial relationships.

Nevertheless, the 2 previous years of frustration and defeat in language skills seem to have left Erik with a smoldering anger. His eruptions are occurring with dismaying frequency. And they're interfering with the success he's beginning to achieve.

Theory into practice

My success with Erik this morning and on a few earlier occasions comes from the reading and research I've been doing. Gaining clues from new theories about the brain and different learning styles, I've tried some new approaches with him. And they seem to be working.

Research by behavioral scientists Jerre Levy and Marylou Reid suggests that the hemispheres of the brain mature at different rates in boys and in girls up to about age 10 or 11. In boys, the right hemisphere matures more rapidly than the left, hence boys' earlier interest in play materials requiring spatial perception and large-motor skills. In girls, the left hemisphere develops more rapidly, hence girls' earlier progress in verbal and fine-motor skills.

Beginning reading programs usually focus on the left-hemisphere specialty of putting letters into correct sequence to form words, and words into order to form sentences. This emphasis could well account for the disproportionate number of boys in low reading groups and in remedial reading classes in the primary grades.

Many boys catch up with girls in verbal skills at around age 10, and many excel after that. But by then, some boys, like Erik, may have failed so often that their self-images and even their attitudes toward school have suffered dramatically. Studies also show that if, in learning to read, children aren't taught with materials and methods geared toward their hemispheric maturation and learning style, they *may not* catch up later.

Certainly the right-hemisphere approach I'm trying with Erik is no panacea for all learning problems. A child may face many other obstacles such as visual or auditory problems, emotional upsets, chronic illness, a different cultural or language background. But as long as putting Erik's language studies in a holistic, visual context works, I'm going to keep it up.

More practice

November—It's math time. My students are thrilled to discover that skip-counting can produce a times table. I pass out copies of the empty form, and the children begin filling in the squares. Suzanne almost explodes with excitement as she realizes she already knows the 10s, though we're only on the 5s.

Suddenly Erik pounds his desk with a fist that sends books and papers flying. "Where are we?" he shouts. "What are we doing?"

I can't make the other children wait while I deal with Erik. But if my guess about his abilities is correct, he'll be able to comprehend the times table as a whole. I hand him a completed table. He takes it to his desk to study, and I can almost see the power surge as he figures out the system and begins to fill in his own paper.

December—Virtually a nonreader in September, Erik now reads successfully and happily in my middle reading group. I'm not using the same step-by-step program focusing on letters and words that he had in first grade and his previous second grade. Now he's in a reading group of five or six children for whom I select narrative material with high story interest, especially for boys.

Few pictures accompany these stories, but the visual imagery of the writing seems to suggest whole scenes to Erik. He somehow manages to come up with the right words, even though he may not recognize them later in a word list. The group's responsiveness to his dramatic ability in oral reading helps satisfy his great need for peer recognition.

Putting it all together

February—I'm convinced now that what works for Erik works for some of my other students too. Adjusting my teaching style to accommodate different learning styles has helped. I try to include visual and spatial activities in every school day's work. Our lessons involve movement or music or imaginative thinking, as well as the more traditional linear material. Here are a few of my strategies.

• I extend the "two meanings" idea and have students draw up lists of antonyms, homonyms, and words that become something else when you add "e" to the end of them, such as *pin* and *tub*.

• I encourage impromptu dramatizations of stories in text or trade books. One child becomes the narrator, and others read words between the quotation marks. When a child actually plays Billy Goat Gruff or Curious George, all the children get a clearer idea of what the words mean.

• I ask the children to visualize stories we read and then write about them. I ask, for example, "How would you feel if you were 3 inches tall like Tom Thumb? Imagine yourself arriving home this afternoon." They do lots of chuckling, drawing, *and* writing.

• I welcome first drafts of stories even with grammatical or spelling errors. (Polishing can come later.) I give students many chances to show and read their work to classmates. With encouragement, stories blossom into books—each page with an illustration.

June—By nurturing holistic and creative thinking along with the sequential and logical, I find that all my students are doing well. As for Erik, his scores on the year-end achievement tests were comfortably above grade level in all verbal and language skills except spelling. His math is more than a year above, and science and social studies are 3 years above. His outbursts have given way to improved self-confidence and the willingness to ask for help before the blast-off stage. Adjusting to his learning style has certainly paid off—for all of us.

Alice V. Shelby, a retired teacher who has taught all elementary grades and has participated in early education research, is now a free-lance writer in Yorktown Heights, N.Y.

DO YOUR ACTIONS SUPPORT AND MOTIVATE?

In their book, *Looking in Classrooms* (Good and Brophy, 1978), the authors identified fifteen separate instructions that educators recognize as supportive and motivating. Researchers have consistently observed these interactions in classrooms noted for high achieving students. These vital interactions relate to response opportunities, feedback, and personal regard.

Review the list below to identify classroom behavior that could help improve motivation in your students.

Response opportunities

Objective: To provide response opportunities to all students in the class.
- To provide response opportunities to perceived "low achievers" as frequently as to other students in the class.
- To give low achievers feedback about their class performance as often as you give it to others.
- In a friendly manner, to be within arm's reach of low achievers as often as of other students.

- To provide individual help to low achievers as often as to other students.
- To praise low achievers' learning performance as frequently as that of other students.

Feedback ✓

Objective: To provide positive feedback to all students in the class.
- To use courteous words as frequently with low achievers as with other students; and as frequently with all your students as with adults.
- To give low achievers as much time to respond to a task or question as you give other students.
- To tell low achievers as often as you tell other students why their classwork is acceptable or praiseworthy.
- To give personal compliments to low achievers and to express personal interest in their outside activities as often as to other students.
- To help all students to respond to questions by providing them additional information.

Personal regard ✓

Objective: To show personal regard for all students in the class.
- To listen as attentively to low achievers as to other students.
- To touch low achievers in a friendly manner as frequently as you touch high achievers.
- To challenge the thinking abilities of low achievers as you do other students by requiring them to do more than simply recall information.
- To convey to all students that their feelings are understood and accepted in a nonjudgmental manner.
- To be as cool, calm and patient when stopping the misbehavior of low achievers as you are with high achievers.

2

REVIEW CLASSROOM STRATEGIES

E ven the most experienced teachers sometimes have difficulty in bringing daily classroom reality in line with educational goals. How to be the teachers they want to be? In this chapter, experienced teachers offer practical classroom-tested suggestions that can make teaching easier and more certain to help students learn. Read on for some hands-on methods they have found helpful for improving effectiveness in the classroom.

Can you keep quiet for three seconds?

Classroom teachers are inclined to see educational research as something done not *for* them or *by* them but *to* them.

Classroom teachers—almost always the observed rather than the observers—are disposed to post-invasion mumblings about ivory towers, pies in the sky, and never-never lands. "What," they'll complain, "did all that have to do with me?" Sometimes they'll wonder wistfully why they couldn't have been left some useful memento of the research—nothing to solve all their problems, surely, but just a little evolutionary something to help them *do* better in the real classroom world.

Mary Budd Rowe's research has produced just such practical help. This distinguished educator is well known by admiring teachers as "the Wait Lady" because of her emphasis on the deceivingly simple notion that classroom teachers didn't give students enough time to answer questions. Years of applied education research have supported the now well-known theory, demonstrated in hundreds of classrooms and demonstrable in thousands more, that can be simply put this way: Young people will think more effectively and self-reliantly if teachers interrogate less, prod less, cue less, reward less, and listen more.

How to experiment with *wait-time*

The only equipment required for classroom experiments in wait-time is an adequate tape recorder. The teacher should select a 15-minute segment of any lesson period in which students are expected to think beyond simple recall of facts or skill steps. Science, social studies, and language arts are among the subject areas that offer such conditions of recitation or discussion. The experimenting teacher should turn on the recorder and attempt to observe the following procedures as closely as possible:

1. Wait at least three seconds after asking a question to let the student begin a response. (Say to yourself: one thousand one, one thousand two, one thousand three. It sounds simple, but the silence can be deafening the first few times.)

2. Wait at least three seconds after any response before continuing the question or asking a new one. (This second wait-time recognizes the possibility that the student may wish to elaborate on the initial response.)

3. Avoid verbal signals—positive or negative—in asking questions. Among the most common are: "Isn't it true that…?" and "Don't you think that…?" A common negative cue is the prodding: "Think!"

4. Eliminate mimicry—repeating the response a student has just made.

5. Eliminate verbal rewards ("OK," "Fine," "Good," "Right") and negative sanctions (the typical "Yes, but …" pattern, in which the teacher completes the answer or restates the question).

Steps 1 and 2 are the foundation of the wait-time theory and may be as much as the teacher can handle in a first experiment. The core of the experiment is the teacher's objective assessment of the tape recording—being the "detached observer" of what has just happened in the classroom. Were wait-times indeed maintained at three seconds or more? If so, what effect did this have on the lesson?

In most classrooms where wait-times have commonly been disregarded, the changes brought about by including them—both in student and teacher behavior and in the nature of the lesson itself—are likely to be profound. (Any teacher wary of self-fulfilling hypotheses might stop reading and try a wait-time experiment now.)

Inquisitory teaching style

Wait-time research grew directly from the observed prevalence of inquisitory teaching styles in subject areas that were supposedly oriented toward inquiry. Inquisition, by Rowe's definition, is a highly structured "bombing" of students with cognitive questions, delivered at such rapid pace that students have no time to think and teachers have no time to evaluate students' responses.

The first 300 tape recordings collected in Rowe's study disclosed that the average teacher waited just 1 second for students to begin a reply, and just 0.9 seconds after a student response before moving on to the next question. The average teacher asked from three to five questions a minute. Some packed in as many as ten a minute—or almost 400 questions in a short class session.

The tapes revealed other types of persistent teacher behaviors, some measurable and some not. Mimicry made up a considerable proportion of what teachers said; some teachers repeated *every* student response exactly. Verbal rewards—"Wonderful," "Very good"—made up as much as 25 percent of some teachers' words. Such rewards, furthermore, were often given randomly and indiscriminately, whether the student's answer had high merit or none at all. Many teachers, as if they were simple teaching machines programmed to accept just one answer in a prescribed form, rejected perfectly plausible student responses. Student responses, plausible or not, were terse and fragmentary—and often inflected as if to say, "Is this what you want to hear, teacher?"

Why was (is) the inquisitory style so persistent and so apparently strong in tradition? Perhaps sheer pace is equated with efficiency in many classrooms, and teachers invent devices to dispel the slightest appearance of "dead time." Some teachers see inquisition as a method of maintaining control—a position that often turns out to be self-defeating as question-battered children tire and lose interest in the lesson. Finally, whether the outcome is intended or not, inquisition, which effectively focuses all attention on the teacher, tends to divert attention from the subject matter itself.

Inquiry: a powerful alternative

"Inquisition," Mary Budd Rowe wrote, "is something teachers do to students. Inquiry is something teachers and students may do together."

What happens when the teaching method begins to shift from one to the other? Evidence was drawn from more than 900 classroom tapes made by teachers trained simply to increase wait-times to at least 3 seconds. The data showed desirable effects on both students and teachers. Consider these changes in student behavior:
- The length of the students' responses increased.
- The number of freely offered and appropriate student responses, unsolicited by the teacher, increased.
- Failure to respond—"I don't know" or no answer—decreased.
- Inflected responses decreased; students thus appeared to be more confident in their answers.
- The number of speculative responses increased; students thus appeared to be more willing to think about alternative explanations of the subject matter at hand.

- Students worked together more in comparing data.
- Students made more inferences from evidence.
- Students asked more questions.
- The frequency of responses by students rated relatively "slow" by their teachers increased.

The wait-time tapes also demonstrated important changes in teacher behavior:

- Teachers became more flexible in their responses—more willing to listen to diverse answers and examine their plausibility.
- Teachers' questioning patterns became more manageable; questions were fewer but showed greater variety and quality.
- There was some evidence that teachers raised their expectations of students who had been rated as relatively "slow."

Bringing it home

For all the evidence, no two classrooms are alike. The challenge of verifying the worth of such research findings still falls on each teacher individually. But detached self-evaluation is likely to be difficult for any teacher. Furthermore, once it is accomplished and teaching patterns are changed, many teachers may find old anxieties appearing in new forms. The inquiry process does, after all, undermine a number of cherished practices that teachers tend to regard as both valuable to children and important to their own sense of self-worth.

Consider, for instance, the matter of looking students in the eye. Rowe's work suggests that discourse is better stimulated when the teacher joins a student group without comment, at eye level but with *no* sustained eye contact with any individual student. Why? Because teachers are likely to have a "silent committee" of dependable students counted on to sustain the business of the classroom and called into ac-

tion by such devices as eye contact. When the teacher stops depending on such devices, the "silent committee" is likely to grow.

Giving praise in response to student answers is another example of the kinds of teacher sanctions that extend from wait-time research. In the original studies, teachers' verbal rewards often appeared as a kind of random "noise" which detracted from students' time to think and respond. Many teachers are likely to see that judgment as an unkind cut at a practice they suppose offers students encouragement and higher confidence in what they are doing. However, this research suggests that a pattern of high verbal rewards may have exactly the opposite effect. High-reward classrooms, she observes, are characterized by great waving of hands and competition for the teacher's attention. There is far less evidence in such classrooms of children depending on learning materials or on one another for ideas and information, comparing results, listening to and building on each other's ideas. Only the teacher matters, and the teacher's management problems, under those circumstances, are almost bound to increase.

On the other hand, when the teacher keeps quiet....

Craig Pearson was a special projects editor for *Learning* magazine and the author of numerous articles about teaching.

60 activities that develop independence

Encouraging independent study is a reachable goal only if students have the appropriate attitudes and skills. This cannot be achieved overnight; it is evolutionary and demands repeated evaluation. Because one of the best ways to learn is "by doing," students first should be encouraged to achieve limited objectives on their own. Some may be hesitant and others will be fearful, but eventually most, if not all, will begin to feel the wonderful sense of independence, responsibility, and accomplishment that accompanies success. "Nothing succeeds like success" will come to have real meaning for students who were previously unmotivated or apathetic.

The following list of 60 activity and reporting alternatives may be used to develop options for all students. Identify those activities that would be motivating for your students, adapt and rewrite them so they're appropriate for the specific unit or topic being studied, and use them as part of an individualized assignment contract, prescription, or "free choice" activity list. They may also be used as learning station "task cards" or placed at interest centers, little theaters, or other instructional areas to task-orient the learner and to help him become independent and responsible.

Activities and reports

1. Make a miniature stage setting with pipe-cleaner figures to describe part of the information you learned about your topic. Display the stage setting and figures and give a 2-minute talk explaining what they represent and why you selected them.

2. Make a poster "advertising" the most interesting information you have learned. Display the poster and give a 2-minute talk explaining why you found the information interesting.

3. Design costumes for people or characters you have learned about. Describe to a group of classmates how you decided what the costumes should be, how you made them, and the people who would have worn them. You could also hold a fashion show with the help of friends.

4. Prepare a travel lecture related to your topic. Give the lecture before a small group of classmates. You may also tape-record it for others who are working on the same topic.

5. Make a "movie" by drawing a series of pictures on a long sheet of paper fastened to two rollers. Write a script and show your movie to one or more small groups of classmates.

6. Describe in writing or on tape an interesting person or character that you learned about and dramatize something he or she did. Ask a few classmates to tell you what they think of the human being you portrayed.

7. Write or tell a different ending to one of the events you read about. After sharing your thoughts with a classmate or two, ask them to think of other ways the event could have ended.

8. Pantomime some information you found very interesting. Let a few classmates try to guess what you are pantomiming.

9. Write and mail a letter to a friend recommending that he study this topic too, and explain why.

10. Construct puppets and use them in a presentation that explains an interesting part of the information you learned. Have a friend photograph your presentation. Display the pictures and the puppets.

11. Make a map or chart representing information you have gathered. Display the map or chart and answer questions about it.

12. Dress as one of the people you studied. Answer questions in an "interview."

13. Broadcast a "book review" of your topic, as if you were a critic. Tape-record the review and permit others to listen and tell you if they would now like to read the book, and why.

14. Outline a biography of one of the authors you read and tell about his writing on tape, in writing, or orally. Give your report to a small group of students.

15. Make a clay, soap, or wood model to illustrate a phase of the information you learned. Display the model and answer questions as a museum guide might.

16. Construct a diorama to illustrate an important piece of information. Display the diorama and answer questions as an artist might.

17. Dress paper dolls as people or characters in your topic. Give a 2-minute talk about the doll characters.

18. Make a mural to illustrate the information you consider interesting. Display the mu-

ral and answer questions which may arise.

19. Build a sand-table setting to represent a part of your topic. Explain the setting to other students. Ask them to evaluate your effort in a few short sentences.

20. Rewrite an important piece of information, simplifying the vocabulary for younger children. Develop a project with the children around the information.

21. Make a time line, listing important dates and events in sequence. Display the time line and be prepared to answer questions about it. Ask a few people to "explain" your time line to *you*.

22. Write a song including information you learned. Sing the song in person or on tape for a small group of students.

23. Make up a crossword puzzle and let other students try to complete it. Check and return their answers to them.

24. Make up a game that uses information from your topic. Play the game with other members of your class.

25. Direct and participate in a play and/or choral speaking about your topic. Present the dramatic or choral creation to a small group of classmates.

26. Write a script for a radio or television program; produce and participate in this program. Present the program for a group of classmates.

27. Develop and present commentaries for a silent movie, a filmstrip, or a slide showing.

Use your own photographs or slides, if possible.

28. With others, plan and then participate in a debate or panel discussion on challenging aspects of your topic.

29. Conduct for your classmates an interview on your topic with an adult or students from upper classes. Ask specific questions.

30. Prepare and make appeals before another class on behalf of school or community drives that can be related to your topic. Contribute whatever monies or goods you receive to the proper agency.

31. Write a news story, an editorial, a special column, or an advertisement for the school or class newspaper explaining your views concerning any one aspect of your topic. Mount and display your writing. Ask three students to write "letters to the editor" praising or chastising you as a reporter.

32. Correspond with hospitalized children (particularly at holiday seasons). Share interesting information about your topic that you have learned.

33. Design and then display an unusual invitation to a class party or program centered around information on your topic.

34. Write a letter to an imaginary friend about fictitious travels concerned with your topic. Mount and display the letter.

35. Take a character from a story such as *Robin Hood* or *Cinderella* and rewrite the story in a setting suitable to your topic. Mount and display the story.

36. Write and then display an imaginary letter from one story character to another. Tell about something that might have happened had they both lived at the time and place of your topic.

37. Make up and tell "tall tales" about your topic. Either write or tape-record at least two of the tales you create. Illustrate them and permit others to react to them.

38. Convert a story you have written into a short play on your topic. Ask a few of your classmates to take parts in the play. Tape-record it and present it as a radio program to a group of younger children.

39. Keep a make-believe diary about your memorable experiences as you lived through the period concerned with your topic. Read a portion of your diary to some of your classmates. See whether they can identify the period concerned with the topic. Add the diary to the resource alternatives available for other people who are studying the topic.

40. Write stories about different phases of your life as they might have happened had you lived in your topic time and place. "Important Happenings During My Life," "Important People in My Life," "My Library" (kinds of books I like and why), or "The Most Exciting Thing That Ever Happened to Me" might be some choices. Combine the stories into a book entitled "My Autobiography" and show it to your teacher, parents, and a group of classmates. Add your book to the resource alternatives available for study of your topic.

41. Make a magazine for the classroom by compiling voluntary artwork and composition contributions on your topic. "Publish" the magazine and distribute it among your classmates.

42. Develop for classroom display collections of colloquialisms or "regional" expressions related to your topic.

43. Collect folklore such as rope-jumping rhymes, counting-out rhymes, legends, or folk songs related to your topic. Write (or type) them neatly and combine them into a book of resource materials. List yourself as editor. Use proper credits. If you are uncertain about the format, ask the librarian to show you samples of edited books.

44. Make a collection of myths, legends, interesting mottoes, and proverbs on your topic. Cover the collection with an attractive jacket and display the booklet as a resource alternative.

45. Try to find original manuscripts, old page proofs, first editions of books, book jackets, taped interviews with authors or other interesting persons in the community, autographs of authors, or any other documentation related to your topic. If the material cannot be brought to school, organize a small group trip to visit the place where you found the items.

46. Document some original research you've found on your topic using bibliographies, footnotes, and quotations.

47. Search the library card catalog and periodical index and list all the books and articles concerned with your topic. Add the list to the resource alternatives for your topic.

48. Make constructive evaluations of a TV program related to your topic. Mount the evaluation on a sheet of construction paper and display it. Discuss your thoughts with someone else in your group who saw the program.

49. Make a comparison between getting information by listening or by reading. Compare the devices used in the two media. Which do you like better and why? Write your answers. Compare your findings with those of another student who selected the same activity alternative. Discuss your reasons for selecting one method as being more interesting than the other.

50. Study the speeches and written work of a particular public figure, determine his motives and find possible hidden objectives, if any. List any clues which indicate the author's real beliefs.

51. View a television program of your choice. Check the facts presented in written materials with those on the program. Put your conclusions into written form and share them with your teacher and two other classmates who have seen the same program.

52. Analyze the point of view of an author of a particular book. Read about the author in order to explain why he believes what he does. Tell at least three other classmates something you learned about the author which might account for his point of view in writing the book.

53. Write an article persuading people to your point of view by using biased words and appropriate propaganda devices. Analyze words with similar meanings to differentiate shades of meaning. List at least 20 such words.

54. Organize a file box for new words, arranging them under headings such as "Descriptive Words" or "Words With More Than One Meaning." Compile a list of words overused in class discussions, such as: *fantastic, man, great, cool, uptight, pretty,* and *tough.* Find substitutes for these words and make a compilation for class references. Add the file box to the resource alternatives for your topic as appropriate.

55. Compile a reading notebook containing excerpts which are unusually expressive and make use of similes, metaphors or alliterations. Use the figures of speech to describe some aspect of your topic.

56. Describe a character in a story. Describe how the author developed the character and influenced the sentiments of the reader. Through a written, taped, or oral report, share your thoughts with at least two or three classmates. Ask for their reactions to your findings.

57. Attempt to understand the behavior of characters in a book by analyzing possible causes. Evaluate the choices made by characters and think through possible alternatives. Write a short (one or two sentence) description of the character. Write a short description of the character's behavior. Write three possible alternative behaviors the character might have shown.

58. Compare the illustrations in different editions of fairy tales or in various types of books. Draw alternative illustrations for three stories you've read.

59. Catalog your own books and records or the books and records in the classroom library. (Topic, value, reading levels, etc.).

Plan a personal library. List the books and records related to your topic that you'd like to own. Display the list attractively mounted and suggest that others obtain the books or records which you liked best.

60. Form a poetry club. Members can bring favorite poems to discuss or compose poems based on their topics. Have the club members present a series of recitations.

In carrying out the above activities, students should be free to learn through a wide variety of multimedia resources—tapes, films, filmstrips, transparencies, books, games, records. Experience with these materials will increase the pleasure of learning and often lead to the discovery of additional options for building independence and responsibility.

Dr. Rita Dunn is professor of education at St. John's University School of Education and Human Services, Jamaica, N.Y. **Dr. Kenneth Dunn** is professor and coordinator of administration and supervision in the department of educational programs at Queens College in New York City. They are authors of the book *Practical Approaches to Individualizing Instruction: Contracts and Other Effective Teaching Strategies* (Parker Publishers).

Underachievers: What to do when they can but they won't!

"Billy has an IQ of 168, but he isn't that exceptional in class," says Ann Reynolds, his third-grade teacher. "He constantly disrupts the class. Sometimes he won't keep his mouth shut and tries to be the class clown. Other times, when he gets in a rebellious, hostile mood, watch out! He's ready to punch someone. And he can't work in a group unless he gets his own way."

"Sarah's not gifted," says her fifth-grade teacher, Bob Masters, "but she's certainly competent. Still, she's performing well below grade level. Most of the time she daydreams, fiddles with books and pencils, talks to classmates, or passes notes—does anything but schoolwork.

"When I assign classwork, Sarah either dawdles the time away or is the first to be finished, having dashed off almost anything and calling it 'done.' She gives up quickly and resists explanations or help. Once in a while, though, Sarah turns in work that indicates real ability. It shows she can achieve. But she just won't."

Billy and Sarah are underachievers—students who perform more poorly in school than their mental abilities indicate they can. Though educators and researchers have paid the most attention to *gifted* underachievers, some children at various levels of ability perform far below their potential.

Many underachievers go unnoticed by teachers and parents; others are hard to miss, they're so troublesome. Some are shy; others are rebellious. Many are falling through the cracks of America's schools.

Who are the underachievers?

Deciding who's an "underachiever" is somewhat arbitrary. But basically, it's a student whose grades are substantially below what might be expected on the basis of IQ, aptitude, or achievement test scores. Though in theory underachievers don't have identifiable learning disabilities, some learning disabled children *are* underachievers. Their failures make them think they're less capable than they actually are, and they stop trying entirely.

Whatever the specific definition, among underachievers, boys outnumber girls about two-to-one. Though the seeds for underachievement are often sown in the early grades, the problem may only become apparent in late elementary and junior-high school when teachers start giving more homework.

No single set of characteristics applies to all underachievers, but here are some signs.
- *Underachievers don't try.* They don't do their homework and are behind in assignments. They either don't complete projects, or they try to get away with doing as little as possible as quickly as possible.
- *They appear lazy.* At home they spend hours watching TV or just hanging around. They expend more effort getting out of doing something than they would if they did it. But occasionally, when they're interested in an activity, they can sparkle.
- *They're immature.* They get upset when things don't go their way or when they're criticized. They act up in class or appear very shy. They don't accept responsibility for personal failure but blame it on the teachers or say the subject matter is "stupid."

• *They lack self-confidence.* They feel they should be perfect; because they can't achieve perfection, they won't try. Some continually criticize themselves and their work. Others brag all the time but deep down feel they are "dumb" and incapable of doing anything right. Still others are painfully shy and go unnoticed because they don't bother anyone. Almost all underachievers have poor self-concepts.

• *They're rebellious.* They know their parents value achievement, and they're not going to play that game. Instead, they have their own game. They may "lose" or "forget" the assignment or not take the books home. They may deliberately fail to turn in completed work. They may, on purpose, miss test questions that they "knew cold" before the test. Many of them corral their parents into spending hours each night "helping" them or actually doing their homework *for* them.

What about their parents?

Gary Jones, a junior-high school teacher particularly concerned with underachievers, says, "Parents of the kids who are having problems rarely take an interest in the school. They don't show up for conferences. They may be concerned, but they're not very involved.

"Those who *are* involved are usually one of three types: There are the parents who want the school to get tough and force their kid to learn. Their attitude is: 'If my kid's not doing what he's supposed to, hit him.' They're sincere but misguided. Many simply don't know what else to do.

"Then, there are the parents who are trying everything to get their kid to study. But that's the problem—they're doing everything *for* him. They sit him down; they go through each problem, each chapter, everything with him. It never works.

"The third type of parents seem to be saying, 'I'm not perfect; the school's not perfect. We've got a problem here; what can we do to solve it?' Unfortunately, this type is rare."

How to help underachievers

Ideally someone in the school or district should be responsible for identifying underachievers, marshaling the school's existing resources to help them, and creating new programs to alleviate and perhaps prevent the problem. You can support a school- or district-wide program or even work to start one. But whether or not you have one, your attention to the underachievers in your own classroom could make the difference for them.

Various combinations of the following strategies have helped many students.

1. Stress success. Only an experience of real success will improve the low self-esteem and lack of confidence that plague many underachievers. Simply telling these youngsters that they have the ability to do well doesn't work. Instead, it reinforces the idea that you have extremely high expectations for them and increases their fear of failure.

Keep those goals and expectations appropriate. Since many underachievers believe the standards for them are too high, ask *them* to set goals for a specific period (for example, turning in all homework for a day or a week). Celebrate success by repeating the goal a few times before asking them to raise it.

Try to find assignments, projects, and tasks that particularly interest the underachiever so he has a better chance of success. This isn't as easy as it may sound. Trying to teach a student who is bored and resistant can be extremely frustrating.

When nothing seems to work, think of the child on a personal basis. One teacher says she finds out about students' interests by making a point of talking to them casually on the playground, at lunch, in the hall, and at after-school activities. Then she creates projects for them related to those interests—even if the topics are outside her usual course content.

For example, a history teacher discovered at a parent/teacher conference that an underachieving student's hobby was toy soldiers. She encouraged him to construct a diorama of a battle for his Civil War project. The resulting success was a turning point for him.

Similar efforts are especially crucial for underachievers who aren't supported and encouraged at home. You might even change the parents' attitudes simply by showing off their child's accomplishments at a parent/teacher conference. Some parents are surprised at what their child can do, and they become eager to help. Others, sadly, do not care—all the more reason for you to provide opportunities and reward accomplishments in activities that the student values.

2. Ease into step-by-step homework. Since underachievement usually becomes a more serious problem when homework is introduced, don't leave homework skills and responsibilities to chance. You can "shape" them systematically by breaking down the introduction of homework into small, progressive steps. For example, begin by assigning all students one math problem to do in class and bring back to class the next day. The next day, ask them to do a math problem at home and bring it to class. Later steps might include longer assignments, writing answers to questions about a short reading passage, and ultimately studying for a test.

Have an assignment sheet available for each student. When you assign homework, make very clear to students exactly what they're expected to do and specifically how to do it. Be sure you reinforce its importance by grading and checking all the work. Tell the parents about your homework program and whether and how you want them to help. This kind of program can nip problems in the bud by helping you identify children who tend to skip homework.

3. Be firm. Many professionals insist that the teacher should react immediately when children fail to complete work or perform substantially below their ability. Waiting until the end of the grading period—or worse, the end of the year—only allows time for confidence to fade and a sense of failure to increase.

Your role here is crucial. Don't let students get away with skipping assignments. Instead, you might keep them after school for "special tutoring" until they complete missed homework. Or ask their parents to cooperate by

HOW TO USE A PERIODIC PROGRESS REPORT SYSTEM FOR UNDERACHIEVERS

1. Schedule appropriate conferences with the parents and the child (separately or together, depending on the situation). You may want to include a counselor at times.

• *Identify the problem* (for example, not doing homework, disrupting the class, not mastering certain skills).

• *Ask the student about self-confidence* (Do you think you can't do the work?), motivation (Are you trying as hard as you can?), and independence (Do you feel your parents are always on your case, telling you what to do?).

• *Consider a thorough medical, psychological, and educational evaluation* if physical or learning problems are a possibility. If your school is already overloaded with testing special ed or LD students, the parents may want to consider outside evaluation. At the very least, look carefully at the child's cumulative file to get any clues you can.

• *Explore topics and activities that interest the student* so you can incorporate these into school projects that are likely to lead to successes.

• *Set modest, attainable goals,* preferably with the student (for example, turned in homework, got passing scores, stayed in seat, raised hand and refrained from calling out answers).

• *Identify rewards.* Determine activities (like television, video games) or commodities (like snacks) that the student values and the parent can provide as a reward for achieving goals.

2. Use a weekly or daily report card (see sample).

• *Select only a few behaviors to monitor,* based on the goals you set, and make up the report card.

• *Write an agreement in simple, clear, definite language* stating specifically what reward will be earned for what performance. Have the parent and student sign it.

• *Tell the student that he's responsible for filling out the report card,* getting teachers to sign it, having it checked by a counselor or advisor, and taking it home. Make it clear that if the card is not filled out or brought home for any reason, there will be no reward. Explore having the student evaluate his *own* progress, perhaps weekly, with a teacher or counselor who can also represent him if there are misunderstandings. In a team-teaching situation, you'll want to make one teacher—probably the homeroom teacher—responsible for checking up on the report card.

• *Encourage the parents to praise accomplishment;* they shouldn't comment on failure, nag, or monitor the child's homework. But they must carry out the consequences for failing to live up to the agreement. Parents *should* be available to help with homework *if* the student asks.

• *Suggest privately to the parents that they try to plan to do something together with the child* each week to build up their relationship—regardless of the child's school performance.

3. Schedule another conference a month later to review progress.

• *If the child's performance hasn't improved, reevaluate the goals and criteria.* Inquire about how consistently the parents carried out the procedures, and reconsider the nature of the reward (Is it valuable enough to the student? Can it be obtained without doing the work?).

• *If the child* has *made progress, set up steps that allow him to work his way off the reporting system.* Perhaps he can go to weekly reports after 3 weeks of perfect daily reports and then off the system entirely after 2 months of perfect weekly reports. If his performance slips, return to earlier procedures.

SAMPLE REPORT CARD

Progress Report for John Smith Week of October 18 Teachers: Please indicate progress by marking YES or NO in each area.					
CLASS	Prompt to Class	Quiet in Class	Stayed in Seat	Contributed to Discussion	Teacher's Signature
Reading					
Math					
Science					
Social Studies					
History					

From "Parent's Guide to the Periodic Progress Report," published by The Boys Town Center, Boys Town, NE.

holding a weekend home study hall in place of a favorite TV show. Some schools hold Saturday morning or after-school "special opportunity tutoring" or "the homework club" in the place of academic detentions or punishments.

4. Report regularly. Periodic progress reports help many serious underachievers who consistently fail to do homework. You could send home a daily or weekly report card that indicates grades on homework and tests, behavior problems in class, and future assignments. (See "How to use a periodic progress report system for underachievers" on page 43.) Parents help by rewarding good reports with privileges or special treats (for example, television time, outings).

This periodic report system gives students immediate feedback and encourages them to improve their performance. It also helps parents relax and stop nagging.

Some teachers and parents are leery of giving rewards for schoolwork. True, mature students shouldn't *need* special rewards—doing a good job is its own reward. But underachievers are immature; they *do* need extra incentives; praise alone is *not* enough. Better to have them work for rewards than not work at all. Besides, the periodic progress report system usually provides a way for students to "earn" their way off the reward system and, through success, to gradually learn to value themselves and their work.

5. Counsel the parents. Research shows that counseling the parents of underachievers can be effective, sometimes more than counseling the children. The parents benefit from knowing others are in the same boat and from hearing what others have done about the problem. Counseling can also help them realize how much their children need successes and rewards for accomplishments. It can show parents that creating a set of clear rules and consequences will encourage their children's independence and responsibility—and free them from constantly reminding, nagging, or directing their children. For parents whose children feel they're loved only if they perform well at school, counseling can suggest doing things together just for fun. Some families may need private counseling and therapy.

6. Give extra support. Some underachievers benefit from special classes during the year or in the summer. For example, the San Diego schools operate a Basic Skills Supplementary Assistance Program for elementary students who are underachieving in reading or math.

Besides special classes, some schools use individualized educational plans (IEPs) similar to those required for students who have learning disabilities. These plans can provide a structure for adjusting the curriculum to the underachievers' special interests and need for successes. Of course, you can do the same thing without a formal IEP, but it may be more difficult.

7. Try peer tutoring. In the Boise, Idaho schools, a peer-tutoring program for special ed students improved the performance of both pupils and tutors. Having older underachievers tutor younger underachievers or other special students could work wonders. With training and supervision, student tutors get a taste of the purpose, effectiveness, responsibility, and success that they need.

Help for underachievers is no frill

Some educators suggest ignoring underachievement and counting on the students eventually "getting their acts together" on their own. That does work...but only for a few. Underachievers who are rebelling against parents and who have a reservoir of successes—social, athletic, extracurricular—may get going educationally once they leave home and lead their own lives.

Unfortunately, most underachieving youngsters will not recover spontaneously. Those with serious self-esteem and self-confidence problems need more help. And that help will come only if teachers and parents take an interest in underachievers.

"I know budgets are tight and teachers are overburdened and dumped on for everything," says parent Sally Randall, "but this is not a frill—this is basic education for the capable."

Robert B. McCall, PhD, is a child psychologist, Director of the University of Pittsburgh's Office of Child Development, and a contributing editor and monthly columnist for *Parents* magazine. He's currently studying the educational and occupational future of underachievers.

Make memorization work in your class

Use the word *memorize* in the teachers' lounge, and you're likely to be regarded as a relic. Today, we're more interested in problem solving and other creative and productive thinking techniques. But maybe in discarding rote memorization, we've thrown out the baby with the bathwater.

Take math, for instance. In our rush to teach the *whys* and *hows* of math, we've failed to teach the *whats*. And when you're trying to compute costs, mortgage interest, or gas mileage, you need to know *what*, say, 6×9 equals. That means somewhere along the line, "$6 \times 9 = 54$" should be memorized.

The greatest thing my fourth-grade teacher did for me was to insist that I memorize the multiplication facts through 12. This made long division a lot less painful. She also had me memorize "30 days hath September...," "*i* before *e* except after *c*...," and other helpful rules. I don't think I'll ever forget them.

Make memorization a game

You may shy away from memorization because you think it's just boring repetition. But it doesn't have to be. Approach memorization as a game rather than as an assignment. Involve the whole class. And be ready for smiles when students find they *can* remember things.

The following six techniques show that memorization can be fun. The key is to use imagery; the more vivid and dramatic the images, the easier the memorization process. And the more it's done, the easier it becomes.

Run it up the flagpole (for lists)

Number 1 to 10 on the chalkboard. Then write 10 grocery items suggested by your students. Turn your back to the board, chant a word like "abracadabra," and name the items in perfect order. Your students will be amazed and impressed.

Now teach them the secret: First, give each number an image that recalls that number. I use these examples: The symbol for 1 is a flagpole, 2 is a bicycle, 3 is a tricycle, 4 is a hearse, 5 is a pentagon, 6 is pickup sticks, 7 is 7-Up, 8 is an octopus, 9 is a baseball team, and 10 is a big fat hen.

Be dramatic when you explain how to remember the grocery items. For example, if the first item is milk and the second is eggs, you might say: "For the first item on the list, I see the flagpole in front of the school. It looks like a big *one*. Run your eyes from the ground to the top. What's at the top? No, not a flag but a carton of milk. Look out! It's spilling! Here it comes! Oh, no! Right in my eyes!

"Number 2 is a bike with *two* wheels. I see a blue 10-speed, and the principal is riding it. Oh dear, he broke the eggs he's carrying. What a mess! The seat and handlebars are all slimy and yellow. His hair and mustache are all sticky. Yuck!"

Continue through the list in the same manner, spending a minute on each image. Be sure the images are striking and clear—that's what strengthens the memorizing. Stick with whatever number associations you use. When recalling, prod students with questions such as "2—What was the principal carrying?"

Ask students for other ways to use this memorization tool. Suggest remembering assignments, books, and things to do. Once you teach this technique, use it yourself. Remind students before they go home to put conference slips (or whatever) "on the flagpole." Your return rate should improve substantially.

Ham with grape juice, please (for pairs and matching)

Make bizarre associations to memorize two items that go together, such as states and capitals, Roman and Arabic numerals, books and authors, people and places. Again, the more farfetched the images, the better the students will remember. Here are a few examples:
• To remember that the capital of New Hampshire is Concord, think of the ham in *Hamp*shire as covered with Concord grape juice. Picture it: pink and purple.
• To remember Roman numerals: D = 500 (In*dy* 500); C = 100 (a *c*entury is 100 years); M = 1,000 (the *M*ilky Way has thousands of stars).

Tell me a story (for poems, lines in a play, and lists)

The biggest problem with memorizing a sequence is recalling what comes next. But it's easy if you create a simple story that uses key words from each line or sentence of what you're trying to memorize. Say you want students to remember these opening lines of "I Hear America Singing" by Walt Whitman.

I hear America singing, the varied carols I hear,
Those of mechanics, each one singing his as it should be, blithe and strong,
The carpenter singing his as he measures his plank or beam,
The mason singing his as he makes ready for work, or leaves off work,

The boatman singing what belongs to him in his boat,
the deckhand singing on the steamboat deck,
The shoemaker singing as he sits on his bench,
the hatter singing as he stands....

Here's the story you can tell: "I went to a *mechanic* to have my *car(penter)* fixed. He put it on *mason*ry blocks. While I waited, I took a *boat* ride, but the *deck* was covered with water and my *shoes* got wet. I took them off and carried them in my *hat*."

You can also make up a story to memorize a list. For example, you may want students to remember that of the four food groups, the meat group contains meat, nuts, poultry, fish, beans, seeds, and eggs. Try this story: "One day I had my friends *meet* (meat) me at the *nut* tree outside my house for a *pull-tree* (poultry) contest. We began to shake the tree. I thought something was *fish*y when *beans* started to fall on us. Then I thought the beans were really giant *seeds*. But they turned out to be *eggs*, and we were all covered with goo."

Crazy phrases (for ordered groups)

Create a phrase or sentence in which the first letter of each word corresponds to the item being memorized. Use this technique for remembering word spellings and musical notes, and for lists like the Great Lakes and the 13 original colonies.

Examples: To spell *arithmetic*, remember this sentence: "*A rat in the house may eat the ice cream.*" To remember the Great Lakes (Superior, Michigan, Huron, Erie, Ontario): "*She makes Harry eat onions.*"

Ask students to invent crazy phrases or sentences to remember things that give them trouble. Their creativity will amaze and delight you.

Sing a memory song (for very long lists)

Use melodies to help teach lists and facts. Remember the simple tune that's used to recall the alphabet? Other songs might list the 50 states or the order of the U.S. presidents. Perhaps your class could compose songs for the multiplication tables.

Repetition (when all else fails)

Even repetition needn't be boring. Use repetition games with the entire class as a fun way to learn short facts. For example, here are three games I've used to teach multiplication facts.
• *Password for the day.* Select a multiplication problem—for example, $6 \times 7 =$. Then call for the answer at set times, such as when students want to leave the room or sharpen a pencil, and at odd times when they're not expecting it. Encourage each student to call for the answer from three other students during the day.
• *Spell a message.* Spell a problem ("s-i-x t-i-m-e-s s-e-v-e-n") and ask the class to spell the answer.
• *Hand math.* Show six fingers, cross your arms, and then show seven fingers. Students respond by flashing 42 (10 fingers four times, then 2 fingers).

Using these techniques

Encourage students as they learn to memorize. You'll find they want more things to memorize and will be willing to try new techniques.

Once something's been committed to memory, be sure to use it. For example, when your class has learned what the five Great Lakes are, incorporate them into various activities that make students use what they've learned.

Memorization doesn't have to be boring. If you use the right approach, it can be fun. And it works.

Beverly Schreifels is a fifth-grade and gifted resource teacher at St. Francis School in St. Francis, Minn.

Why don't they follow directions?

For years of my teaching, I wondered why my students seemed to be so lousy at following directions. They'd get an assignment from a textbook or a worksheet and seem to have no idea of what to do and no view toward referring to the directions supplied. I'd give directions for some activity to the entire class, and no sooner were my directions complete than several hands would go up to ask, "What do I do now?" So I'd repeat my directions in that slow, distinct tone of voice I hope I never let slip out at a dinner party with friends.

Over the years, I thought about why following directions seemed so difficult for my students. One possible reason was that they just had poor listening or reading skills. Another was that they just didn't pay attention well enough. Television was an easy target for blame—all those hours sitting and watching, without having to do anything with the input. But whatever the reasons, the situation never improved. In fact, one year, things got worse. Much worse. The problem of not following directions was blown to extraordinary proportions by my new sixth graders.

Getting the students to do even one assignment without an enormous amount of direct, step-by-step supervision seemed impossible. It wasn't that they were unwilling or unable to handle the work; they just didn't focus on what they were to do.

I tried my usual tricks. Sometimes I'd give them an assignment and set a kitchen timer for 5 minutes. During that time I wouldn't answer any questions. In the past this technique had helped with students. Not so this year.

One day, I distributed the worksheet that appears on page 50 to my class.

All but two in the class were tricked by the ploy, and I used this exercise as a jumping-off place for a class discussion about the problem. But not much changed, and I was getting more resentful and discouraged. How was I supposed to work with individual students on needed skills if I couldn't get the rest of them going on their own? I complained to any and all.

Then one day a thought came to me: I was seeing the students' inability to follow directions as *their* problem. I thought that if they would only change, the problem would go away. Suddenly I saw it all differently: Yes, there is a problem, but it isn't the students who have it. It's *me,* and the sooner I stop blaming them and do something positive, the sooner I'll lick it.

A change in attitude

My objective became to teach students why reading and listening to directions is important, and how to do it. I decided to teach this in the same way I teach any new concept— by providing a variety of firsthand experiences the children could easily relate to. And I decided to focus on the positive. Children learn and grow from being in a supportive environment, where they have many opportunities for developing new understandings—not in a punitive, negative classroom that's a battlefield between teacher and students.

For starters, I gave the class a writing assignment: Write directions for making a peanut-butter-and-jelly sandwich. (That's my idea of drawing on real experience.) Later I collected the papers and chose one to use for a class demonstration. The next day, I brought in the ingredients called for in the directions

WORKSHEET: FOLLOWING DIRECTIONS

This worksheet is designed to assess your ability to follow directions quickly and accurately. Please complete it as rapidly as possible.

1. Read through all the questions before filling in any of the blanks.

2. What is your birthdate? _____

3. How old are you? _____

4. Write your address. Be sure to include your ZIP Code.

   _____

   _____

5. What is your telephone number? _____

6. Do you have any sisters? _____ If so, how many? _____

7. Do you have any brothers? _____ If so, how many? _____

8. How many letters are there in your last name? _____

9. Which is longer, your first name or your last name? Mark the correct sentence with an X in the box.

   ☐ My first name is longer than my last name.   ☐ My last name is longer than my first name.

10. Put a check mark (√) in the box that describes how you came to school today:
    ☐ I rode the school bus.   ☐ I came in a car.   ☐ I rode my bike.
    ☐ I walked.   ☐ None of the above fits.

11. About what time did you go to bed last night? _____

12. Did you watch television last night before going to bed? _____

13. What's your favorite flavor of ice cream? _____

14. What time is it now? _____

15. Do you have a wristwatch of your own? _____

16. How do you get up for school in the morning? Mark the correct box with an X.
    ☐ You have an alarm clock that wakes you.   ☐ You just wake up automatically by yourself.
    ☐ One of your parents gets you up.   ☐ You get up a different way not listed here.

17. Which do you like better, hamburgers or hot dogs? _____

18. Which do you like better, chicken or pizza? _____

19. How many students are in your class right now? _____

20. Do not fill in any of the blanks for questions 2 through 19. Sign your name to show you've read this entire sheet.

   _____

to make the sandwiches: bread, peanut butter, jelly. (I really do believe there's no substitute for concrete materials!) I explained to the class that I was going to try following one set of directions. I asked the writer of the paper I'd chosen to read her directions, stopping after each step so I could do exactly what she said. I told her not to embellish on the directions, but to read them exactly as she had written them. I also explained that I would not ask any questions, and that no comments could be made during the demonstration.

My goal was to follow the directions accurately but unconventionally whenever possible. I had chosen a sample that fit that goal. Here are the directions that she read and what I did for each:

"Take two slices of bread."
I removed two slices from the loaf.
"Open the jar of peanut butter."
I removed the lid.
"Spread peanut butter on one side of one slice of bread."
Here was my first chance to follow the directions, but not as they were intended. I reached my hand into the jar and scooped out some peanut butter, smearing it onto the slice of bread with my fingers. No knife was mentioned and I chose not to use one. The kids' eyes got very big.
"Now open the jar of jelly."
I did this with peanut-butter-covered fingers.
"Spread the jelly on one side of the other slice of bread."
Back to the hand routine—a sticky mess, but a small sacrifice for inculcating the possible consequences of imprecise directions.
"Put the two slices of bread together."
I did so, putting the sides smeared with the peanut butter and jelly facing out. I tried to hand the concoction to the reader to eat. She wouldn't bite.

I then returned all the papers (after licking my fingers clean) and organized the class into small groups. Each group's task was to write one set of foolproof peanut-butter-and-jelly-sandwich-making directions. This called not only for clear thinking, but for resolution of the different notions some groups' members had about how a peanut-butter-and-jelly sandwich should be made. I kept out of the discussions, agreeing to offer help only when everyone was stuck.

Later, one member from each group read a set of directions out loud. The class discussed the various solutions to the task. I encouraged the students to tell how they arrived at their solutions, and what ideas they discarded along the way and why. We discussed whether the directions would indeed work, or whether they could be tampered with as I had done in my demonstration. We tried several—until we ran out of supplies—then took a break to eat our results.

For those questioning the educational value of including peanut-butter-and-jelly sandwiches in the curriculum, consider the benefits of the exercise: It demanded precise and clear expression; it reinforced children's writing skills; it called for different solutions to a problem and different ways to reach those solutions; and it gave students the opportunity to work both independently and with others. My initial goal—to introduce students to direction giving and following—was accomplished in an involving, nonthreatening, and fun way for the class.

Tic-Tac-Toe and other games

Because I believe it makes sense to give children enough experiences with a new idea so that they have a chance to truly internalize it, I chose to follow up the peanut-butter-and-jelly activity with another exercise whose content the children were familiar with: games. Again I divided the class into small groups and asked each to come up with a list of two-person games (tic-tac-toe, checkers, tether ball, etc.). When the groups began to run out of ideas, I gave them a new direction: "Put a star next to each game that you think is suitable for playing in the classroom."

When they had done their sorting, I compiled a list of the starred games on the chalkboard. Then I had students copy down the list and check off the games they felt they knew how to play well enough to teach another person. I collected their papers and used them to organize the class into groups so that each member knew at least one game in common.

The next day, I had each group choose one game the members felt they could teach. I explained that each group's task was to write the directions for how to play that game. To demonstrate, I asked the class to help me write the directions for tic-tac-toe, a game they all were familiar with. The students dictated while I recorded. As I wrote down their thoughts, changes were suggested, and I had to erase, substitute words, rewrite sentences. It was good for them to see the process of rethinking, editing, correcting. The final directions were left on the board for the groups to refer to when they wrote their own directions.

Then I made a graph of each of the games that had been described and asked each student to choose one game he or she would like to

BETTER LISTENING EXERCISE

Many students have difficulty following directions, sequencing ideas, and speaking in front of peers. With this activity, you combine all these skills into one fun practice session.

Before the lesson, prepare about 10 designs for the students to duplicate *solely* by your oral instructions. Some designs can be recognizable, such as a smiling face; others can be abstract.

Begin the exercise by reviewing such concepts as *first, second, then, next, up, down, right-hand corner, left-hand corner, middle,* and so forth. Then review simple shapes and lines—*zigzag, curve, straight.*

Hand out blank paper and

try to instruct the children to duplicate one of your designs. When you've finished giving directions, have the students share their "masterpieces" and compare them with your original. Encourage them to comment on whether your directions were clear or vague. Repeat the exercise with your other designs.

Next, have each student create a design and communicate it orally to the group. At first, they may be reluctant, but with practice this can be lots of fun. Act as a group member yourself, following each student's directions. If a direction is unclear, a group member can ask a specific question

for clarification.

These exercises provide many learning opportunities and should be done over a series of classes.

learn. Children had to prove they understood the directions by playing the game with someone who had written the directions. This exercise allowed students to evaluate for themselves whether their directions were understandable. If children were confused by any directions, they had to discuss that with one of the group members who had written them.

Following verbal directions

It was now time to focus on verbal directions, to contrast with the heavy emphasis on written work. The activity I chose called for students to work in pairs on either side of a structure (a large book or something) that allowed each student to see the other's face, but not what he was doing. I distributed various construction materials—cubes, Cuisenaire rods, blocks—to the pairs and gave them the following directions: "One student builds a structure using 6 to 10 blocks or cubes. When you've got it built, your job is to describe it to your partner so that she or he can build exactly what you did from your directions. Neither of you may look at the other's construction until you both agree that both structures are identical. Then lift the wall between you and compare structures."

We talked about the directions first. They asked several questions: Could they build any shape they wanted? Could they ask questions? What did you do if you didn't understand the other person? I assured them that they could do all the talking they wanted; they just couldn't peek.

The activity was successful from several viewpoints. First of all, the intensity of communication it fostered between students was startling; the amount of earnest eye contact was fascinating to observe. Students also learned the importance of using precise, helpful words and phrases to explain how to position the materials. They also learned the value of cooperation. One student, for example, complained that her partner made her so nervous she couldn't concentrate. Others talked about how kind and helpful their partners were. Their comments confirmed for me the value of a supportive atmosphere to foster learning. Direction following was at last seeping into my class in a way I felt sure would stay with us.

I continued to assign tasks in direction giving and following. Students made a series of signs about classroom procedures that we posted around the room: how to collect lunch money, where to put finished assignments, how to write a proper heading for a paper. Several students wrote directions on how to study for a spelling bee. For a social studies project on our town, one group wrote directions for one-day tours for visiting tourists.

Things were definitely improving. The students seemed much more able to focus on directions, to refer to them as a useful tool when they were stuck. They certainly listened more carefully and all because I changed my approach from complaining and resisting to exploring positively what I could do to change the situation. I think I learned as much as—or more than—my students did. Isn't that always the way?

Marilyn Burns is the creator of the Math Solution in-service courses, now taught nationwide. She is the author of nine children's books, including *The I Hate Mathematics! Book* and *The Book of Think*. Her latest book for teachers is *A Collection of Math Lessons*.

How to teach listening skills

If you've ever had to repeat the same directions to your class a half-dozen times, you already know about the need to teach listening as a skill. But you may not know how.

As the language development teacher in a large city elementary school, I work daily with students who need help listening. Here are some teaching ideas that have helped me—and can help you—sharpen students' listening skills.

Give the children ample opportunity to listen for pleasure by reading aloud and telling them stories whenever possible. Not only does this help students become better listeners, but it also inspires them to investigate new books and authors on their own. Occasionally, I even catch students searching our library's globe for places mentioned in the latest adventure they've heard.

Listening to vintage radio plays also helps students visualize stories. Start with very short plays so the children have time to adjust to a medium without pictures. I like to offer a sequence, building up to the famous *War of the Worlds* broadcast by Orson Welles. Once they've become familiar with radio, my students love to produce their own dramas, complete with music and sound effects.

Listening to stories is only one way to receive information aurally. Children must learn to listen more carefully to each other, too. With this goal in mind, I have my students conduct interviews for the school newspaper, interviewing each other first, then other students and staff members. Though I require them to write the questions beforehand and the replies afterward, the interviews have to be oral.

In class, riddles help focus attention on the spoken word. I write the riddles and their answers on strips of paper, then have volunteers pull them out of a box and read the riddles aloud. To guess the answers, the students must listen closely to the clues.

Listening skills can be sharpened while teaching virtually any subject. For example, use filmstrips and sound movies whenever possible in social studies and science classes. Sometimes I preview a filmstrip and outline it on the board or a ditto. The students take notes as they watch the filmstrip, then they exchanges views afterward in a discussion.

With a younger group or when using a filmstrip I haven't previewed, I show it twice—the second time without sound—then ask questions about the most important points.

Homework gives students the chance to link careful listening with the sounds they encounter every day. One of my favorite assignments is to have the students list the sounds they hear from the time they leave school until dinner. The next day they use their lists to write poems about sounds.

Another successful assignment is a report on a television program. Each child chooses a favorite show and reports on it the next day. The reports must describe the show's characters, setting, problem, solution, and the part the child liked best. At the end of the session, the students evaluate the reports, telling what they liked about them.

Rainy days are good times for listening activities, as are the odd moments when the class is idle—for example, while waiting to go to the auditorium. On these occasions, I like to have my class play the camp game, Going on a Picnic. Each student tells which item he'll bring, then lists the items the other students have named.

Twenty Questions also encourages careful

listening. Peer pressure weighs heavily on the player who wastes a precious question on information that's already been revealed.

Listening activities don't have to be sedentary. Dancing requires the children to pay attention to both the music and the directions. Nonlisteners quickly fall out of step.

Craft projects help build concentration because they can be taught through step-by-step oral instructions. Teaching origami has a bonus: Novice artisans frequently teach friends and relatives how to make the complicated figures, which helps them learn how to give instructions.

In other art activities, students use listening skills to create visual images. For an exercise in contour drawing, I have the students close their eyes and hold their pencils on a large sheet of newsprint. Step by step, I describe the figure that they are to draw. Keeping their eyes closed and making sure their pencil points never leave the paper, the students draw the images forming in their minds as I speak.

The more outrageous the figure is, the more the students enjoy the exercise. For example, I might tell them to start near the top of the page and draw a round hat with a huge curving feather. Then I tell them the hat is on a tall skinny clown, who is riding on a fat camel, which is hobbling along a tightrope—on crutches. As you'd expect, the drawings are outlandish.

Exercises such as those I've just described are opportunities for children to learn a skill that can benefit them for the rest of their lives. One of the highest compliments any of us can be paid is to be called "a good listener."

Linda Armstrong, formerly a language development teacher in the Los Angeles City Unified Schools, is a free-lance writer and poet. Her stories for children have been published in *Highlights*.

Recognize student strategies

The change from formal to child-centered teaching is intended to make alternative schools places where children can learn in natural ways, with no need for the devious strategies they develop to cope with teacher-dominated schools and other coercive situations in home and society. But the strategies are deep-rooted and can present serious obstacles to learning in the open classroom. In the transition from teacher-dominated to child-centered schools, students bring their institutional bad habits with them.

In a coercive environment, a child's strategies enable him to preserve his feelings of worth and capability and perhaps even his sense of safety. By keeping an authority figure off his back he becomes in a sense the winner in the race.

The implementation of such strategies varies widely from child to child, but all fall within four fundamental categories, any of which can present serious challenges to teachers trying to open up their classrooms. The four distinct types are: the Good Kid, the Saboteur, Dr. No, and the Fun Consumer.

The Good Kid strategy

You'll recognize the Good Kid strategy. A teacher started one day by saying to a group of 10- to 13-year-olds, "If you know how you feel, right now, raise your hands."

No hands.

"I mean, how does your body feel? Do you feel good? Or tired? Or full of energy? If you know, raise your hands."

Eyes searched the teacher's face, trying to

get a clue to the right answer. How were they *supposed* to feel?

Two hands rose weakly.

"Is it possible for anyone else to know how you feel? Who else could know more about it than you?"

"*You* do!" they chorused.

Wanda, the teacher, broke into laughter, and the kids giggled as they recognized for the first time their absurd dependence on psyching out teachers.

They were using the Good Kid strategy. The Good Kid determines what will please the teacher and then does it, or appears to do it. The Good Kid never risks an answer or opinion until he has figured out what the teacher expects. Obviously each kid knew the answer to Wanda's question better than she, but none would risk commitment.

The strategy was frustrating the school's teachers, who wanted the children to assume a greater part of the responsibility for their own learning. The blandness of Good Kids was sapping their writing, their conversation, their art work, and their involvement in learning. Ironically, since the kids liked their classes at the Aspen Community School and wanted to "be good," they strained all the harder to apply the Good Kid strategy.

Immediately after the how-do-you-feel incident, Wanda gamely tried again to elicit some honest answers.

"Let's think about three musical groups—the Jefferson Airplane, Lawrence Welk and his band, and the Supremes. We're going to go around the room, with each of you putting these three musical groups in order, from best to worst. We'll start with Carol."

"Um, the Jefferson Airplane, then the Supremes, then (giggle) Lawrence Welk."

So it went. A few ranked the Supremes first. Welk was a unanimous dead last. Until Wanda's turn. She ranked Welk first.

There were outraged cries. "You're putting us on!"

"Lawrence Welk is the best," Wanda insisted coolly.

Pandemonium. "You can't believe that!" "He's so icky!" "How can you say that?"

Wanda firmly stated the facts. "He's been on TV longer than the others. He has sold more records."

"That doesn't mean anything!" "That's weird!"

"You can't argue with the facts."

But they did argue—long and strong. The teacher's musical values were just too outrageous, adaptive strategies be damned. Without the teacher having to tell them, the students learned that they could state opinions without first figuring out what the "right" answer might be.

So teachers should anticipate that when students make the change to informality, many will need to reacquire natural ways of learning and being with people. Teachers who fail to anticipate this problem commonly become so disillusioned that they enter a phase of thinking that the children can't handle—or are not worthy of—freedom.

If the teacher is as new to the child-centered styles as the students, Good Kids can bait her into returning to the formal-teacher style she is trying to abandon. Some teachers react strongly enough to become quite authoritarian, or try to avoid coercive reactions by going to a permissive extreme, thus being perceived as weak.

The Good Kid strategy is especially insidious because it is so easy to live with. Many teachers will argue, for example, that "good students" aren't using strategies at all but simply like school that way. But evidence seems to contradict this premise.

Haim Ginott quotes a high-school student's description of the Good Kid strategy he developed early in his school life.

It is easy to "snow" teachers. If you appear motivated and don't disturb them, they let you live. I became "school wise" early in the game. I figured out what makes teachers mad: violation of simple rules and "not trying." So, I come to school on time, I don't ask troublesome questions, and I am polite. And, of course, I am never caught "not trying."

Our principal stopped me on the way home and asked an original question: "What did you do in school today?" I was tempted to tell him the truth.

I apple-polished the English teacher.

I faked interest in social studies.

I read comic books during arithmetic.

I cheated on a science test.

I did my homework during recess.

I wrote notes to my girlfriend during Spanish.

I replied: "It was a busy day." He smiled in satisfaction.

Such conscious adaptation is not the worst problem. Unconscious adaptation is far worse. Some students are quite sincere about their deceits. Conditioning starts early. When a small boy was transferred in the middle of last year to the Aspen Community School, his parents told me—the director—that they were disturbed by the effects on the boy of the competition and violence in the public school he had attended. The next day, a volunteer helped the child with reading. After their session, in which he was unable to read, the boy asked the volunteer to tell the head teacher that he had read perfectly. When he wrote or drew, he asked if he could have an A or a gold star. He was only 7 years old, but already well schooled in the ways of the Good Kid.

Contrived incidents can be helpful in rooting out the consequences of the Good Kid strategy. In *Values and Teaching*, Raths, Harmin, and Simon describe the contrived-incident's purpose as "to simulate as closely and as dramatically as possible something that will give students a real feeling or experience or understanding. It cuts through the easy level of words." If the situation seems real—as in the dispute over Lawrence Welk—strategic defenses might drop.

Naturally, a Good Kid strategy works best for a child who can easily get on the good side of teachers. For a youngster classified as a loser, a strategy requiring little or no teacher approval is more effective. Some students are bright enough to win the Good Kid game easily, but their integrity requires that they use recognizably hostile strategies against people, including teachers, they have learned to associate with oppression. In institutions that try to suppress them, such children gain substantial satisfaction through sabotage.

Stopping the saboteur

In a teacher-dominated situation, where a child's assertion of initiative and personal power is difficult, the Saboteur is hard to stop. Saboteurs often talk openly about what they can get away with, and other students, including some of the Good Kids, enjoy it.

But when a child brings the Saboteur strategy into a school situation that the students enjoy, his efforts are likely to annoy most of his peers. The strategy has become inappropriate because channels of assertion are open. The disapproval of peers gives the good child-centered teacher an excellent chance of helping the Saboteur break his habit.

Greta, a blue-eyed sprite of eight, was a precocious creator of chaos. Although her classmates were a frisky lot—anything but Good Kids—they found Greta's disruptiveness excessive and sometimes loudly stated their opposition to her tactics.

When I started an improvisational drama elective, I invited Greta to join. She loved the

CHAOS IS US

class, but she was going to sabotage it anyway because that was what she always did. She came to our second meeting sucking loudly and wetly on *something* that bulged in her cheeks. The other students were keenly annoyed.

Knowing Greta, I recognized a setup for verbal sabotage. If I asked her to get rid of the chewing gum, her slobbery reply would be, "Ik nok choon gum." We could then run through some alternatives. Pistachio shells? Bubble gum? A prune being soaked for recess? By the time Greta had exacted her price and agreed to put her weapon in the wastebasket, the pace and spirit of the class would have sagged.

So I innovated. I grasped the back of her neck firmly in my left hand. With my right index finger, I gouged an amorphous glob from her mouth and flipped it into the basket. Wiping my hand on my jeans, I continued with the class. No words were exchanged. The class promptly regained momentum.

On two later occasions when Greta tried sabotage, the other students gathered and talked about the effect she was having on them and about the improvements they would like her to make. The students did the talking as I cuddled Greta on my lap. It required only a few more class meetings for Greta to become an ex-Saboteur.

The lesson is this: if the teacher reacts to sabotage by becoming oppressive, she loses; if she reacts by being easily duped or allowing some students to interfere with the activities of others, she appears weak and also loses. A mixture of openness and firmness generally wins.

Although sabotage is maddeningly hard to deal with in a coercive situation, it is one of the less difficult strategies to overcome in an open school. Basically, the teacher needs to:

keep her affection for the child and sense of humor intact as she analyzes and breaks up each stratagem before it gets off the ground; see that all students have plenty of opportunity for open discussion of their concerns (which will include their annoyance with sabotage); and help the ex-Saboteur find genuine involvement in alternative ways of expressing himself.

Many Saboteurs—even hard-shell cases—respond dramatically when given opportunities to teach younger children. The experience gives them both a constructive sense of power and some empathy for the plight of the teachers.

Even worse, Dr. No

In the transition to openness, the Saboteur is far less likely to blow the teacher's mind than the Dr. No strategist. Kids using the Dr. No approach implicitly insist: You have to try to make me do something so I can refuse to do it.

Juvenile Dr. No's are common in newly founded, child-centered schools. Having learned the rewards of resisting what they are told to do, Dr. No strategists push against authority as they would push against a closed door. When the door flies open, they often fall. Without adult coercion, they are lost. So in an open classroom, they may find it necessary to try to provoke coercion. For example: "You (the teacher) aren't *teaching* us anything." When the teacher makes the mistake of offering a specific task, the strategist, naturally, immediately says no.

Such kids seem to be prompted by two conflicting fears. First, they are afraid of taking the responsibility of freedom. Second, they fear that if they carry out a teacher's assignments or suggestions, their performance will be found inadequate.

One way the teacher can help is to make decisions about what the students should do to get started, being careful that the decisions are based on the real needs of the students and not on the teacher's plans. Unlimited choice is frightening to some children. The teacher can ease anxiety by offering a child only two or three alternative activities and telling him he may choose the one he is going to do.

The fun consumer

The last of the four strategists, the Fun Consumer, is at his or her best in a group situation.

Everyone has known an "entertainer-teacher." He keeps the attention of students by putting on a good show, though such attention should not be mistaken for active involvement and initiative. Nonetheless, if he has talent and keeps his material fresh, he might be a hit. He is also a particularly easy target for the Fun Consumer, who plays on the ham in a teacher by getting him to entertain—day... after day... after day...

While they manage to avoid working at learning, the Fun Consumers as a general rule are not entirely passive. As they lure the star-struck teacher ever deeper into show biz, they gradually become entertainment critics, which gives them the same sense of power other critics enjoy. After an interlude of applauding the teacher's efforts, the Fun Consumers know the hook is set. Then comes the switch: "This isn't *fun*." "We had more fun last week." "Why don't we do fun things like the time we made the red bubbly stuff and got it all over everything?" "Mr. Berle's class last year was more interesting. He was always fun."

One hears actors complain that drama critics are not creative and so they get their rewards by ripping at the bowels of those who are. A teacher who blunders onto the entertainer track might at first be stung by the sudden criticism. The real hurt, though, comes when he realizes that the kids are making him entertain them, when that was not what he wanted to happen. He wanted *them* to be cre-

ative, not an audience for his creativity. I knew a strong man of 30-plus to howl anguished curses on the day he finally recognized that for months he had been the infatuated dupe of a class of nine-year-old Fun Consumers.

The four strategies are, to repeat, deadening for the students who get away with them. The teacher who would help free them must be willing to part with some of her traditional ways. She must stop dispensing her own knowledge in her own way and instead help the children find their own way to their own insights. She must root out of herself the tendency to continue judging, sorting, and classifying students. She must try to make the classroom so stimulating that students don't need to scheme to avoid the crushing boredom.

When she succeeds in doing that, she will not only have cured the strategists; she will, in the process, have become a far better teacher.

At original publication of this article, **Farnum Gray** was an editor of *Learning* magazine.

Coping with excuses

How many times have you heard students cry, "I didn't do it!" "*He* started it!" "I can't help it. That's the way I am"? Excuse making has become a culturally acceptable way of avoiding responsibility. Teachers who want to help students accept responsibility for and change unacceptable behavior patterns need to learn to cope with excuses. That means learning to discourage students from making excuses and to make their excuses ineffective as a way of avoiding the consequences for their actions.

The first step is to recognize an excuse when you hear one. Because excuse making is so often taken for granted, recognizing an excuse is not always easy. The six most common forms of excuses are:

- denial ("I didn't do it.")
- blaming others ("It's her fault.")
- blaming circumstances ("The glass fell off the table.")
- blaming authority ("But that's what I was told to do.")
- personal idiosyncrasies ("I've always had a terrible temper.")
- self-reproach ("I guess I'm just lazy.").

The last two examples are particularly hard to spot because excuses that take the form of self-criticism give the appearance of the student's accepting responsibility for his actions. Such expressions, however, actually excuse behavior by claiming that the behavior is beyond the individual's control. They also tend to be self-fulfilling prophecies: when students continually excuse their behavior with self-critical remarks, they program themselves to become the very behavior problems they describe.

Responses to avoid

- *Don't ask why.* When a student does something he's not supposed to do, a teacher's response most often is to ask, "Why did you do that?" But the question serves no positive end.

First, students rarely know why they have misbehaved. Second, by asking, "Why?" teachers are actually encouraging excuse making by putting the student in a defensive position. When we focus on the explanation rather than on the behavior, we teach students to think up good excuses instead of encouraging them to change their behavior.

• *Don't moralize.* Most students already understand what is considered right and wrong. They know what they *should* do; they just don't want to know how to do it. Moralizing usually has the effect of making students feel hostile and defensive; it emphasizes the power of authority and minimizes the power and responsibility of the individual to control her or his own behavior. Moralizing tends to focus on what *should* have happened instead of on what *did* happen and what can be done about it. It also tends to induce guilt feelings, which make change more difficult because they convince students that they are bad or that they should feel bad. Guilt feelings reinforce a negative self-image and serve as an excuse for not changing.

• *Don't accept students' statements of good intentions.* Like adults, children express good intentions because they believe they are expected to do so and because they want to please. But good intentions, no matter how sincere, are usually a substitute for action. They are an avoidance of responsibility rather than an acceptance of it. If students truly intend to change their behavior, they must come up with a specific and concrete plan to alter their ways of behaving.

My son recently came to me the night before a spelling test to ask for help with his list of spelling words. After we went over the words, I asked him what he might do to improve his study habits. "Study harder!" he answered. It was a classic statement of good intentions, but provided no specific plan of action. After further discussion, he came up with a simple but concrete plan: to go over his list of spelling words several nights before a test rather than wait until the night before the test to try to learn all 20 words on the list.

By coming up with a specific plan, a student makes a commitment to change his behavior. The plan may not always be carried out, but it has a much greater chance of succeeding than a general promise, which, like a New Year's resolution, may be made sincerely but is rarely carried through.

Positive steps

The goal of learning to cope with excuses is not to eliminate all students' explanations of their behavior, but to make it clear that an explanation, no matter how truthful or accurate, does not absolve students from responsibility for their actions.

How many times have you been confronted with a barrage of excuses, yet have been unable to determine what actually happened? One approach, developed by William Glasser, is to ask everyone involved in the incident to state exactly what she or he did. The question should be posed without pinning the blame and without being judgmental. If one student tries to sidestep your question by pointing at others ("Janet threw the eraser at Gail"), simply listen politely and then ask her, "What did you do?" You are not asking for reasons, excuses or justifications; you are simply asking for a statement of what happened.

When excuses are offered, listen to them but focus on the problem and what can be done about it. Ask: "What could you do to make sure that this situation doesn't happen again?" or, "What can you do to solve the problem?" Questions such as these, when asked in a nonjudgmental way, place the responsibility for the student's behavior back on the student. They neither affirm nor deny the validity of an excuse; they sidestep arguments about excuses and focus on the problem at hand and its solution. By asking students to come up with solutions and to follow through on them, teachers encourage students to consider their actions, to plan ahead and to accept responsibility.

Implementing an approach for solving problems and changing unacceptable behavior patterns in students requires perseverance, assertiveness, and good listening skills. The following dialogue exemplifies an effective approach teachers can take to help students go beyond excuse making and accept their part in solving behavior problems:

Teacher: I see you boys have been fighting. (A statement of fact, not an accusation.)

Jay: Zeke started it. (Blaming others.)

Teacher: What did you do, Jay? (Focusing on Jay's behavior.)

Jay: I hit him back. (Blaming others.)

Teacher: You hit Zeke. (Reflective listening; ignoring excuse.)

Jay: But he started it. (Blaming others.)

Teacher: Zeke, what did you do? (Focusing on Zeke's behavior.)

Zeke: He called me a name, so I punched him. (Blaming others.)

Teacher: You punched Jay. (Reflective listening; ignoring excuse.)

Zeke: He made me. If he hadn't called me a name, I wouldn't have punched him. (Blaming others; avoiding responsibility.)

Teacher: You punched Jay. (Focusing on the problem, not pinning blame.)

Zeke: Yes. (Admitting to his action; accepting responsibility.)

Teacher: What else could you do, Zeke, when someone calls you a name? (Focusing on problem behavior and asking for a solution.)

Zeke: I could hit him. (Testing teacher.)

Teacher: What else could you do? (Staying with problem.)

Zeke: I could try not to punch him. (Statement of good intentions, not a specific plan of action.)

Teacher: Yes, that's a good idea, but I think you need to come up with something specific you can *do* to keep yourself from hitting people when you get angry at them.

Zeke: I could walk away.

Teacher: OK. Why don't you try that next time, and we'll see how it works. Jay, what about you? What could you do instead of calling Zeke names?

Jay: Tell him I don't like it when he plays too rough.

Teacher: OK. Let's see how it goes.

This scenario represents only the first stage of an approach to get students to accept responsibility for their behavior. Such situations may not be resolved after only one encounter, but that doesn't mean that the teacher has failed in her approach. It means only that the teacher needs to go back to the problem until the students clearly see their part in it and accept their responsibility to help find the solution.

Robert J. Martin is the author of *Teaching Through Encouragement* (Spectrum Books/Prentice Hall, 1980).

Try homework without tears

Buckets of children's tears and millions of parents' headaches are engendered each year by "homework." Some parents want less, others want more, and most children would like none at all.

A good case can be made for doing away with homework altogether, since no one seems to be able to demonstrate any great value resulting from the grim sessions with smeared purple dittos on the dining room table. As a fine, traditional "old school" English teacher told a group of parents clamoring for more homework: "I have never found a way to teach a child something when I am here and he is at home." Listening to some parents' demands for more work, one sometimes wonders if they are seeking revenge for all those 3 o'clock feedings and peanut butter hand prints.

Adults need to be reminded that school is really very hard work for children. And if we wonder why children resent homework, consider how their working mothers and fathers would feel if they were met at the time clock with a box of additional electronic components to assemble at home, or a stack of additional typing for unpaid evening work. Of course, all of that could only happen over the dead body of the shop steward or the union representative—and rightfully so. As teachers we have an obligation to be very sure that extra work requirements are reasonable and that they really do contribute to learning. We are the only shop stewards our students have.

So, what is homework good for, if anything? A few things—spelling and some arithmetic skills—can be improved with practice. But it is important to know who needs practice, and

what kind. The students who are successful with those repetitive tasks probably don't need much extra practice, but they may enjoy it as a way to polish the skills they already have. But if it isn't fun, you are courting boredom when you assign much homework of this type. Boredom, in turn, may mean a loss of interest that will actually reduce skills. So, for good students, it is wise to use drill-type homework sparingly, with considerable variety, and be ready to drop it altogether when boredom develops.

Drills and do-mores

Drill homework for students who have difficulty with skill subjects gives mixed results. If the student doesn't really understand the work, he may be religiously practicing errors over and over—or he may simply deepen his confusion by trying a variety of approaches, most of which are wrong. A friend of mine who worked as a reader for correspondence courses showed me the papers of one of her students. It had taken three exchanges of letters to his home at a lighthouse on the Pacific to clarify why 21 take away 1 didn't leave 2.

If a youngster really does understand, some drill may help him develop mastery. But if he feels "dumber" because he has more homework than others, or because his grades are so much lower than others, the homework may do more harm than good.

Why not make the requirements much more adaptable to the child's life? There are times in any child's life when there is something far more important to do than homework—visit Grandma, ride a new bike, go to an auction, or take a stomachache to bed. Rigidly scheduled homework may be unfair. If you feel you must use homework, why not make materials available and allow the child to choose what he will do and, within limits, when?

A different name for homework would help. How about *do-mores?* The assignment might be to complete two or three *do-mores* sometime during the week. This allows the youngster to plan his time—a skill that will probably be far more valuable to him than memorizing spelling words. He can double up and do them all in one night if he has personal projects on other nights that need his attention. It is hardly fair to insist that all his own and his family's plans for the evening be changed abruptly because the teacher decides to give homework at dismissal time.

If allowed to choose which subjects he will work on, a student may, for a time, take home the ones that seem shortest (or easiest) and not hate ones he most needs work on. But, over a period of time, he will discover that he can help himself more by choosing to work on problem areas, or he may ask the teacher for advice on which subjects to do. (When he asks, that is a good time to discuss alternatives, but leave the choice to the student. If he is able to choose, for himself, the harder but more useful material, his grown-up feeling will be a happy dividend.) A student who continues to avoid a problem area is sending a clear message that he is afraid of the material and needs some special help, in which case just carrying the homework home would be futile anyway.

Enrichment activities

There is a second and much larger area of activity that is ideal for homework. This includes enrichment activities, enlarging experiences, opportunities for communication. It is difficult to require that all younsters go to the museum this week—or even this month. Family plans often make that impossible. But a full semester plan, from which one activity is chosen by the child each week, allows him to arrange things so that he gets to do them all without tears or tension at home. It also will add to the classroom experience to have someone speak who has just been to the museum, or the zoo, to see the very latest additions. Reports are much more interesting and enlightening if everyone didn't see the same things on the same day. A semester plan can be as varied and imaginative as you can make it, and it gives both the child and his family time to save up the money or arrange the transportation needed for a particular trip or to locate the special pictures or books or other materials needed. A clever name for semester plans helps, too. I'm partial to "My Tour of the World Plan," but your children can think of a different one.

Do-mores and World Tours are also a magic solution if your school has to be shut down for labor problems, budget disasters, or weather or fuel emergencies. Every child can go home with a pocketful of extra do-mores and make plans to complete his World Tour before school begins again.

Your World Tour should fit your students' needs and the requirements of your curriculum. There follows a collection of possibilities for a variety of age groups and subject areas.

✓ The world tour plan

● Make a map of somewhere you would like to go or somewhere you have been. Put your map up on the bulletin board.
● Visit the zoo (or an art gallery, or a factory, or a museum, or a concert). Tell the class at least five interesting things about your visit.
● Learn a new poem and say it for the class.
● Spend an hour watching a dog, or a bird, or a worm, or any other animal or insect. Write

down four things you discovered.

● Make up a menu for one entire day's meals for your family. Go to the grocery store and find the food you need. Figure out what it would cost to make the meals.

● Think of something you can do that others in the class may not be able to do—or learn something new. Plan how you would teach it to the class when you are ready.

● Make a puzzle. Bring it to class so everyone can work on it.

● Go to work with your father or mother or some other adult and find out what that person does. Write down all the reasons you would like to do the same job and all the reasons you wouldn't like to.

● Choose a country you are interested in and make a scrapbook about the country with clippings, brochures, and pictures. Write a letter to the ambassador from that country asking him to send material for your scrapbook.

● Listen to the national news and read the newspaper. When you come across an issue you feel strongly about, study the issue and write a petition to the proper officer (President, congressman, governor, mayor) stating what you think about the problem. Get 25 people to sign your petition.

● Make a book. Plan a story or an article and write or type it. Find or make pictures to illustrate the story. Make a cover for the book. Bring the book to school so others in the class can read it.

● Build something or make something. Bring it to show the class. Be prepared to show the class how you made it.

● Make up a new game. Make all the pieces you need to play it. Bring it to class and teach everyone how to play.

● Take a pet census in your building or on your block. Go to the library and find what species each animal is. Report to the class.

● Go to the park or some other place where you can quietly watch several people you do not know. Watch for at least one hour. Write down five things you discovered.

● Write a history of your family (or your school, or your neighborhood, or your church).

● Watch a favorite movie or television story. Write a story of your own with the same characters that tells what you think happened to the characters after the show's ending.

● Read a book about a famous person. Make a hat or part of a costume he or she would wear. Wear it to school and tell everyone about the book.

Students will do the more practical do-mores more willingly if they are allowed choices and flexibility in schedules. Of course, educators would never choose a program because it was easier for the teacher—but will you really miss all those extra homework papers?

Jean Gatch, formerly a teacher and associate professor of humanities at New York University in Plattsburgh, N.Y., is now a free-lance writer. She is the author of several books for teachers and of a recent book for small children, *School Makes Sense...Sometimes* (Human Science Press).

How to create learning areas in any classroom

The problem in today's informal classrooms is one of making many things possible and subject to change without engendering chaos; of enabling simultaneous and differing activities without ensuing conflict; of finding ways for children to explore and create on the basis of their own initiative, not someone else's; of establishing social situations in which children learn from children and other adults, not from the teacher alone.

The physical and curricular consequences of this new pedagogy may seem insurmountably formidable to teachers functioning on limited budgets and with outmoded furnishings, who must work within the four walls of an old 1,000-square-foot shell or within a totally undifferentiated open plan stretching the length of an entire school floor. Yet, a few principles of organization, a bit of ingenious scrounging, the supportive labor of children and parents who need possess only basic painting, carpentry and sewing skills, can accomplish most of the transformations.

Each teacher should begin only with those changes that feel comfortable—perhaps just a carpeted reading corner or a cozy armchair at first. Ultimately, however, success in redesigning the classroom depends on the structural supports built into the physical arrangement and on concern for seemingly minute details of design and display.

Organizing the classroom into different activity areas makes it possible to centralize within one physical space the materials, surfaces and people who will be involved in the functions of a particular activity. Work spaces should be located in terms of their functional relationship both to one another (messy versus clean, noisy versus quiet) and to the fixed features of the room (protected and exposed spaces, lighting conditions, exits, primary pathways, closets, sinks). Ideally, some areas should be expandable as interests and numbers dictate, but some should be intentionally small, soft and cozy, thus minimizing interference and cross-area traffic. Others, perhaps those involving messy materials and a great deal of movement, should be open to general access and perusal.

Teachers have found that most areas should be scaled to accommodate about four children comfortably. Physically limiting the number of occupants in an area allows for quiet interaction and discourages the potentially distracting influence of a large group. It also insures that children will be dispersed throughout the room, making maximal use of all the facilities available under conditions of minimal congestion.

As an area is created, special attention should be paid to the organization and display of its materials. Like the store-keeper who arranges his merchandise aesthetically, the teacher may, by the placement and attractiveness of the materials displayed, capture a child's attention and curiosity and entice him to an area and the things within it. Once there, the child should also be able to find and replace easily the materials he needs for his activity.

Since children have little tolerance for searching out and setting up things, it is essential to balance the richness that entices against the clutter that distracts and discourages. The easiest way to encourage use of and a respect for materials, and a cooperative spirit of cleaning up, is to have the attractiveness of the classroom itself convey such respect.

The keys to creating and defining an area are the furnishings and the boundaries or dividers which will hold the materials and physically separate the area from the rest of the room. Wherever possible, the scale (height and bulk) and number of pieces of furniture used should relate to the child's height and size rather than to the teacher's. The environment must not dwarf and dominate the child but should provide him with a feeling of comfort and control, perhaps even of power.

In addition to furnishings and dividers, color, texture (carpets, pillows), lighting, changes in level and in scale, living creatures like animals and plants, and the placement of objects, mobiles or structures from various heights overhead also help establish the tone or mood of an area. They define it in visual rather than physical terms. The distinction is important, for total reliance on defining physical space, while encouraging seclusion and reducing distraction, may also limit the child's ability to keep in touch with other activities going on around him. Since children are often enticed by others to explore unfamiliar realms, possibilities for cross-area "interaction" need the same attention dedicated to privacy and control. In the final analysis, it is the life of the classroom—the children, their inquiries and creations—which should stand out both physically and visually.

Defining areas

When defining special areas for specific activities, consider five elements: location, based on whether the activity needs protection or exposure; boundaries, which can vary in height, mass, and permeability; work and sitting surfaces appropriate to the activity; storage or display of materials that are accessible to children and related to the functional activities of the area; and a mood or personality that distinguishes each one from all others.

This corner of an *art area* fulfills such requirements superbly. Readily accessible are an easel, paper, paints and brushes, smocks to protect clothing; a table plus boards and instruments for working with clay; a plastic bucket in which clay is stored; and (not shown) shelves on which finished products may dry. Reachable by pulley is an overhead rack which keeps drying paintings from cluttering the floor. The easel, which accommodates varying sizes of paper and allows communication between children working side by side, was made from a 4-by-8-foot sheet of Homosote, an inexpensive fiberboard sold by lumber companies. The surface is washable when covered with two coats of polyurethane over two coats of semigloss paint. Homosote panels may be mounted floor to ceiling to create a "painting wall," or cut to fit backs of bookcases and cabinets, providing an excellent bulletin board surface for individual areas.

The table, chairs, shelves and bookracks in a *writing and reading corner* provide the five elements essential to area definition. The single area of the classroom that it's most important to "soften" is undoubtedly the reading corner which, even if it accommodates ten children, should always suggest coziness and quietude. Simple reading corners can be created using a few cushions (or a mattress) placed near shelves that display books and double as area dividers.

A *manipulative-game area* can be designed to incorporate a post (despite its location in open space) to have definition through a playful, coordinated color scheme. An area divider can be constructed from two 3-foot-long fiberboard tubes (available free of charge from most paper companies) cut vertically to support a 4-by-6-foot sheet of Tri-Wall cardboard inserted between them.

Since supports are free standing, both sides of the panels may be used to define areas. Interesting entrances and views can be designed by varying the shape and height of the panels. Plywood, coated with chalkboard paint and placed between such posts, will make a blackboard immediately available to reading and writing areas.

Easy-to-make furnishings

Tables of varying shapes and heights can be built from telephone spools or from fiberboard tubes topped with plywood. (Counter-height tables make especially good work surfaces for some activities.) Stools made from tubes can be individually decorated by the children and used for personal storage. A carpeted board can be slung between a window sill and a bookcase of the same height, creating spaces above and below.

Platforms and risers

Low, carpeted platforms and risers can be constructed by placing boards, or two layers of Tri-Wall cardboard, across a series of fiberboard tubes cut to desired height. This has proven to be one of the simplest yet most dramatic ways to add cozy areas and additional seating, reading, and working spaces to a uniform expanse of classroom. Such variations in height afford individuals and small groups a measure of separateness. Two tiers of risers in a corner enable large groups to gather intimately, improve the quality of group meetings, and let all the children see the teacher and the activities. Depending upon construction and size, risers may double as storage compartments.

A slab of wood only 8 inches off the ground provides new perspectives on paint, clay, or construction activities and helps young children "get on top of" their work.

Private spaces

Small, portable private spaces for reading, resting, or just getting away from it all can be provided anywhere in the classroom by means of cardboard barrels obtainable free of charge from chemical companies and hospitals. Available in several heights, the barrels must be a minimum of 2 feet in diameter to accommodate an elementary school child. Different decorations and openings add variety, and linings such as foam, Mylar, or fake fur provide interesting textural experiences, especially for the very young.

Supplementary resources

1. Olds, A.R. "Designing Developmentally Optimal Classrooms for Children with Special Needs," in *Special Education and Development: Perspectives on Young Children with Special Needs* (edited by Meisels, S., University Park Press, 1979), for a comprehensive, step-by-step guide to planning classrooms for children.
2. Drew, W., et al. *Motivating Today's Students* (Learning Handbook, October 1974).
3. Alexander, C., et al. *A Pattern Language* (Oxford University Press, 1977).
4. For information on purchasing Tri-Wall material, write to Tri-Wall Containers, Inc., Plainsville, N.Y.; Butler, Ind.; Pinedale, Calif.
5. "Building with Tubes" and "Building with Cardboard," Education Development Center, Newton, Mass.

Anita Rui Olds, PhD, teaches in the Department of Child Study at Tufts University and is principal of Anita Olds & Associates, Consultants, Environmental Facilities for Children in Cambridge, Mass.

3
BOOST SELF-ESTEEM AND MOTIVATION

Today's teachers understand the importance of students' psychological well-being in the learning process. Vital to such well-being is their self-esteem. With this in mind, teachers consider the potential impact on self-esteem of classroom events and interactions a major concern. They know that helping each child see himself as a worthy person helps create enthusiastic learners.

Read on for some classroom-tested strategies other teachers have found useful to help their students strengthen a positive sense of self.

You can't have learning without self-esteem

A poster with a bright yellow-and-orange flower proclaims to a fourth-grade class,

I am so glad you are here.
It helps me to realize
how beautiful my world is.

A gray poster with a weed that has produced an exquisite, vibrantly colored flower says to the children,

You don't really know
how great you can be,
how much you can love,
what you can accomplish—
what your potential is...

The school bell rings. The class president steps up and calls the class to order. The vice-president determines absentees. The secretary records the lunch count, then goes to the blackboard to write down "needs" and "problems." The class members raise their hands and indicate their needs for the day. After a brief discussion, the class translates its list into a meaningful schedule to meet those needs. The teacher will accept the schedule if he feels comfortable with it; if not, he will express his discomfort and suggest a compromise. The planning meeting is adjourned. As the children set about their agreed-upon tasks, the noise level begins to drop. The record monitor selects and plays a record.

The atmosphere in this fourth-grade classroom is one of quiet contentment and curiosity, of children, working in small groups or alone, who want to learn and succeed and who have chosen their own course to accomplish these things. The teacher moves from one group to another quietly asking, "May I help?" To another he gives a "warm fuzzy," consisting of a hug, a touch on the shoulder, or a smile, trying to make contact with each child.

A group of five boys has formed a "dinosaur center." Here they read about dinosaurs, write letters to editors of dinosaur books, consult the encyclopedia, make models, and draw pictures in preparation for teaching the class.

Judy and Alice are playing cards, not with spades and diamonds, but with word cards. Judy is bright; Alice is a borderline educationally handicapped child.

Alex greets a visitor and offers to show him the various interest centers. He quietly and confidently explains how each area is set up and proudly shows the visitor his own work. Last year Alex experienced headaches, stomach cramps, and tears each school-day morning. This year he comes to school happily, confident that he will succeed.

In one corner of the room, four children are sitting on comfortable old couches, reading and spelling. Sometimes they help each other; sometimes they work alone. They seem confident and happy.

A different classroom

What is different about this classroom? The children are learning to accept *the responsibility for their own education*. This classroom is a microsociety in which the children learn skills of decision making, communication, self-management, self-motivation, and problem solving. And they are learning these skills as a normal process of living. The goal here is to create learners by helping each child to see himself as a worthy individual so that he can realize his full and unique potential.

When using traditional methods, the teacher is "in charge of" the children and generally considers learning to be the dissemination of information. He tells, decides, judges, and tests. He employs competitive techniques; he passes some and fails others. When a class is taught as a whole, the needs and feelings of individual children are rarely met, and their uniqueness is usually denied.

Typically, with the use of traditional methods, only a few children become actively involved in their own learning and thus motivated to learn or to direct their own energies. Newer methods are more effective for creating classroom learners.

Self-esteem vital

The development of self-esteem is the primary prerequisite to learning. Children must be heard if they are to feel that they count and are worthy people. When we say to a child, "I *like* the way this is done," "I'm *pleased* with the way this is written," "I *like* the way you answered," we recognize something that has been done as being worthwhile, and we reflect this worth in a *specific* example. In "reflecting" his worth we enhance his well-being.

When the child feels good about himself, he can begin to invest in the world of people and things. He can risk learning something new, meeting new friends, playing new games. But he will not risk a new venture if he fears rejection or failure. Thus we must establish an environment that is consistent in nurturing and honoring the special worth and value of the child. When the child begins to develop self-esteem, he is saying to himself, "I am comfortable with myself; I won't be hurt or fail; I know I have an environment of love, affection, and warmth; *now* I can do what I need to do!"

Planning limits

Working successfully with children in a free learning environment requires adequate planning and a basic understanding of the essential tools to be employed. First of all, stable limits must be established. Sensible limits for behavior allow the students maximum freedom while protecting their psychological and physical well-being. Very early in the year, rules for the class as well as for the teacher can be agreed upon and posted. Our fourth-grade class, for example, agreed upon the following rules for the classroom:

Rules for the Class
1. Do not yell.
2. Do not cheat.
3. Do not hit or bite.
4. Do not interrupt.
5. Do not be critical of others.
6. Treat others as you would like to be treated.

Rules for the Teacher
1. Do not yell.
2. Do not hit us.
3. Do not tell us what to do.
4. Do not be mean.
5. Do not keep us after school.
6. Do not keep us in at recess.

Planning student involvement

Involvement is a key to success in programs of self-enhancing education. Involve the children in active co-planning and in self-management as early in the year as possible. Allow them to make their own decisions within the established structure of the classroom. Allow them to express their feelings, to solve problems, to communicate with their peers, and to relate to other people. This is affective teaching—accepting, listening, honoring, and trusting. But keep in mind that the environment that makes it safe to risk these things must be firmly established.

Planning for change

An ideal vehicle for initiating change and for creating a classroom environment that is responsive to the emotional as well as intellectual needs of children is the classroom meeting.

Basically, there are three kinds of classroom meetings:
(1) *open meetings* designed to give vent to covert feelings;
(2) *problem-solving meetings* to resolve obvious conflict;
(3) *decision-making meetings* to determine a course of action.

The setting for all classroom meetings is simple. Students and teacher sit in a large circle with one of them designated as discussion leader. In the beginning, the teacher will be the discussion leader, but as the children learn, they will be able to take over the role.

Consider this scenario as it unfolded in our fourth grade class. This meeting solved a problem every teacher can recognize. As the children flood into the room after recess, Mark strides up to the teacher. His usually amiable face is set in grim lines, and tears smudge his chubby cheeks.

Mark tells the teacher that the other kids called him names on the playground. He is particularly upset with Jon, who teased him about being overweight.

"If you and the class will help me, I'd like to tell Jon how angry I am. I want an open class meeting," Mark requests.

During the preceding months, this class held many classroom meetings, and now every child in the room knows he is safe in saying just how he feels. He will be listened to, his feelings respected and his suggestions acted upon. An open meeting is warranted by Mark's anger at Jon.

The open meeting

Within minutes of the call, the class has regrouped in one corner of the room. The teacher checks the chart and finds that Peggy is listed as this week's discussion leader.

"Peggy, would you be comfortable leading the meeting today?" inquires the teacher. Peggy nods assent.

"Who called for this open meeting?" Peggy asks.

"I did," Mark swivels around to face Jon. "I'm really angry with you, Jon, for calling me Fatty. It makes me feel bad. I know I'm overweight, and I don't need you to remind me of it every minute."

Jon squirms uncomfortably. "I was only kidding."

Peggy interrupts to remind Jon that he is to reflect Mark's statement first. Jon faces Mark again. "You're angry with me for teasing you about your weight, right?" Jon repeats.

Mark looks down. "My mother has been after me about losing weight. Every day she bugs me about eating. I just don't know what to do about it."

Larry's face is sympathetic. "I feel the same way you do. The guys call me fat, too. I try not to pay attention to them."

Brian, Jon's friend, enters the conversation. "But you are chubby, Mark."

Jon chuckles and addresses Mark again. "I like to get a rise out of you and have you chase me."

The discussion leader has to intervene again. "Do you feel you've been heard, Mark?" Mark shakes his head no. "OK," says Peggy. "Jon, please think about how Mark feels."

As he backtracks and voices the other boy's words, Jon tries to get in touch with Mark's feelings. "You wish I'd stop teasing you, Mark?"

Mark sighs with relief. "I think you've really heard me now, Jon."

Although the dialogue has been primarily between Mark and Jon, it has created an air of acceptance in the classroom. Soon the other children begin to contribute their perceptions and feelings. The hurt feelings have been soothed and new understandings arrived at. Hate and anger have mellowed into compassion and concern. Jon is sobered. He doesn't apologize to Mark, but he promises, "Mark, now that I know how you feel, I won't tease you anymore."

Despite the fact that the subject matter in an open meeting is unstructured—i.e., nothing is taboo—the meeting itself follows a definite format. First, the person calling the meeting states his concern. Mark, for example, said, *"I* am angry..." He didn't say how his friend felt, or how the class felt. Because young children derive strength from parental authority, they are prone to say "we" or "my mother says" rather than "I." It is important that the concerned individual states how *he* feels and what triggered his reaction.

The next person speaking has to "reflect" (restate in a nonjudgmental way) what the person before him has said, and hopefully reflect that other person's feelings, too. Then he may offer his own views.

The discussion leader plays a crucial role. He keeps the discussion on the topic and makes sure that everyone reflects and that everyone feels that he has been heard. Furthermore, the leader has to see to it that a dialogue, once begun, is completed without interruption. He does this by simply asking if the dialogue is complete before he calls on someone else.

It takes time to train discussion leaders and the class as a whole; it may take several weeks or several months before everyone functions effectively in the meetings. Even while the group is learning, however, the time spent in discussion is not wasted. The experience of participating in these sessions helps students to grow emotionally. Eventually they realize both that they are competent human beings themselves and that others have thoughts and feelings. They become more open, more trusting, more caring. They learn to express their emotions constructively.

The problem-solving meeting

While the open meeting clears the air of hostile feelings, the problem-solving meeting attempts to resolve other kinds of conflicts. The setting for problem solving is the same as in the open meeting. The problem is stated by the person calling for the meeting—in the following example, the teacher. He doesn't like a disorderly room and states his concern.

"The clutter in this classroom disturbs me. I'm really upset. Can we talk about my problem?"

Class members raise their hands, eager to discuss the teacher's problem. They are called upon by the discussion leader. Kenny is the first to speak.

"You're upset by this messy classroom?" Kenny is checking back to make sure he's received the correct message. A nod assures him, and he continues. "I've cleaned up my mess, but the others haven't."

Lisa concurs with Kenny. "I agree that the room looks terrible."

Kenny realizes that Lisa has heard only part of his statement, so he clarifies the point: "But I've done my part of the cleanup."

Lisa offers a solution to the problem. "I

think we should have a 10-minute cleanup after our projects, and everyone should help."

At this juncture, the discussion leader interrupts. "Lisa, don't you think you're giving a solution? Can you wait with your suggestion until we talk about solutions?" Lisa agrees.

Steve reflects Kenny. "You've cleaned up your mess, and I've cleaned up mine. I don't see why we need a classroom meeting to discuss this."

Chris raises his hand. "Are you saying, Steve, that this isn't a problem since you've cleaned up your part?"

Steve affirms that is exactly what he is saying.

Chris nods. "Well, I don't agree with you, Steve, because there is junk all over the room where it doesn't belong. I think we should have some rules about cleaning up."

The discussion leader again has to put the discussion back on the track. "I'm wondering if we are trying to solve the problem before we know what that problem really is."

Kathy looks thoughtful as she admits, "I left some of my brushes in the sink because I wanted to get back to my desk. I forgot to wash them."

Brad perks up. "Kathy, you forgot to wash your brushes. I left some paper lying around because I forgot. Sorry about that."

The discussion continues in this vein. After a time, the leader asks if anyone can define the hidden problem. The hidden problem underlies the stated problem and generally gives rise to it. The children realize that they were so excited by their individual projects that many forgot about their responsibility for the classroom. The leader states this generalization and asks if there is a consensus that it is the real problem.

Now it is time to think of solutions that will be acceptable to all those involved. Lisa re-states her earlier solution—that there be a 10-minute cleanup after art work. John agrees with Lisa. Now Rebecca reflects John and Lisa, then adds to the original idea. "I think 10 minutes is enough cleanup time. I'd be happy to wash brushes. I enjoy doing that."

Deanne's face lights up. "I really like the idea of you doing the brushes, Rebecca. I hate that job. But I'll clean up my side of the room."

Many children volunteer to take responsibility for part of the cleanup. They are all set to agree that they've solved the problem to everyone's satisfaction when Allen breaks in with a divergent idea. "I don't think we ought to waste 10 minutes cleaning up. We won't have enough time for PE. Let's clean up after PE."

For the first time since he stated the problem, the teacher speaks. He discusses his discomfort at the idea of leaving a messy room. Allen reflects the teacher, and then adds, "I don't like the idea of taking 10 minutes to clean up, because I work slowly and won't ever finish my project."

Pat has been sitting morosely in the circle. Now he says, "I agree with Allen. I like doing projects, but I'm slow, too, and just barely finish in the hour we have."

Shelly has an inspiration. "Why don't we each do our own cleanup as soon as we finish, and those of us who have time will take care of the rest of the room during the last 10 minutes. Those who have to can use the whole hour. A few people shouldn't make that much mess."

The discussion leader sums up the solutions and asks, "Do you all feel comfortable with these solutions?" All do.

The teacher is pleased, too. "You've come up with some good solutions to my problem. I'm also delighted about the problem-solving skills you've used during this meeting. Shall we try these solutions and see how they work?"

The class is enthusiastic. A 1-week trial period is set to evaluate how well this approach will work. At the end of that time, another class meeting will be held to assess the progress.

Looking back, we can see five steps involved in the problem-solving meeting:

1. The problem is stated by the person with the problem.

2. The hidden problem is brought into the open by the discussion leader's questions.

3. Many solutions are proposed, and these are incorporated into an action plan.

4. A trial time period is set.

5. At the end of the trial period, the solutions are evaluated.

Decision-making meetings

While the subject matter of both the open and the problem-solving meetings can be whatever bothers a particular individual, the content of the decision-making meeting is highly structured. This is the meeting that decides how to go about doing that which must be done and generally pertains to matters brought up by a governing adult—a state law, the school board, the principal, perhaps the teacher.

Although the state may set the curricula for a particular grade, it does not specify in what manner this material should be covered. This leaves room for innovation. In conventional classrooms, the teacher decides which projects and activities are best. Often these result in good learning experiences for the children. But the teacher is only one resource, one person. The class is comprised of many individuals, each with his own background of expertise.

Who knows better what interests the child than the child himself?

Learning requires involvement. A child can sit before a lecturer for hours or be in a library surrounded by thousands of books, but he won't learn until he takes the responsibility for learning. Involving him in the decision-making process is a basic first step in this direction.

The setting, format, and skills necessary for this type of meeting are similar to those used during the open and problem-solving meetings. Students and teacher work together to discover different ways of learning. There may be as many ways as there are children. During the decision-making meeting, each child generates his own ideas about how he wants to approach learning, and the teacher agrees that these are valid ways. A joint decision is then incorporated into a contract. Sharing the responsibility for how he is to learn motivates the child to learn. In effect, the decision-making meeting gives the student back to himself.

It is a good idea to keep a written or taped record of all classroom meetings, but it is vital that records be kept of the decision-making meetings. Just as a discussion leader is listed for each week, a recorder should also be listed. The recorder takes notes or operates a tape recorder. These notes are then put into a binder, posted on a bulletin board or stored on cassettes accessible to all the children. These minutes not only record what has been agreed to or accomplished, but also enable the children to see for themselves the steady growth they have made in the acquisition of skills.

All kinds of classroom meetings encourage change, as well as showing children how to cope with change. Youngsters, unhampered by traditional modes of viewing things, think in surprisingly original ways. As they come to believe in themselves and in their own abilities and worth, they become more flexible and evaluative, which makes effective change possible.

But it must also be remembered that change is painstakingly evolutionary. All too often, administrators and principals agree that an emphasis on the development of self-esteem produces healthier and happier children, but they are afraid that innovative teaching methods will "rock the boat" and incur the wrath of parents. Thus teachers trying to help children in new ways must be prepared to defend their programs at every step.

The truth is that change occurs only when the parents of the community allow it. Administrators are generally not free to educate in the way they feel is best. The community, therefore, must be educated about the nature and necessity of the changes taking place.

To sum up, we must teach three basics:

We must further the respect of each child for his own identity—the knowledge that he is important, that he counts, that he is part of the community.

We must teach the skills of communication.

And we must teach the skill of decision making, allowing children to decide for themselves and thus grow in their own uniqueness.

We must, in short, educate children to educate themselves. Our old methods have failed; we have no choice now but to seek and use the new.

Jerry Vogel teaches fourth through sixth grades in an alternative program at Monta Vista Elementary School, Cupertino, Calif.
Annette Smith, formerly an elementary school teacher, is a free-lance writer.

Every child has high worth

Wouldn't it be wonderful if every child learned in school that he was important, cared for, listened to, loved as a person who could also extend himself in loving ways? Certainly there would be less failure, fear, and hatred for school and instead more personal growth, intimacy, and happiness. But this need not be an idle wish. It will happen when teachers care as much about, and work as hard at, nurturing healthy self-respect in their students as they do about educating them.

We teamed with the staff of a school for children with learning problems to develop some strategies to promote feelings of self-worth and well-being in elementary school students. These kids were variously described as "difficult to reach," "uncontrollable" or "outside the reach of the normal classroom." They come to regard themselves as "stupid," "dumb," "weird," "crazy," "creepy." We felt that through values clarification and validation strategies we could counter feelings of failure, shame, and fear, and enhance creative growth and feelings of love.

We developed these strategies to treat troubled, failure-oriented children, but we recommend the same strategies as preventive measures as well. Too many schoolchildren, even those who aren't "difficult," feel helpless, confused, and angry, often at a very early age. Even by first grade many can't separate "I'm not very good at reading (or writing, or arithmetic)" from "I'm not very good." And then so much of what they do grows out of negative self-esteem and continues to prove to them how bad they really are.

The elementary school teacher can easily use some of these techniques in her own classroom. None of the strategies requires a child to read or write, so all can be used at the earliest levels of education.

Strategy 1: "What Is Important?"

This activity is really a direction setter. In a rather enjoyable way (certainly a nonthreatening way) it helps us as teachers learn about our kids' priorities and identifies areas for follow-up where the potential is high for us to have a positive, meaningful impact.

The teacher plays the simple song "What Is Important?" on guitar or piano as the class sings. When the children reach the line, "Tell me if you know," any student may fill in the following line with a word he feels is important. The song is repeated as long as the children have ideas.

As each new word is offered, it is recorded on a sheet of newsprint or on the blackboard. Our "sing-along" produced the following important words: *food, school, birds, pets, people, ducks, math, buses, we.*

After discussing the list and the reasons for some of the choices, the children rank-order their top four items. Our group voted the following:

1. *We,* each of us, are important.
2. Other *people* are important, too.
3. *Food* is important.
4. *Pets* are important.

Now, with a freely chosen set of our students' affirmed values, we sought ways to integrate them into a child-centered program. For the first two priorities—*"We* are important" and "Other *people* are important"—we developed specific strategies (see Strategies 2 and 3). We didn't develop strategies using the other two priorities, *pets* and *food,* but instead built them into the daily life of the classroom.

What is important?

Words and Music by Marianne Simon

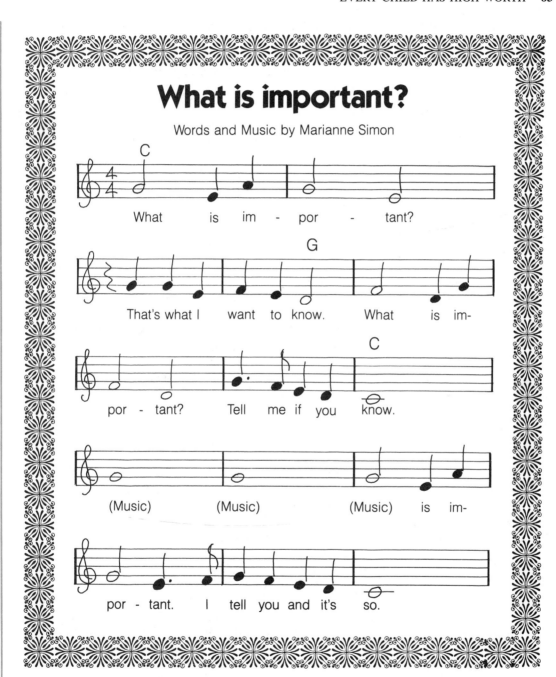

We set aside a room for pets, with lizards, insects, gerbils, fish, crawdads, all lovingly brought from home, cared for, and housed, with parents' happy consent.

As for food, we planned our own menus and did our own shopping, cooking, baking. When a child had the urge to nibble, he could go to a cupboard supplied with fruit, cookies, and cereal. And we had a regular snack time every day.

From our own experiences we believe the values, needs, and expressions of these troubled children closely parallel those expressed by children in the regular classroom. We do recognize, however, that priorities will vary. For example, in poverty areas "food" might well be the first consideration; in urban areas, children might not list "ducks" and "birds." (Our children happen to live by the Rocky Mountain Flyway, a well-traveled route of ducks, geese, and other migratory birds.)

Strategy 2:
A love and care group

We've made it a practice to begin values-clarification workshops by asking if there is anyone in the group who is anxious about a personal problem. These concerns are then discussed, and closure is sought through the considertion of alternative solutions so that the participants are, from then on, more able to function without the anxiety of unfinished business cluttering their minds. Children also are not free to learn if they have such inter-ferences. So each morning a short session of 10 to 15 minutes was devoted to children's needs:

Has everyone had breakfast? If not, we feed them.

Does someone's neck hurt? Massage may help.

Is there an unsettled argument? Let's talk about it.

Does someone need a hug? A pencil? A new start? A rest period? What?

Children soon learn that there are people willing to help them and they become less and less inhibited in asking for what they really need.

Strategy 3:
A sharing time group

The last 15 minutes of each day concluded with small groups sharing some of the day's experiences:

What, for you, was the high point of the day?

What new things did you learn about yourself? About others?

Did someone do something nice for you today?

How did you help someone?

Is there anything you would like to change?

We also included in this period strategies for discovery:

"I learned that I..."

"I wonder about..."

"I wish..."

These experiences provide simple ways for children to clearly state a belief and urge others in gentle, caring ways to give consideration to an idea that may be new to them and thus afford an opportunity for change and growth in their lives. There is no "you should" or "you must" implied, but instead a simple invitation to express oneself.

As an extension of our end-of-the-day sharing group, each Thursday morning an hour called "Validation Time" was set aside for the staff and children to meet in a circle to consider their personal strengths and values. It has been our conviction that as we consider good aspects of ourselves, we learn to develop and grow even more in healthy directions; we make ourselves better people. We feel this accent on the positive is more productive than thinking only in negative, diagnostic terms: "What's wrong with me? I must change! Quick, tell me how, write a prescription." Strategies 4 through 8 promote these concepts of validation and growth.

Strategy 4: A good things list

As the children sit in a circle, a sponge ball is thrown to a child to catch as a signal for him to sit in the "spotlight chair." Then the other children spontaneously suggest things the child in the chair already does well. These things (we usually limited these to two or three items so that the session would move rapidly enough to include every child) are used to begin a list—"A Good Things List"—that is posted in the hallways, on the doors and in the classrooms for everyone to see. Each day the children are encouraged to think of the good qualities of their friends, and when they think of something, to ask a teacher to help them write it down. The list can include what a person does well at home, alone, with friends, at school or other places. Periodically the children tour the building to check all the lists and take pride with each other in their accomplishments.

Strategy 5: Things I love

Tom T. Hall is a storyteller and composer. In one of his songs, "I Love," he sings about all the simple things he has found in his life that are lovable. We introduce this strategy by either playing "I Love" or reading the lyrics. Among the things he loves are: "old pickup trucks," "slow-moving trains," "sleep without

dreams," "pictures of my friends," "Pepsi in a glass," "onions" and, above all, "you."

We then ask the children to draw a picture of something they love—a person, something in nature, an object. After they finish their drawings, they share their pictures and tell *what* they love and *how* they give love in that particular instance. After each child's explanation the teacher summarizes on newsprint "Ways We Love":

"What do you love?"..."I love birds and flowers."

"How do you love?"..."I would never shoot a bird or pick a flower."

Teacher writes, *"Caring is a way of giving love."*

Our list showed these ways of loving: caring, giving gifts, protecting, hugging, sharing those things we love, considering others' feelings, smiling, helping, talking, and being friendly. Each is a special way of saying, "I love you."

There are many other questions and activities to help children consider love:

How have you been loved this week?

Who loves you?

What loving things have you done these past few days?

Notice how others respond to your love.

Care for a plant or an animal for one week and list the different ways you showed the plant or animal love.

Choose a particular tree to really know. Draw a picture of your tree throughout the year. Note the many seasonal changes. (To love deeply we must know deeply; in this deep relatedness we experience valuing.)

Strategy 6: Peak experiences

In this strategy we interview each child individually and ask him to remember a time when he was really happy, a time when he felt good and was having a lot of fun and really enjoying life. We jot down each detail as the child dictates his experience, then quickly sequence the details into a short paragraph that is read to the child for his additional comments. We then ask the child to keep his story a secret because, with his permission, it will be read to the group later and the children will be asked to guess who told the story. (An interesting variation is to tape-record the interviews for playback later.)

When the group meets, the teacher reads each story and asks the class to guess who told it. Then the question is asked, "From the story, can you determine what each person values?" Example: "I remember a time when I was six years old and we went to visit my grandmother in the summertime. She lived out on a desert. They caught me a horse and I rode him all by myself. It was my first time ever to be in the desert and I saw squirrels and lots of birds. It was also the first time I ever rode on a horse and that's what made me feel happy."

This child values: grandmother (older people); deserts, summertime, squirrels, birds (nature); riding by herself (independence, adventure).

The child is then told by the group that her values are accepted and valuable because they came from her own experience and were freely chosen as being good for her at that time. In this way each child gets in touch with his own valuing process and has the experience of validating life itself as being good.

Strategy 7: Animal metaphors

We ask each child to close his eyes and think of a particular animal he would most like to be, and why. As the child tells about his an-

imal, the other children think why that child might be especially good at being the animal of his choice.

"I would like to be a whale 'cause they can swim out real far and dive deep." (A 10-year-old expresses the values he places on strength, freedom, and the need to be alone.)

Validations: "You are big and strong, too." (Like a whale.) "We know that sometimes you like to be alone." (Swim far.) "Someday you'll be free, really free, if you really want to be." (Dive deep.)

There are a variety of ways to extend the metaphor activity: Read stories of animals and on a particular day attribute a new name to each child according to the animal he identified with—"Big Bear," "Running Horse," etc. At the same time, review the strong qualities of the animal.

Fantasize and act out what might happen, for example, when Big Bear meets Running Horse in a secluded valley.

Many movement exercises can be presented: "Move like an elephant... now like a deer... now like an eagle." Appropriate mood music can simulate the slow, heavy movements of an elephant; the grace and speed of a deer; the soaring of an eagle.

Children need affirmation

Difficult children don't just happen. They have to learn from life's many experiences that they are "bad." To some degree this is true of all children. They hesitate and find it very hard to list their strong points. Our whole society seems to lean more toward criticism than toward praise, perhaps fearing that praise leads only to pride and arrogance. This is rarely true. Most people (adults as well as children) simply do not receive enough validation and affirmation to nourish their lives. For this reason alone it seems necessary to develop strategies aimed at making children aware of their strengths.

How can a person feel good about himself until someone else feels this way about him, too, and makes a point of telling him so?

How can someone grow if no one offers him any invitation and support?

How can a person feel successful unless he has achieved success in a few important endeavors?

Growing, developing children must be involved in what is going on around them and in some way feel they can shape their own future. Values-clarification and validation methods are one way to inject into the educational setting opportunities for all children to think, choose, affirm, and act with feelings of success and thus learn a process that can guide them the rest of their lives.

Dr. Sidney Simon is a professor in The Center for Humanistic Application of Social and Behavioral Science in Education at the University of Massachusetts. **Robert O'Rourke** is a psychologist of Ft. Collins, Colorado currently directing retreats and workshops on meditation and relaxation. "What Is Important?" and other strategies were adapted from Values-Clarification by Simon, Howe, Kirschenbaum (Dodd-Mead, 1985).

Improve students' self-image 10 different ways

Here are 10 great ideas that have helped students be more successful and feel good about themselves and their school.

1. Interesting awards assemblies. At monthly awards assemblies, the principal honors students for academic achievements, citizenship, sportsmanship, and personal traits such as generosity or kindness. For academics, both high-achieving and "most-improved" students get awards. They receive certificates signed by their teachers and the principal.

2. Prize drawings for extra excitement. Each day, teachers have three tickets to give the students for outstanding work, good behavior, or other accomplishments. Students write their names on the tickets they receive and put them into a box. At the monthly school assembly, the principal selects tickets randomly from the box and awards prizes. Prizes include used books, pencils, erasers, records, toys, games, money, and free ice-cream coupons. (During an October assembly, the principal gave out over 200 pumpkins.)

3. Special Eagle Grams. Teachers write notes daily to students who've done something special in class. These 5½ × 8½-inch Eagle Grams are printed in the school colors, with the school mascot (the eagle) on them.

4. An active student council. Elected student representatives from grades three to five meet weekly with the principal to discuss school problems and improvements and to make plans for monthly awards assemblies.

5. Student-written school newspaper. Central's newspaper publishes *all* student-written articles. The principal believes that children who make the effort to write articles should see them in print. The newspaper is published whenever enough articles are submitted to fill an issue.

6. Peer teaching for added prestige. A middle-grade student becomes a reading and writing "teacher" for a primary-grade student. The peer-teaching program is most successful for developing language experience stories. As the younger student dictates his story, the older student writes it down. Then the two of them reread it several times until the "author" has mastered his story. At the end of a peer-teaching experience, the older student is given an award certificate.

7. Personal attention during "Happy Hour." The principal sets aside an hour each week to meet with individual students. Teachers select the students for Happy Hour and are encouraged to send both outstanding and unmotivated students. After the meeting, the principal sends special notes to participants.

8. Shared experience stories. Every month, each class creates a chart or poster based on classroom projects, field trips, holiday vacations, or original stories. These are displayed in the halls for all students to read and enjoy.

9. Birthday greetings in person. On their birthdays, students go to the principal's office for congratulations and personally signed cards.

10. Reaching out with Christmas certificates. Students complete Christmas certificates with a promise to do something special for their families. In a school where a majority of students are from low-income families, this project helps students understand that a valuable gift doesn't have to cost money.

Dave E. Borbe is principal of Central Elementary, an inner-city school in Allentown, Pa. **Susan Ohanian** is a staff editor for *Learning* magazine.

WAYS TO RECOGNIZE EVERYONE

Student of the Day

- Try to honor one student each day for something—academics, citizenship, positive attitude, or a trait he can personally be proud of.

GREAT STUDENT AWARDS

- Academic excellence is easy to recognize, of course. You can acknowledge high test scores; exceptional papers, themes, and projects; or completion of all assignments.

Magnificent Mustang Member

- For students displaying commendable personality traits or positive attitudes toward school and classroom responsibilities, set up a special honorary "club" and award formal initiation certificates.

ATTENDANCE CLUB

- For students with perfect attendance and no tardies for each term, establish another club and have special prize drawings.

Set a "go team" spirit for your academic players. Trophies and cheering fans are honors usually reserved for athletes. But at New Martinsville School in Wetzel County, W.Va., they go to students who show academic, rather than athletic, prowess.

As part of the "academic coaching" program, students are honored both for excellence and for improvement in their schoolwork. Those who get straight "As" or who raise their grades by 5 percent during a marking period receive trophies and certificates at school assemblies attended by peers, parents, and teachers. (The media is on hand too; local newspapers publish the names and photos of honored students.)

Teachers serve as "coaches" in the program—encouraging students and planning academic fairs and contests. By all reports, the program is a success.

Use photos to develop self-esteem

Formal portraits, class composites, candid snapshots—there's no self-image like a photographic one. And there's no end to the ways that photos of your students can be useful in classroom activities, for in addition to their other functions, pictures can play a vital role in building a sense of identity.

Most schools have class composite photos taken each year. Just a few extra prints—or even photocopies—of the class picture will provide you with material for several projects with a personal touch. Try these candid ways to develop each child's self-image.

Photo votes

Here's an activity in which children use photos as "votes" or claiming devices. Cut apart a class composite photo into individual portraits and post the pictures on a bulletin board with pushpins. Then prepare a collection of sentences about class members:

She has the longest hair in the class.
Who gets milk for us this week?
"I have a new puppy at home!"
Who moved into a new apartment?
His hamster is missing.
"I lost a tooth!"

Use a variety of sentence forms and write each sentence on a separate strip of paper. Post three or four sentences at a time on the bulletin board near the children's pictures. As children read the sentences, they will notice that the statements and questions apply to students in the class. Children claim sentences they feel apply to them by placing their pictures next to those sentences. Some sentences may apply to several children and can be marked with several pictures. If it happens that more than one sentence applies to a child, he or she may choose another sentence to claim. (Help young children to use pushpins carefully to avoid injury—and to save photos from pincushion syndrome.)

Continue to collect information for sentences as children share bits of news. Change the sentences fairly frequently to maintain interest but leave them long enough for less-confident readers to become comfortable reading them. Most of the class will enjoy re-reading the sentences anyway when the items have been personalized with pictures.

Phototoons

This project starts with a class composite photo. Have about ten copies of the photo made—or make them yourself if your school copier handles photos well. Cut the copies into individual portraits, then provide each student with an envelope containing ten pictures of himself or herself. Also provide scissors, glue, plain white paper, markers or pens, pencils and crayons.

Invite students to imagine their smiling everyday faces attached to cartoon figures in action—chinning themselves, cheerleading, climbing a volcano, chasing dinosaurs. To inspire imaginations, suggest themes, such as "great feats I've accomplished" "once I dreamed that...," or "a funny thing happened at..." Students may plan for single-frame cartoons or a multi-frame sequence.

Students may want to sketch a few situations before settling on a final plan. When students are ready, have them prepare each of their photo faces by removing the head from the background and cutting carefully around the hair and chin. The face may then be positioned on the paper and the stick figure added, or the figure may be sketched in first. Remind students planning their artwork to save space for speech balloons.

Some students may enjoy collecting pictures of classmates and putting them into a larger cartoon scene—a riotous party, "big game" action, a science fiction setting. Others might try making a comic strip using a cast of class members. Or consider the possibilities in "ads": Students become celebrities endorsing various products, services, and organizations—real or imagined.

Photo graphs

A reader suggests using photos of children to introduce graph reading. A cut-apart class composite photo provides the necessary material, or have each child bring in a favorite picture. The graph can be constructed on a large piece of posterboard or chart paper, or you might use a portion of a bulletin board.

For a beginning graph, place all the children's pictures in a single horizontal row at the base of the graphing area. Label this row "people in our class." Have the children count the pictures, adding numbers to the graph as they move along this horizontal axis.

Add a vertical axis perpendicular to the left-hand end of the row of photos. Discuss possible subgroups within the people-in-our-class group—for example, subgroups based on eye color, age, or number of brothers and sisters. Choose one of these categories and label the vertical axis accordingly: eye color—blue, brown, other. Reorganize the photos according to subgroup designations and arrange them in rows opposite the appropriate labels to make an instant bar graph.

Use this photo-graph setup to present other information about the class, including such data as results of surveys about various "favorites" (foods, animals, games, etc.). The open-graph format also comes in handy for keeping track of milk buyers and lunch buyers, absentees and other such accountables. All of these "pre-graphs" are especially informative and fun because they show not only *how many* but also *who*.

Photo rules

Try using photos of class members to help communicate class rules. With all the regulations that children have to learn—bus rules, cafeteria rules, playground rules—classroom rules may need special treatment if they're to make an impression. Begin by asking students to think of rules that are important for the classroom—for safety, for convenience, for learning. Settle on no more than eight or ten specific rules, then divide the class into groups to act out those rules. With your camera close at hand, help students decide how they'll demonstrate each idea. You might take several shots as each rule is acted out so that you and your students will have a selection of pictures to choose from. (The dramatics can be fun—and rule reinforcing too.) Finally, prepare a colorful poster or bulletin board showing the class rules illustrated with the photos. Students enjoy seeing themselves, and at the same time they're reminded of the rules they chose for their room.

Photo tokens

Here's an idea that gives students the opportunity to stroll the lanes and pathways of their favorite board games "in person." Full-length pictures are needed for this project, but they can be obtained quite easily and without the expense of 30 individual photos. Simply take several group shots with students standing close to one another but not touching. The prints can then be cut apart to separate the individuals. Mount each student's photo on a rectangle of posterboard or a slice of 3-by-5 card. Open a paper clip by bending the inner loop up and the outer loop down to form a right angle; this way the clip can stand by itself. Tape an opened clip to the back of each mounted photo. Now every student has a personal "stand-in" token ready to take off on a board game adventure or to play a scene or two on a puppet stage.

Photo brag books

Photos can also be memory joggers and motivational devices. Photographic records of class projects in progress can help students remember steps in a process, and reviewing the photos allows students to relive successes, to reconsider mistakes (what went wrong, what was done to correct matters), and to take note of personal work habits, as revealed in the appearance of the work area, for instance.

Photo histories of projects can be captioned or embellished with speech balloons that elaborate on the action and the feelings.

Photos of each project can be assembled in a small "brag book" photo album that can be circulated among the students and sent home with each person in turn to be shared with his or her family. Sharing school experiences, a problem for some students, can be somewhat easier when photos serve as prompters and discussion starters.

Keep the photo histories available for frequent review of past activities and to aid in planning future projects. Reliving their achievements through pictorial histories may

help some students gain a more positive sense of their capabilities—and may help them develop confidence for trying something new.

Photo stories

Photos can aid in oral expression. Take a special photo of each child, allowing the child to choose the setting and the "props" with which to be photographed. (Sharing the stage with the class gerbil may be just the conversation starter a particular child needs.) Mount each photo on colored paper and arrange time to share the picture with the "star." You might ask the child to talk about where the photo was taken, to describe his or her outfit, and to supply other details.

After the photo has served as an language stimulator, write a few sentences from the conversation below the picture and post the paper for all to enjoy. The star should almost be able to "read" the story written in his or her own words.

Photo comic strips

Here's a photo project that's especially helpful for children who need an "image lift." The finished products are short photo stories, each starring one or several children in a three- or four-photo sequence—in comic strip style.

Start by taking a set of photos without a specific story line in mind. To do this, assemble a group of "stars" (being selected for stardom is image lifting in itself, of course) and invite them to discuss the best and the worst food they've ever eaten, a close play in a recent game, how to balance on a skateboard, or anything that evokes animated conversation with gestures and facial expressions.

Along with the children, explore the finished photos for story possibilities. Imagine what the characters might be saying as you study their expressions. Does one shot suggest a punch line or surprise ending? Arrange and rearrange photos to discover a productive sequence. (Although you may need to direct these activities at first, later the children should be able to choose pictures and to write dialogue for stories on their own.)

Mount the selected photos in their final order on black posterboard and put speech balloons in place. Or assemble materials and slip them into clear plastic page protectors. The results can be quite satisfying and "professional looking."

After having some successes with stories of this spontaneous, ad-lib sort, children may want to develop photo strips for a specific story line. You might have children browse through paperback collections of comic strips or follow the comics in daily newspapers to develop a sense of the compact story told in a few frames. The children may also discover the story often is conveyed in the speeches while character action is minimal. This realization can be a boon to photo-story creators when they are "staging" their shots.

Producing a photo comic strip calls for a variety of creative skills and technical operations. It also enhances self-images as well as puts them on paper.

From the class ham (who is constantly "on camera," even when nobody is taking pictures) to the camera-shy blusher (who will never pose but doesn't mind showing up in an occasional candid shot), it's fun to have everyone on film. Make the most of class composite photos, group shots, and individual pictures in ways that add personality to the activities in your room.

Ideas for these activities were suggested by readers of *Learning*.

Motivating children to learn: What you can do

A while back, my colleague Richard Ryan and I were invited to conduct a workshop for elementary school teachers. The topic was "Motivating Children to Learn." We'd researched that topic for some time and had these four points to emphasize.

1. *Children are intrinsically motivated to learn.* Preschool children, with their continual experimenting and questioning, are the most striking evidence of this. But school-age children are also eager to learn, provided they can follow their own interests.

This latter point is especially important because behaviorists have long asserted that learning must be prodded by external reinforcements.

2. *Intrinsically motivated learning is better than externally controlled learning.* Our research showed that understanding is deeper and more integrated when children learn something because they're interested in it. Standardized tests work against this idea. A form of external control, they promote rote learning more than conceptual understanding.

Free from external pressures, children are also more creative. Teresa Amabile, a psychologist at Brandeis University in Waltham, Mass., has shown that intrinsically motivated children produce more creative work than those who are externally controlled.

3. *Rewards, deadlines, surveillance, and threats of punishment actually decrease intrinsic motivation.* For example, in our research we've observed students working on puzzles or other interesting activities. When

we offered these students rewards for doing the same activities, or threatened punishment for not doing them, they lost interest. Instead of doing the activities spontaneously, they did them only because of the rewards or threats. The result? Conceptual learning suffered and the quality of their overall learning declined.

4. *The way teachers deal with students can greatly affect learning.* Some teachers believe *they* should control what children do and how they do it. Other teachers believe children can learn by solving their own problems and making their own decisions. These teachers support the children's autonomy by being good listeners and good questioners. When they set limits, even the limits allow the children some autonomy (see insert, *Setting "Autonomy-oriented" limits in your class*).

In our studies, we measured the intrinsic motivation and self-esteem of children with both kinds of teachers. Those with supportive teachers scored higher in each category than those with controlling teachers.

What we learned at the workshop

We'd thought the teachers at our workshop might resist these ideas, but that wasn't the case at all. They seemed to know these points from intuition and years of experience. In fact, they seemed more interested in talking about their *own* motivation. So, instead of lecturers, we became listeners. What we heard were the same points we'd intended to make, but on a different level.

First, they said when they began teaching, they were highly—intrinsically—motivated to teach. Second, they thought they performed better and felt better about themselves when they were intrinsically motivated. Third, such pressures as standardized curricula and standardized testing have decreased their sense of autonomy in the classroom and have sapped much of their interest and excitement for teaching. Fourth, they said that school administrators differ substantially in their style of administering. Some are very controlling; others tend to support their teachers' autonomy. And when their administrators are more controlling, they feel less motivated and less good about themselves as teachers.

Finally, though they acknowledged the need for structures and constraints, the teachers still wanted some flexibility, some control of their own. If they had to do something they didn't like, they at least wanted their feelings acknowledged.

Though the focus of the workshop had shifted, the substance hadn't. The principles of motivation are the same in any relationship that involves different levels of power—administrator/teacher, teacher/student, and so forth.

As part of our earlier research, we'd once asked teachers how they thought *they* should be treated by their supervisor if they did something wrong—perhaps failing to turn in a report on time. All seemed to agree:

- They'd like to have the problem pointed out.
- They'd like to know the *real* consequences of their action.
- They'd like their supervisor to understand why they missed the deadline.

None suggested that they be punished, have their privileges withheld, or be pressured to conform. Yet, when asked what they thought would be an appropriate response if a child handed in a late assignment, several teachers suggested imposing a punishment, withholding privileges, or forcing conformity.

People frequently fail to take the perspectives of others into account. Yet it's clear that, just as teachers would be more effective if they took their students' perspective, administrators would be more effective if they took the teachers' perspective.

Why are teachers controlling?

All of this led us to a piece of research that seemed to round out the picture. We wondered: If children are less intrinsically motivated, feel less good about themselves as students, and learn conceptual material less well when teachers are more controlling, then why are teachers controlling? Part of the answer, of course, lies in teachers' personalities—some are simply more controlling than others. But because of our experience in the workshop,

Setting "autonomy-oriented" limits in your class

When we suggest supporting children's autonomy, many teachers ask, "But what do you do when they misbehave or aren't interested in their work?" The answer? Set autonomy-oriented limits, the kind that provide children with choices.

Setting the limits

Setting these limits isn't easy. First, you have to decide what the limits will be. Some limits— such as "no fighting"—don't allow any latitude. But many limits can still allow a choice.

For example, if the children have three projects to work on before recess, why not let them budget their own time rather than tell them when to do each? If some children finish their class work early, why not let them do whatever they want as long as they don't disturb others? In each case, you've given a limit—"work on three projects, don't disturb others"—but within that limit you've given choices.

Next, you'll need to establish the reasons for the limits. If you don't want fighting in the classroom because you're not willing to risk someone getting hurt, tell the children that. If you want them to be quiet so you can finish writing a lesson plan on time, let them know that. These are legitimate reasons. On the other hand, "Because I said so" is not a legitimate reason. It's a power maneuver and only invites defiance.

Don't punish with consequences

For limits to be effective, you have to state clearly what the consequences of going beyond them are. Be careful, though, that the consequences aren't actually punishments. Ask yourself: Are the consequences I'm proposing intended to control the students or get even with them, or are they just the realistic outcome of certain behaviors? Note the difference between these two examples:
• "I told you not to do that; now you'll have to stay in your seat while the other children go to recess." This teacher is probably angry and wants to get even with the child. The consequence is a punishment.
• "When you finish this assignment, you can go out for recess." This teacher has expressed a limit (finishing the work) and a consequence for noncompliance (not having recess). The consequence is a realistic outcome. If a child doesn't finish, the consequence simply follows—no one-upmanship, no power struggle.

Freedom to transgress

Another important part of setting limits is allowing the child to transgress those limits if he wants to (except, of course, when harm might result). That way, he'll understand that keeping or transgressing the limits is his own choice, and if he chooses to transgress, he has to take the consequences.

When you stop to think about it, what more important lesson could children learn? *Life consists of choices, and choices entail consequences.* It's a lesson that all the controlling of children, all the supervising, directing, evaluating, punishing, or rewarding doesn't teach.

Finally, when you set autonomy-oriented limits, acknowledge children's feelings. Whenever children face limits, they're likely to have contradictory feelings. They must learn that these are okay. It's all right to feel angry about being limited; it's all right to not want to do what the limits require.

Suppose you have a boy who didn't complete his assignments and is angry now because he can't go to recess. You might say, "I understand that you feel bad about being here while the others are at recess, but you need this time to complete your work." Or, if a girl is staring out the window because she's obviously bored, you might say, "I know you don't find this very interesting, but now is the time to attend to this material; you can daydream after the lesson is finished." Here, you've acknowledged the child's feelings, plus given her an opportunity to do what she wants at another time.

Children aren't wrong for feeling what they feel, though they may be wrong for doing what they do. They can't—and shouldn't—be forced to change their feeling. But if that feeling is acknowledged and accepted, they'll find they're able to behave in ways they don't really want to.

we wondered whether the degree to which teachers control students depends in part on the degree to which *they* feel controlled—or at least pressured or stressed—by the situation.

To test this, we set up an experiment in which teachers helped students learn to solve puzzles on spatial relationships. To simulate the pressures reported in our workshop, we told half the teachers that they were responsible for their students' performing up to high standards. We said nothing about performance standards to the other half.

The effect of this simple manipulation was remarkable. The teachers we stressed performance to spoke three times as much, were more directive, and used more words like "should," "must," and "have to" than did the teachers in the other group. They also spent so much time instructing their students on how to solve the puzzles that the students had little opportunity to explore, to experiment, to discover. Though these students assembled twice as many puzzles as did those in the other group (because they were told the solutions), they independently solved only one-fifth as many.

When other people listened to tape recordings of the teaching sessions, they rated the teachers quite differently, even though they knew nothing about the experiment. The teachers who'd been given "performance standards" were rated as less effective, and the raters said they would like these teachers less than the other teachers.

In short, the pressure created by mentioning performance standards led the teachers to be more directive and controlling. And in line with previous research, when the conditions were controlling, the students seemed to comply with the controls. In other words, they did what they were told—but they didn't have the opportunity to learn for themselves and to gain a real grasp of the material.

The moral of the story seems to be that we live in a culture obsessed with achievement. This pressures school administrators who in turn put pressure on teachers. The teachers then pressure the children. The pressure tends to ripple throughout the educational system, resulting in achievement that is neither creative nor humane. However, as we've observed in classrooms, some teachers can remain relatively free in the midst of these pressures and create environments that support autonomy—and real learning.

Edward L. Deci, PhD, teaches psychology at the University of Rochester, New York. He is coauthor with Richard Ryan of *Intrinsic Motivation and Self-Determination in Human Behavior* (Plenum Publishers, 1985).

TEACHER'S GUIDE TO CLASSROOM PRAISE

Used correctly, praise is a powerful reinforcer of positive behavior and a motivator toward student achievement. Ineffective praise can demotivate and cause confusion. Check the lists below to evaluate your own use of praise.

Effective praise	Ineffective praise
Is delivered contingently	Is delivered randomly or unsystematically
Is specific and detailed	Is global and nonspecific
Shows spontaneity, variety, and other signs of credibility; suggests clear attention to the student's accomplishment	Shows a bland uniformity, suggesting a conditioned response made with minimal attention
Rewards attainment of specified performance criteria (which can include effort criteria, however)	Rewards participation, without considering performance or outcomes
Lets students know about their competence or the value of their accomplishments	Provides no information at all or gives students information about their status
Orients students toward better appreciation of their own task-related behavior and problem solving	Orients students toward competition and comparisons with other students
Describes present accomplishments in context of students' own prior accomplishments	Describes students' accomplishments in context of peer's accomplishments
Recognizes noteworthy effort or success at difficult (for this student) tasks	Is given without regard to the effort expended or the meaning of the accomplishment (for this student)
Attributes success to effort and ability, suggesting that similar successes are possible in the future	Attributes success to ability alone or to external factors such as luck or an easy task
Fosters endogenous attributions (students believe that they work at the task for internal reasons because they enjoy it and/or want to develop task-relevant skills)	Fosters exogenous attributions (students believe that they expend effort on the task for external reasons—to please the teacher, win a competition or reward, etc.)
Focuses students' attention on their own task-relevant behavior	Focuses students' attention on the teacher as an external authority who manipulates them
Fosters appreciation of and desirable attributions about task relevant behavior after the process is completed	Intrudes and distracts attention from task-relevant behavior

Using computers can help students grow

I've always been skeptical about anything touted as a panacea for school problems, so I wasn't exactly ecstatic when two computers arrived in my third grade classroom at the start of the school year. True, I was prepared; I'd had 2 weeks of intensive training during the summer. Still, my first impulse was to push both machines into a corner, cover them with dustcloths, and proceed with business as usual.

I didn't, of course, and what began with reluctance blossomed over the year into enthusiasm, even fondness.

Why the change? Because I saw how computers could help me be a better teacher of 32 youngsters struggling to learn and grow through the year. I also saw that working with computers gave my students a better understanding of the tools that already are reshaping their world.

Computers and individualization

The first benefit I discovered was that computers could help me provide the right level of materials for each child. As I became familiar with the computer programs our school system had available, I could target materials more accurately to each child's level of achievement and keep better track of how that child progressed.

For some children, 15 intensive minutes of well-chosen math drills on the computer were as helpful as 40 minutes of work in our prescribed math workbook. That's because the computer program presented only one problem

at a time, so it didn't confuse those children who, after brief lapses of attention, couldn't relocate their work on a page dense with print. Also, some programs use the cursor to guide the student through the steps of a problem. That feature gave comfortable support to students who weren't comfortable with how work is organized on a printed page.

Besides individualized skills work, I could use the computer to provide challenging programs that responded to the children's personal interests. Franklin loved to go fishing with his grandfather; I found a fish pond simulation program that also challenged his problem-solving abilities. Laura and Thomas came from families that run small businesses, and they helped out in their respective stores. A simulation program about operating a lemonade stand was just the ticket. It engaged them in cause and effect thinking, and in estimating and calculating.

Computers and motivation

Most of the children seemed willing to work harder at the duller tasks of learning when they could do them on the computer. Claims of "I'm finished" when the drill assignment was only half done became a thing of the past. Spelling words were typed over and over without complaint. Rather than "Do I have to do *all* this?" I was more likely to hear, "Could I do just one more, *please*?"

When someone needed a little extra drill and practice in a particular skill, I put an appropriate program in the computer and scheduled a solo 10 or 15 minutes a day for that child. This worked especially well for Sharon, my "special needs" child. She'd always had trouble paying attention to paper and pencil tasks for more than a few minutes. With the computer, she would stay focused for as long as 15 minutes. The success she experienced made subsequent tasks more inviting.

Computers and creativity

Of course, I used the computers for more than just drill and practice. With the help of LOGO, a special programming language designed for children, I got my 8-year-olds to try their hands at writing their own programs.

Even with LOGO, programming demands a lot of inventiveness and problem solving. Having the students work in pairs allowed them to help each other. But the biggest help came from seeing shapes appear on the screen in response to their commands. This made the students eager to learn; I was amazed at how fast a new programming idea could spread through the group after I'd taught it to one or two teams.

The children wrote programs that produced geometric designs. I could see their understanding of angles and shapes grow as they struggled to make squares and triangles and accidentally discovered pentagons, hexagons, and other shapes they hadn't recognized before. Soon they were grasping geometric ideas I'd never thought possible for third graders. They were learning, and so was I.

Computers and personal growth

As I looked back over the year and prepared to say good-bye to the class, I could see that some of the children had changed noticeably. I don't mean to suggest that these changes happened only because of the computers, but I can't help feeling that the computers were a significant factor. Having the machines, a selection of programs, and someone to help me when I ran into problems allowed me to provide a wider range of good learning experiences for more children. And nothing helps a child's self-esteem more than succeeding in interesting, worthwhile activities that make sense to him and earn him the respect of others. Let me tell you a few examples of outstanding personal growth.

PAUL. Paul turned out to have a flair for programming and invented two games that the class loved to play. That was great. But even greater was Paul's learning to work with other children. Whenever he was stuck, he'd gratefully accept anyone's suggestion—even if it was just a wild guess—and would then let that child work with him. Whenever he succeeded, he willingly explained to his classmates what he'd done or discovered, and basked in their admiration.

Paul's newly developed capability made a difference outside of school, too. Paul's parents were divorced, and he harbored resentment toward his father. Now, because of their shared interest in computers, Paul and his father enjoy their weekends together. Paul no longer has a chip on his shoulder—or if he does, it's a computer chip!

FRANKLIN. A year ago, the second grade teacher had looked at me with pity when she heard Franklin was in my class. His school record reinforced her gloomy forebodings. But doing skill drills on the computer helped Franklin concentrate and apply himself for longer periods. What's more, he found tapping on the keyboard easier than wielding a pencil. And his embarrassment at working on second grade skills in a third grade classroom was mitigated by his mastery of a sophisticated machine.

Franklin gained recognition as the class authority on fish behavior by excelling at the fish pond simulation program. This made him less surly and defensive than he'd been the year before. By admiring his fund of practical information, the other children and I helped Franklin realize that valuable knowledge wasn't limited to what you learn in school.

LAURA. At first, Laura seemed to be one of those children who just disappear into the crowd (especially in a class of 32). But she gained the attention of her peers when the simulation about the lemonade stand was introduced. Suddenly Laura was the authority on the fine points of buying and selling, and her popularity soared as children vied for her as their partner. Buoyed by this sudden boost to her self-image, she began to voice her opinions about other matters, too. Soon she was an active participant in class discussions and playground activities.

ME. Yes, using the computers helped *me* grow as well. Though I'm usually eager to try new ideas, I was reluctant at first about the prospect of computers in my classroom. Mostly, teachers teach things they themselves were once taught, which gives us something to fall back on if we falter. But few of us have computer experience in our background. For us, as for most adults, computers are a new experience and rather frightening.

When I actually confronted a computer in our summer training session, all sorts of fears welled up inside me. I worried about pressing the wrong key, about making mistakes and looking foolish, about what the instructor would think of me, and about my ability to learn what was expected of me. Later, this experience of facing a totally new learning situation made me think much more carefully about the first few weeks of school for my students. After all, for them *everything* is new. So I'm a lot more careful about how I introduce new materials and ideas.

Because my class of 32 eager users had only two computers and a limited collection of programs, I found I had to be quite selective about which child used what program, when, and for what reason. This encouraged me to think much more about my students as individuals. I've become more responsive to their personal interests, learning needs, and lives outside of the classroom, and this has made life in school more interesting for all of us. It's also encouraged me to spend less time looking to the text and teacher resource books for interesting ideas, and more time looking to my students. Of course a teacher doesn't need computers to become more sensitive to students. But wanting to make maximum use of the computers forced the issue, and I think I'm a better teacher because of it.

Finally, there comes the bottom-line question: If computers are so great in the classroom, won't they threaten the role of the teacher? I, for one, am not worried. For all my enthusiasm, I know that computers are just machines. Someone has to make an informed decision about how to match programs, purposes, and pupils. And that someone is the classroom teacher. You can understand, then, why I was delighted, the following fall, to welcome to my classroom not just the new students, but two more computers.

Mari E. Endreweit, formerly a faculty member at Bank Street College of Education in New York City, is now educator and director at the Montclair Cooperative School in Montclair, New Jersey. She worked on developing the *Bank Street Writer,* a word processing program (Broderbund and Scholastic), and is co-author of *Bank Street's Family Computer Book* (Ballantine, 1984).

Tips For Testing & Evaluating

4

TIPS FOR TESTING AND EVALUATING

Tests are a major thorn in the classroom rose garden. Students worry about them to the point of panic. Teachers wish they could avoid giving them and the tedium of marking them. But until we find another objective way to monitor progress in learning, tests are here to stay. Read on for some better ways teachers have found to deal with classroom and standardized testing.

How to give a test that teaches

Some time ago, one of the authors of this article, a teacher, gave his students a difficult test. The next day, he graded the tests, returned them, and asked for questions. There were none, even though many test questions were missed. The next day, he gave his students the same test again, offering them the higher of the two grades. Astonishingly, only two students did better the second time; two did worse.

As he had done before, the teacher passed back the tests and asked for questions. A few were put forth unenthusiastically. The next day, he gave the test a third time. This time, three students improved. At that rate, the teacher calculated, it would take 22 days of retesting to get improvement from the entire class. Most students, it appears, take a test, wait until the teacher "gives" a grade on it, and then proceed to forget it.

This is unfortunate, but students alone are not to blame. They have merely accepted the notion of tests as the means of giving students a grade, and nothing more. But tests can and should do more. Here are a few suggestions for giving "tests that teach":

- **Test/retest.** Try the experiment described above. It should encourage students to ask more questions about tests and to look up answers to missed test questions. To provide incentive for seeking correct answers, include on new tests the questions from previous tests, especially the troublesome ones.
- **In-class test/take-home test.** Following an in-class test, give the students the same test to complete at home. Let the grade be the average of the two test scores. You should expect a near-perfect score on the take-home test, but that is completely in line with the goals of tests that teach.
- **Individual test/group review.** The day after you give a test, organize the class into groups of students of varying abilities. Ask the groups to review the test, discuss the questions, and decide on the correct answers. Then have the students *individually* retake the test. If the group average on the retest exceeds a predetermined score—say, 90 percent—every member of the group earns bonus points.
- **Student-written test questions.** One of the best ways to get students to learn material is to have them write their own test questions on it. Ask each student to make a list of true-false or multiple-choice questions based on the material you wish to test. Collect the lists, select the best questions (modify them as needed), and include them on the test. Students will feel proud to see their questions selected, and they'll usually get them right too. For essay questions, have the students work in groups, assign one unit or lesson to each group, and ask each group to write one essay question that covers the major points in the unit. Then collect the questions, modify them as needed, and give them to the class as study guides. Tell the students you'll choose two of the questions for an essay test. What's to be gained? Students will know what will be on the test and will be less anxious about it. But they'll still have to prepare for it, because only you will know which questions will be on the test.

These are just a few ideas for using a much-overlooked but highly valuable teaching and learning tool. Implement the suggestions, and you may find that tests keep on teaching.

Dr. M. Mark Wasicsko is Dean of the School of Education at Texas Wesleyan College in Fort Worth, Tex. **Dr. Steven M. Ross** is Professor of Education at Memphis State University in Memphis, Tenn.

Help your students do better on standardized tests

The scenario is all too familiar and its implications all too often ignored. The announcement goes out to the students: "Tomorrow is standardized test day. Get a good night's sleep and report in in the morning, fresh and alert, ready to do your best work."

Morning comes, but are the students relaxed and ready to go? Not too many of them. A good number of students enter a testing situation experiencing panic in its truest sense— heavy perspiration, tensed stomachs, minds drained blank. The tests are given, the students (not surprisingly) perform poorly, and one more disastrous notation is added to the cumulative records that will follow them throughout their lives—slotting them into "average," "slow," or "special" ability groupings and, soon enough, discouraging or disqualifying them from going on to higher education. What's worse, students tend to take test results as total definitions of themselves, unchallengeable verdicts on their personal value.

The irony of all this is that even if the testing environment were ideal, the scores would be very deceiving. Analysis of many tests purporting to measure IQ or reading achievement, for example, reveals that what is actually being measured is little more than skimming skill and eye-hand coordination. Often students do well because they are good test takers, not necessarily because they are bright. Similarly, the reader who works through every paragraph of a book fares worse than one who can appraise a table of contents and glean pertinent information, digesting only what is useful for exam taking. Seeking exactness, imagining alternatives, and consulting one's own experience make for true learning but, alas, for poor standardized test scores.

Students who perform badly can be helped through very simple techniques to raise their scores. But why bother? If standardized testing does not measure true learning, why not simply campaign for its abolition? Eventually, standardized tests in the form we now know them may be replaced. But today's students are still having to take these tests and we should teach them the skills for taking those tests successfully.

I want to suggest three distinct steps to follow: first, make students comfortable in the test-taking situation; second, show them how to complete tests efficiently; third, help them see standardized tests for just what they are. In short: the Warm-up, the Dry-Run, the Follow-Through.

Step 1: The warm-up

Before getting to the test itself, familiarize students with the mechanics of the testing situation. Pass out facsimiles of the answer sheet, and have students practice filling in their names and other information. Do this often enough, outside of a testing context, so that they feel easy about the beginning of the job. And when you rehearse the preliminary instructions, use the exact language the manual advises (i.e., "Complete the information called for at the top of this page" or "Fill in the blanks asking for your name, school, date of test, etc. Be sure to write clearly"). Hearing the same formula over and over in an unthreatening situation will help the students relax when they hear it before an actual test.

Practice arranging the seats; test makers usually suggest a seating plan that will keep

students from copying from each other. Decide jointly on such an arrangement, and have the class adopt it whenever they rehearse for the real thing. After a while, this maneuver becomes part of the game, a relaxed rather than anxious moment. Remember to tell students to clear their desk tops so that they have nothing but pencils and answer sheets in front of them.

Distribute No. 2 pencils for practicing on the answer sheets. Each student should get at least two *dull* pencils, which last longer, don't break as easily, and require fewer strokes to mark a box. The thicker the pencil, the greater the comfort of the students. Teach them to make only one stroke when marking a box; the machine will pick it up. If this makes students too anxious, tell them to mark the box as quickly as they can, with as few strokes as possible. It is a waste of time to fill in an answer box neatly. Although care and accuracy are good qualities in real work, they are of no use on a standardized test, where speed is essential.

After you've distributed answer forms several times to practice filling in information and marking boxes, devote some sessions to rapid drill. Briskly call off "right" answers for the students to mark: "1-E," "2-D," etc.

Examine the placement of the answers. Is the form arranged vertically? horizontally? Encourage the students to find a comfortable posture and their own best placement of paper and handling of pencil. Watch out for those who tend to lose their place or have trouble marking the proper boxes. Teach them to use their hands, spare pencils, erasers, or whatever as markers. Above all, help them realize that the ability to mark boxes has nothing to do with their store of knowledge or their intelligence.

Next, before dealing with an actual test, type up a list of easy questions. It doesn't matter what their content, as long as they're a cinch to answer.

1. How many students are in this class?
   A. 30   B. 14   C. 18
   D. 25   E. None of these

2. What season is this?
   A. Winter   B. Spring   C. Summer
   D. Fall   E. All of the above

The students should answer the questions on a separate sheet, identical to the one they will use during the actual test. This will help them perfect the dozen little motions involved in reading on one page and answering on another. It will also help to isolate performance from thought and content—a vital stage in test taking.

Step 2: The dry run

Test makers do not expect their clients to be naive or ignorant of procedures; back copies or sample questions of tests are usually available from the publisher. But never use items from the upcoming test itself—students need to be competent, not unethical.

Let them become familiar with the question format, the vocabulary of the directions, and the general appearance of the test. Some directions are so complicated that students spend more time decoding the questions than finding the answers. Then again, some answers offer such intricate choices that students will get lost unless they've been over similar terrain.

Students should devise their own best strategies for test taking and then share their ideas with one another. A sense of community arises when everyone confronts a problem together, not when students are pitted against each other in a destructive, competitive atmosphere.

Use the passages in former tests to help students devise effective strategies for answering questions. Some examinations are organized so that the correct answers fall only within a particular section of a passage. A long poem, for example, might be sectioned off into portions which are numbered. The answer boxes might then be numbered to correspond with the sections. Even if a student judges that a correct answer is located in a particular section, the answer boxes might not contain the number of the segment the student has selected. Therefore, the students should be taught to read *only* those segments for which there are possible answer boxes. They should also learn to match wording in the questions with wording in the passages.

The teacher should look through the test to determine any special skills required. Some tests employ graphs heavily. Some require students to look at many charts. Sufficient practice with these special devices is useful, so that students will feel comfortable with the material.

It's important that the teacher be familiar with each test's scoring system. Some tests use the instruction "Do Not Guess" to signal that every wrong answer will be subtracted from the total of right answers, so you should discuss with students the risk of guessing. On the other hand, if you know the score consists only of the number of right answers, then students might do well to guess when necessary, and fill in every blank. If, in a timed reading test, speed and comprehension are scored together, the student must skim the passage and complete it. In other cases, it may not be necessary to read the whole passage to answer the questions on it.

In general, skimming is a vital skill. Have students practice reading passages both aloud and silently, stressing only key words. Newspaper and magazine articles, stories from basal readers, passages from social studies tests—almost anything will do. Students will grasp soon enough the difference between real understanding and test-taking comprehension. Extracting the main idea from a test passage means looking at the first or last sentence and matching it with the suggested answers. It does not mean reflecting and summarizing. The same technique holds true for determining a title for a passage.

The best way to locate specific information on a test is to skim the passage with the question and answers in mind. Have students practice this procedure until it becomes automatic. Sometimes the passage itself is not even necessary; the answers are apparent in the question.

At the end of the practice session, discuss with students the following "Rules for Test Taking":

● Complete the entire test or section as quickly as possible, answering at first *only* those questions you are sure of and those with obvious answers. Lightly mark the questions that make you pause and return to them later.

● Leave a minute at the end of the test to fill in any blank boxes. This is the time to guess—to mark all of one number, or to follow some other system. But leave no answer blank—unless incorrect answers are deducted from correct ones for the final score.

● Refuse to get interested in the reading passages, or in any of the information contained in the questions. Standardized tests are not for thinking and learning, they are for gauging how well students take tests.

● Recognize that the "right" answers on standardized tests are not always the only answers or, indeed, even the best answers. They are simply the ones predetermined by the testing agency. Arguing with the answers is futile. In fact, a proportion of failure is built into most tests, because, from the agency's point of view, it would be calamitous if too many people scored 100 percent. So there are tricks, confusing wording and obscure answers. Students aren't *expected* to answer every question correctly.

Step 3: The follow-through

The first requirement in all this is to try out these techniques for yourself. Take a test the students will be subjected to. See if skimming and matching get you the right answers. Try some of the mechanical skills, such as box-filling and racing through the entire test. Then set up a timetable for working with your students. Keep it light. Keep it fun. And let them know you are convinced they'll swim, not sink.

Students need to know that their scores reflect only their ability to take tests, and are no cause for pride or shame. In the course of a school year, you will naturally focus on their own real work as a measure of ability. The students must know why they're practicing test-taking skills in order for these procedures to be successful.

Masha K. Rudman is a professor in the School of Education, University of Massachusetts at Amherst, and the author of numerous books and articles about education.

10 shortcuts to grading papers

Some teachers find it easy to assign writing often, and to edit all student writing quickly and effectively. These teachers live in an ideal world of small classes, well-motivated students, and lots of preparation time. Such a world exists in some schools, but not many. The other thousands of merely mortal teachers *know* they should have their students writing often, but are swamped by the task or the prospect.

Teachers should not be martyrs to their work. If you are a grim-faced, conscientious clutcher of batches of yet-unevaluated student writing, you may well become a difficult person to live with—difficult for your colleagues, your spouse, your students, and yourself. So the question is: How to teach writing without anguish. The answer: Use shortcuts. Here are ten of them, all moral, divided into three categories: shortcuts for preventive care, shortcuts for evaluation and editing, and shortcuts for following up on writing.

PREVENTIVE CARE

1. Foresee difficulties and preteach. If your assignment involves writing dialogue, teach a quick review of how to punctuate, capitalize, and paragraph this writing form. If it involves a series of actions, teach how to avoid the then-then-then syndrome by demonstrating how to write smoothly flowing, varied sentences. If it involves organization of thoughts or materials, discuss ways to handle this and give a few examples. If students are likely to have to spell *embarrass* or *government* or *character,* or even

its/it's, teach them ahead of time. Preteaching has two advantages over mop-up teaching: it allows students to practice doing things right, and it saves you a lot of correcting time.

2. Teach, and teach again, how to proofread papers. Much of your time is wasted proofreading for your students, marking errors they could have corrected before handing in their papers. Show students how to make themselves "strangers" to their own writing and then to read it with a cold, objective eye or, better, to read it *aloud* so that they can hear the mistakes they don't see. Demonstrate this process several times early in the year, basing your demonstrations on specific examples dittoed and distributed to all. Recommend that your students save at least 10 minutes' time for proofreading their papers. Permit them to cross out and neatly correct the errors they find while proofreading. Remember that writing, not calligraphy or precise margins, is the first priority.

3. Have students read and edit one another's papers. Have the students group into threes and pass their papers around the group, with each student marking the two papers that are not his own. Allow some time (perhaps overnight for the students to consider the editing and suggestions that have been made by their two classmates and to revise their papers. Then collect the papers, probably much improved (with no time spent by you).

EVALUATING AND EDITING

4. Resist overcorrecting. Let students know that you will correct *selectively*. Then mark only those errors and needs for revision that you think the writer can and should address efficiently. If a two-page paper contains 30 spelling mistakes and 20 punctuation mistakes, choose for marking only the five to ten of each from which you think the student can learn most. No rule or sense of integrity requires you to mark *every* error, and students should not get back papers that look more as if they had been attacked by a disease than worked on by a teacher/editor.

When evaluating papers, you use grades primarily as a quick way to instruct students. A single grade on a paper, however, is often uninformative, since it lumps your evaluation of content, spelling, and mechanics—three areas that are quite distinct. Try giving separate symbols and grades for each area. You may devise other symbols, depending on what needs emphasis in a certain written lesson, such as *O* for organization, *T* for transitions, *SV* for sentence variety, and *L* for logic.

5. Teach a lesson on common problems. Quickly scan an entire set of papers, making no marks on them but picking out five or six significant common problems. Next day teach a lesson on these problems, typical of which might be: spelling words ending in silent e; transitions; getting off the subject; writing that is general when it should be specific; not backing up statements with evidence. Before teaching the lesson, hand back the papers so that students can evaluate their own work in relation to the points being discussed.

6. Teach from examples written on the board or duplicated. Read enough of a set of papers to find out what the main problems are. Then underline selected sentences and passages on certain papers that serve as examples. The next day ask the students who have marked papers to write the underlined passages on the board *as is,* and use these sentences as a basis

for teaching a lesson. If you have the time and facilities, it works even better to duplicate the passages on which you are going to base the lesson and distribute a copy to each student. Have students revise their papers in the light of the lesson and then file them.

7. Project some papers. If you are fortunate enough to have an overhead projector, use it to project a few typical papers and passages in front of the entire class. Discuss the strong points as well as the weaknesses within the individual papers. (Of course, you should not project a paper without student permission and you should not project papers that will embarrass the writers.)

8. Have groups of students read and evaluate papers according to selected criteria. Work out a dispersal routine for the class so that students can quickly divide into groups of about five. Each student will then read his own paper aloud and ask for the group's reaction, based on particular items you have written on the board (such as: interesting beginning, good description, needless repetitions, choice of words). Two or three items are enough for the average class. Sometimes it is well to ask each group to choose the best or most interesting paper and to have these papers read, perhaps the next day, to the entire class. With all this attention having been given to the students' writing, it may not be necessary for you to spend time correcting and editing the batch of papers.

FOLLOW-UP

9. Devise and follow through on a complete revision process. Teacher effort in correcting and evaluating papers is fruitless unless it results in further student effort to improve the papers. It is better to mark a few assignments with some care and have the students revise and correct them than to slave over every paper and be satisfied to have the students merely glance at what they "got." If you have evaluated a paper thoroughly, you and the writer should consider the work unfinished until the writer has dealt with every item you noted—spelling mistakes corrected, mechanical errors fixed, awkwardnesses revised, etc. Correcting and revising papers should "count." Grade students not only on their first efforts, but also on how well they handle your marks and comments. Circle those items that are still a problem when papers are handed in a second time, so that you and the student can easily see what's still to be done. Only when a student has completed all revisions and corrections should the paper be marked OK for filing.

10. Establish a reading and consultation period. Schedule it definitely, perhaps once a week. Students should be prepared to do independent work or to read silently during this period as you hold one-on-one conferences with students whose written work needs special attention. Write on the board a list of the names of the students you need to see, or let students sign their names on the list if they need to see you. Thus, without any waiting in line, students can confer with you on problems of correction and revision.

Intelligent, discriminating uses of these shortcuts, plus others you invent, can help all of your students feel that their work has been read, appreciated, and improved. They'll be encouraged to write more and better, all without your becoming a miserable martyr or a dull drudge.

Eric W. Johnson, a teacher of English and sex education for over 30 years, is the author of *Teaching School,* 3rd edition, 1987, published by the National Association of Independent Schools, 18 Tremont Street, Boston, Mass.

Checklists for evaluating instructional materials

Have you ever used an instructional material that didn't live up to your expectations? Or a material that was obviously not getting across to certain kids? According to what the publisher's representative told you, it should have fit your requirements and the needs of kids beautifully. But somehow it turned out to be a misfit. On the other hand, have you ever used a material that you found worked even better than you'd expected with certain kids?

Have you ever felt that there ought to be a way for what you have found out about specific materials to be shared with other teachers and other schools—and information about their experiences made available to you and other teachers in your school? If you have ever wanted to, or would like to, take part in such an exchange of information, or if you want to know how you, as an individual teacher, can affect the judgments and procedures the publishers of instructional materials follow in developing and revising materials, then read on.

The things you can do have been organized into two checklists. The first will help you keep publishers and other producers of instructional materials pointed in the direction of better quality control in the development and revision of their products. The second will help you select and use materials in such a way that you get the best possible "materials-teacher-learner fit." You may already be occasionally doing many of the things on both checklists, but it's important that they be done

systematically and persistently.

Checklist 1: Quality control

After a sales representative has finished his prepared presentation and you have asked the usual pro-forma questions, go on to ask these:

● *Have the materials been systematically tried out with learners* to identify and correct any specific difficulties kids might have in using the materials?

● *If so, what were those difficulties* and *what was done about them,* either with the materials themselves or in the teacher's manual? (Don't fall for displays of data and tables assertedly drawn from "nationwide field tests." Ask whether the producers ever used the data to identify how the materials needed to be improved. Were the improvements made?)

● *What problems have teachers reported* when they used these materials? What kinds of kids were affected? What have you done to eliminate the problems or help me deal with them?

● *Do I need special training* to get the best results with these materials? If so, does your company provide it? Free?

● *Does your company maintain a communications network* that continually gathers information from teacher and student users of these materials? If so, how is that information used?

● *Do these materials have a clearly specified set of objectives and a set of achievement measures* that I can review? If so, do you have evidence that kids like mine have achieved those objectives using these materials? Can

NEW COMPUTERIZED RESOURCE

During the last 10 years, EPIE has worked on designing computerized systems for organizing all the various types of information about instructional resources. By 1986, this work resulted in the Integrated Instructional Information Resource (IIIR), an electronic data-base that helps a school to identify specific materials that best fit its curriculum requirements and the needs of its teachers and learners. During 1986, school districts in 12 states used IIIR to help select textbooks in relation to local and state curriculum objectives, to identify supplementary materials (e.g. computer software) that will compensate for a textbook's shortcomings, and to learn whether a particular test correlates well with a school's curriculum objectives and/or textbooks. In addition, some schools are also using IIIR's curriculum information to design or to redesign a curriculum before they select textbooks, other teaching materials, and tests. Currently, the IIIR database is being extended to include teacher information on the classroom integration of specific materials in specific ways to achieve specific learning outcomes. This information is being gathered in the form of exemplary lesson plans and teaching strategies, which are being correlated to specific materials as well as to specific curriculum goals and objectives. Teachers may use this database to access information about exemplary ways in which a particular material they know about may be used to meet the needs of learners and the objectives of a curriculum. Other teachers may use it to identify new materials that may meet their needs more effectively than the familiar ones.

---

you give me the names of schools and of teachers who have used these materials? Can I call them?

Some suggestions about using this checklist:

Be as specific and detailed as you can in asking these questions and insist that the company representative offer specific and detailed answers. Problems with a material are almost always specific, so try to anticipate as many of them as possible and get detailed answers *before* you make a final selection.

Examine the stated objectives carefully. Ask yourself whether the objectives spell out what your students should be able to do after having put the required time and effort into use of the materials. After you've done that, look carefully at the achievement measures and ask if their questions, problems, and activities really measure the learning that has been set forth in the objectives. Do this conscientiously, and you'll have the answer to a question of fundamental importance: Did the producer state ambitious objectives but test for modest objectives, particularly for those that are easy for the learner to master and for the producer to measure?

Checklist 2: Improving the "fit" of instructional materials

Keep in mind that the only real reason to use an instructional material is to facilitate learning. Then ask the following questions about any materials being considered for use in your instructional program with your students:

● *Am I satisfied that this material has been*

developed for and with feedback from kids like those I'm teaching?

• *Does the publisher seem willing to give me concrete help* in getting the best results with these materials? Especially after the sale has been made?

• *Do the materials fit my "teaching style"?* Do they feel right? Are they too systematic for me? Are they too loosely organized? Do they require me to do things I know perfectly well I'll never do? Or would be uncomfortable doing? If they don't fit my style precisely, can I adapt them without destroying their instructional design?

• *Can I learn something about instruction from these materials?* If so, am I willing to learn?

If your answers to these questions leave you with a positive feeling about the material, you're probably looking at a product that is "your size." But if you're going to get a really good fit for both you and your kids, you must pay careful attention to the product's instructional design before, during, and even after using it. These are the key design elements: goals and objectives, scope and sequence of content, teaching/learning methodology, and evaluation and measurement procedures. None of these interrelated elements is a thing unto itself, and you must therefore check how well each relates to the other—and to the learners who use the product.

A satisfactory teacher-learner-materials fit also requires that attention be paid to how you, as the teacher, adapt to each major design element, or adapt each of them to you. That means you recognize in which elements the material is weakest and on which you will therefore have to work hardest. It also means

knowing where the material's design is stronger than you are (e.g., the developer really does know how to structure a methodology along Piagetian lines, and you're only just learning). In that case, it makes sense to lean heavily on that design element.

You probably do some of these things already. Many teachers do, but it's often only at a highly intuitive level. All teachers can benefit from doing them more consciously and systematically. Instructional materials, after all, are the tools of a teacher's trade, and every teacher should know how to use them well.

Kenneth Komoski is executive director of the EPIE Institute (Educational Products Information Exchange).

5
HELP STUDENTS WITH SPECIAL PROBLEMS

In today's classrooms, teachers must take into account the effects on learning of their students' various and complex problems. Teachers need to consider, know how to recognize, and cope correctly with the effects on their students of child abuse, divorce and other family problems, physical and mental disorders and handicaps, and in some areas poverty and the inability to speak English. Read on for other teachers' experiences in managing such problems.

Two teachers' work with students who don't speak English

No matter how important you feel the mastery of the English language is to the foreign student, your drive, your enthusiasm, your energy will not "learn him English," as the expression goes. It is up to the student to take on the responsibility of reaching out, of communicating in English. But this will happen only as the child develops a sense of security in his new environment. Your job as a teacher, then, is to create situations in which the student feels comfortable attempting to function in the second language. Some suggestions:

• Be aware that your tone of voice, your facial expressions, your gestures will relay far more information to the child than your words. Your actions and attitude will tell the child that you are happy to see him, that you care about his welfare. Remember, too, that speaking very slowly or loudly doesn't help one bit. On the contrary, it tells the child that you don't credit him with any intelligence.

• A simple but often overlooked way to show the new student your regard for her is to learn to pronounce her name correctly. Learn to say it as she says it; don't try to anglicize it or, heaven forbid, give her an English name. Teach her to pronounce your name as well. Then teach her name to the other members of the class, and have them introduce themselves to her. Name cards on desks can be very helpful.

• Provide plenty of opportunities for the other students in the class to help the new child— in learning English, in finding his way around, in adapting to classroom routine. You might introduce a sign-up sheet on which students volunteer for 15- or 30-minute teaching stints. Ask the students about suggestions for language learning activities; they come up with some interesting ideas. You might also want to appoint a "buddy"—on a weekly basis, perhaps—to oversee the daily sign-up sheet and to make sure the new student goes to special activities.

• Be sure to allow some necessary "free" time for the student to observe and listen to regular class activities. Let him work on guided activities of his own while others are engaged in individual or group projects.

• Be consoled by the fact that most foreign students learn English quite rapidly. You may not see evidence for this in the first month of school, but you should begin to see signs of understanding soon thereafter. (You'll generally see it first on the playground; children feel less threatened with peers in a relaxed setting.)

• As soon as possible, set up a conference with the child's parents—both of them. If you must use an interpreter, be sure to find someone who will convey your words accurately, but remember that a great deal of information can be communicated nonverbally. The goal of this initial conference is twofold: First, you want to let the parents know that you are pleased to have their child in your room, that you are eager to have him speak English as quickly as possible, and that you need their help in encouraging the child to learn English. Second, you want to glean as much information as possible about the child's school and family background—the kind of school he attended, the age he started, the subjects he studied, number of members in the family, when they came to the U.S., and current living situation. Record the information you learn; it will serve as a valuable reference.

• Allow time for the parents to ask questions too—about their child's schoolwork, his daily schedule, special activities. Show them their child's desk, his books, his work folder. Let them know that parent conferences will be a regular procedure, and that you will be available should problems arise.

• Above all, remember that the most valuable resources you can draw on are your own intuition and teaching experience. Trust yourself and your own good judgment.

Joan Donnelly is coordinator of the ESL program in the Mamaroneck Public Schools in New York and has written many articles about teaching foreign students.

Audrey Weitkamp recalls her family's experience of living for a year in Switzerland. She used it to guide her in her own classes with non-English-speaking children:

We arrived in Switzerland at the end of August and immediately enrolled our four children in the local public schools, where the classroom language was German. At first our children were scared and overwhelmed by the new environment and alien language. Then came a period of greater self-confidence and a tremendous learning rate; I knew from observing and listening to them how much they were learning, even though their teachers might not have been aware of it. After this exhilaration came depression and discouragement. By November, all four children were ready to pack up and go back to the U.S.

December saw a change that we didn't really notice at the time. The kids seemed more self-confident and spoke with pleasure of sharing experiences with their classmates. By January they were mostly comfortable in their new environment and finally could profit from classroom teaching.

As a teacher, I have thought a lot about that experience and have tried to apply what I learned in my own classes. Some advice:

• Relax. The newly arrived child may not look

it, but he's probably learning more and faster than any child in your room. He won't be ready for your "teaching" for quite a while, because he is too busy mastering his own "survival curriculum." His basic instinct tells him what to learn and in what order. Trying to impose your own order on his learning will waste time and frustrate the child.

• Help the child relax as well. Your easygoing attitude and reassuring smiles will convey to him that he is in friendly surroundings. Benign neglect is what he needs from you at this point.

• Seat the child next to a helpful and patient classmate and encourage him to mimic his neighbor's actions. This is the best way to teach appropriate behavior and classroom routine.

• As the child begins to understand those words and simple directions that are most frequently used in your classroom—"go," "sit," "lunch," "gym," "Get out your books," "Number your papers"—write down the words so that he can begin to read them.

• Give the child, even an older one, a picture dictionary. It will provide hours of productive browsing, both at school and at home.

• Don't be a stickler for proper pronunciation or syntax when the child begins to speak English. The important thing is to encourage him.

• Understand that the tendency to "tune out" occasionally is usually a matter of exhaustion. Learning a new language and adapting to another culture require diligent concentration; the information overload can be tremendous.

• Finally, pay attention to the ego battering the child may be suffering getting lost because he can't read directions, standing up when everyone sits down, taking out the wrong book. You can help by showing sympathy and also by educating classmates to be empathetic.

Audrey Weitkamp is a teacher in Seattle, Washington.

Mainstreaming handicapped children

We have all heard about children who have been shut away from the world, cloistered by their parents. These children, like those who have been placed in institutions, have been kept away from us—saving *us* from facing our own ambivalence about people whose appearance or actions are different from our own.

Of those few handicapped children who, in the past, made their way into the public school systems, most were "identified" and placed into special classes far away from the mainstream of "normal" children. They still were set apart, reinforcing stereotyped notions about how odd handicapped children really are.

Since the Education for All Handicapped Children Act of 1975, called Public Law 94-142, these children are entitled to be educated and their education must be paid for by the local school district, no matter what their handicap. The law gives them a chance to be evaluated (or reassessed, if they are already in special classes) and to be educated in "the least restrictive environment." In most cases, children with handicaps go into regular classrooms for at least part of their school day. Whether they go for only a specific activity, such as art or recess, or for a full morning or afternoon, most of these children who were once set apart have joined the mainstream of American children.

Public Law 94-142 provides for a wide range of supportive services to make mainstreaming workable and effective. Individual Educational Plans (IEP), written by teachers and special education personnel working together to come up with the best plan for each student, specify what the teachers *think* a given student can accomplish in a specific amount of time. The goal may be as nonacademic as just being able to sit quietly and listen to a story; it may be a list of three or four math objectives or a whole reading book. The IEP is only a projection of what we believe a child can achieve, not a statement of what we know he will do. We cannot be held solely responsible for the child's performance if we try our best but goals still are not met. We *are* obliged to reassess the situation and to define new goals—and then to go on from there.

The IEP lists not only what we will try to do in the classroom, but also what we and the child will need in terms of special help and materials. Most of the time, special education teachers work with the children who are mainstreamed into regular classrooms, and they are available for needed support.

Mainstreaming is working well, with obvious benefit not only to the handicapped students but to the regular students as well. Children with spina bifida, cerebral palsy, or other physically limiting conditions find that the many things they *can* do in a regular classroom help them develop a stronger sense of independence and their own potential. Their non-handicapped classmates benefit in learning patience, understanding, and tolerance and the special joy of helping others. The successful integration of a handicapped child into the regular classroom depends not only on the child's and parent's attitudes, but also on the attitude and preparation of the teacher.

Teachers find it easy to welcome the mainstreaming of children with physical handicaps that do not impair the children's abilities to learn or to get along with their schoolmates. These kids can be taught relatively easily, and they provide the basis for broader human experiences for the students. Children whose handicaps cause them to be slow learners and those whose emotional problems generate antisocial or disruptive behavior are not welcomed as readily by teachers. It is definitely easier to accept a child whose handicap is obvious—confinement to a wheelchair, for example—than one who is physically like all the others but who behaves differently. The teacher who helps mainstream a child with learning and behavior problems will need a lot of support from special education and administrative personnel.

But after talking with teachers who have been involved in mainstreaming, I am confident of one thing: *Teachers make mainstreaming work.*

***

Barbara Hendrickson is a former elementary school teacher and is a full-time free-lance writer.

Orienting the blind student

The majority of blind children in the United States are now being educated in public schools. Many of these children are in regular classrooms and are given resource (or itinerant) help on an individual basis. Larger schools may also have access to specialized teachers, known as peripetologists, who teach orientation and mobility skills to blind children. But for many students, contact with these specialists is limited. Therefore, all school personnel—not just the classroom teacher—must reinforce orientation and mobility skills that are introduced in the specialized setting. However brief your contact, you can enhance the blind child's learning of independent orientation and travel skills. These guidelines will help you ease the blind child's ability to move freely in the classroom and throughout the school.

● Identify yourself by name when you walk up to a visually handicapped student. Do not walk away without telling the child that you are going.

● Use the sighted-guide technique for helping the blind student through unfamiliar territory. Have him grasp your arm just above the elbow with his four fingers on the inside of your arm and his thumb on the outside. Walk a half step ahead with the blind student's left shoulder behind your right shoulder (or vice versa). When going through doorways or other narrow areas, drop your guiding arm down behind you to let the student know that he should step behind you.

● When describing the location of an object on a flat surface, use clock directions. "Your book is at 3 o'clock."

● If you give the blind student verbal directions to a specific destination, make certain the directions are nonvisual and are given from where *he* is. Use compass directions and left-right cues as well as familiar landmarks. "Turn left by the drinking fountain."

● Don't leave *any* doors ajar, and if there has been a rearrangement of a particular classroom corridor, advise the blind student of the change.

● Guide the hand of the blind student to an object if it is near and in danger of being knocked over.

Specific tips for the teacher: The classroom teacher's responsibility to help the blind child develop orientation and mobility skills includes orienting the child to the classroom, arranging movable items in the child's immediate surroundings, following through on travel skills being learned, and fostering positive relationships between the blind child and her classmates.

Be sure to point out the following classroom landmarks to the blind child during his first day in the room: your desk, his desk, book-shelves and permanent cabinets, storage places for paper and writing equipment, wastebasket, bulletin board and chalkboards, windows, interest centers, doorways, pencil sharpener, and any other miscellaneous items used frequently in the classroom.

Take the child from the classroom entrance to each landmark and back again. Ask him to start at the entrance and, using the back of one hand and the knuckles of his fingers to touch surfaces lightly, to "trail" the perimeter of the room. Encourage the blind student to explore the classroom by himself until you are confident that he has a mental "picture" of it.

When furniture has been changed around within the classroom (and the teacher should feel free to do this), simply tell the child that the rearrangement has taken place and then reorient him. Place objects that are easily upset out of his line of travel. Try to give him a desk with easy access to the door, his books, and any special equipment. If the child has some vision, it is important that he sit in an appropriate place. His desk should not be next to any source of noise (a banging radiator, for example). Bulletin boards should be within arm's reach, particularly if they hold braille or large-print notices.

The blind student should be expected to clean up his own working area and his share of the entire room. When he becomes proficient in traveling around the school building, call on him to run errands as often as you call on other children.

To foster good peer relationships for the student who is visually handicapped, ask students to guide him on field trips to unfamiliar places and to tell him about visual activities. Be certain, too, that the blind student has opportunities to help other students in ways that will bolster feelings of self-worth and mini-mize feelings of dependency.

Myrna R. Olson is a professor and chairperson of special education at the Center for Teaching and Learning at the University of North Dakota.

Helping the deaf student

Proponents of mainstreaming make some basic assumptions about the advantages of teaching deaf students in regular classrooms rather than in special schools. One is that if such students have a chance to interact with the kind of people who will make up the world in which they will ultimately function, the students' communication skills will be increased, and they will maintain basic skills in reading, math, and other school subjects at a higher level. They further assume that hearing impaired students will develop social skills similar to those of hearing students.

Opponents to mainstreaming, however, disagree that integrating disabled and nondisabled students in the same classroom has these benefits. Although these educators agree that disabled children should receive the best educational experience possible, they believe that mainstreaming is not the solution because disabled students should have special attention geared to their individual needs. Regular classrooms and teachers, the argument goes, are just not equipped to meet these needs.

There is also a great fear that the disabled student will be misunderstood and possibly ridiculed by the other students. Deaf students attain different levels of language development depending upon their age at the onset of hearing loss, the degree of the loss, whether or not the child has deaf parents, the child's communication training, and how early the deafness was discovered. Severely inhibited language development can create special problems, because a major criterion for success in most American classrooms is written or oral fluency in English.

Preparation helps: We offer the following suggestions for coping with changes that hearing impaired students will make in your class. Often, these suggestions can enhance the education of all students.

• *Do not allow initial awkwardness to develop into lingering, uncomfortable feelings.* Acquaint yourself with other deaf persons before meeting your new students for the first time. Many cities have schools for the deaf that would welcome a visit from an interested teacher. You may meet teachers, many of whom may be deaf themselves, who work with deaf students. Visit their classrooms and interact with their students. A call to your local vocational rehabilitation agency might provide you with another opportunity for meeting deaf persons. It may even be possible for you to meet with a local deaf club member who may be willing to accompany you for a visit to a local club. These interactions can help you become familiar with deaf students and adults. Occasionally, one or both parents of a hearing impaired child may be deaf, and these experiences will help you develop positive relationships with both students and parents.

• *Understand that all hearing losses are not the same.* They can be mild or profound and involve one or both ears. Different kinds of losses produce different effects on students. Find out about each student's problem and learn the best way to deal with the individual.

• *Do not assume that deaf students are mute.* Most deaf people have no physical problem with their sound-producing mechanisms. But because they cannot monitor their voices, they may sound different with respect to loudness, pitch, tone, and discrimination of specific sounds. Many deaf people do not like to use their voices because they lack training or fear

embarrassment. Differences in speech and communication modes can create the misconception that deaf persons are less intelligent. This, of course, is nonsense—intelligence is distributed normally among deaf students.

• *Do not expect all deaf students to speechread (lipread) well.* Not every deaf child learns to be a good speechreader, and even those who are highly skilled cannot depend on speechreading alone. Good speechreaders can comprehend 25 to 30 percent of the spoken message.

• *Be ready to accept a wide variety of communication skills from deaf students.* Students who come to you from "oral" schools (that stress speech and speechreading) have different skills from those who use sign language.

• *Do not expect all deaf students to be exceptional readers.* And don't think that deaf students will understand a concept by merely reading it. Most deaf children do not read as well as their hearing peers, and just giving a deaf child reading material will not guarantee understanding any more than it will with most children. In fact, deaf youngsters might have difficulty with reading comprehension because of poor vocabulary development and problems with English sentence structure.

• *Reject all the other misconceptions, such as deaf people see better, cannot appreciate music or dance, cannot drive.* These give false impressions about deaf students and can limit what might be done to meet their needs and educational requirements.

Some specific suggestions: Ideally, before a deaf child enters your classroom, your school system will have provided faculty and administrators with in-service training about the impact of deaf pupils on school programs and the communication processes that will be used in teaching the deaf. In addition, resources for communication training and consultation should be readily available. Finally, the school system should have considered curriculum modification, adaptation of the environment to include visual media as supplements to instruction, and provision of support services including note-taking, tutoring, interpreting, and counseling.

Here are ten practical suggestions for meeting the challenge of teaching a deaf child:

1. *Get the student's attention when you speak.* Tapping loudly on a desk or lectern or waving your hand will help. In a group discussion, have the speaker point to the next person to talk. If an interpreter is present, he or she will do this. The main purpose is to ensure that the hearing impaired student knows the visual or auditory source of information. Be aware, however, that continuous visual attention could lead to visual fatigue; allow time for a rest.

2. *Using a normal tone of voice, speak clearly at a moderate pace.* Exaggerated speech can interfere with lipreading. To facilitate speechreading, look directly at the student as much as possible. Try to maintain eye contact with the student and to avoid moving around the room too quickly. When you use the chalkboard, wait until you are finished before speaking so that words directed to the board are not lost to the hearing impaired child. Try not to block sight of your lips with a book, pencil, or other object when you are speaking.

3. *Rephrase a thought or question to make it more understandable to the deaf child.* Give test directions, homework assignments, discussion notes, and any important instructions *in writing.* You may have to clarify questions and repeat them during fast-moving discussions. If an interpreter is involved, translating may cause a slight time lag that can make it difficult for the hearing impaired student to follow a discussion. If aides are not available

for note-taking and tutoring, ask a hearing peer to volunteer. Although the deaf student will need assistance to gain information initially, allow him to show independence and creative thinking abilities.

4. *Use as many visual aids as possible,* including overhead projectors, captioned films, slides, newsprint, and the chalkboard. Avoid having the source of information (including yourself) in a poorly lighted area or in an area in front of a bright light. Pacing around the classroom or changing sources of information rapidly can hinder understanding.

5. *Obtain feedback from the student so that you know he understands.* Be aware of any vocabulary limitations or difficulties with English idioms. Present new vocabulary in advance. If the student does not seem to understand, repeat or rephrase the information and ask the student to demonstrate his understanding. You may need to slow the pace of communication.

6. *Encourage development of communication skills, including speech, speechreading, finger spelling, and manual communication.* Encourage the use of any residual hearing the student may possess. Work with your committee for the handicapped to get needed resources. Encourage the student to ask questions by developing a nonthreatening atmosphere in which the hearing impaired student does not feel embarrassed by what she perceives as inappropriate questions.

7. *Seat the student where he will have visual access to the instructor, other students, and visual media.* Allow the student to change seats to gain this access in all situations.

8. *When critical information is presented, be sure the hearing impaired student understands.* Be sure someone repeats loudspeaker announcements, such as early or late bus arrivals. If you know there will be a practice

fire alarm, share the information with the hearing impaired student so that he is not thrown into a panic. If critical information is announced or a fire alarm sounds, flicking a light off and on can gain the student's attention.

9. *Become knowledgeable about hearing aids.* You may be able to replace hearing aid batteries, to reduce certain kinds of noise levels, and even to make minor repairs. Be aware of changes in hearing caused by colds, chronic ear infections, or other illnesses.

10. *Work closely with the support personnel available to you.* Provide the interpreter with an outline of the classroom presentation and notify her of any materials requiring special lighting arrangements. Reproductions of charts, graphs, and diagrams in the form of hard copies and transparencies can help note-takers, tutors, and the deaf student. A profile of the course content, resources, and methods of evaluation can help give the student realistic expectations for the class.

These suggestions are merely a start. Your own creative approaches can add to a basic understanding and awareness of the needs of a deaf student and diminish the initial apprehension both you and the student may have.

Barry R. Culhane is chairperson of the academic department for general education at the National Technical Institute for the Deaf and a psychology teacher. **Richard L. Curwin,** a faculty development specialist at the same institution, has worked with Barry Culhane in presenting workshops about mainstreaming deaf students.

What not to do for the deaf student

Stronger, more powerful hearing aids, earlier identification and treatment, proliferation of special education programs—all have paid remarkable dividends in the education of deaf children. Because their sensory impairment often results in a language problem, they need special consideration if they are to have the best chance of being assimilated into the neighborhood school.

Many school systems provide in-service education about working with the handicapped child; many experts advise you about what you should do. But it's also important to learn a few things you should not do. The following is a list of ten things teachers should *not* do when teaching a deaf child:

1. *DON'T SHOUT!* The child probably will have on a hearing aid or an auditory trainer that amplifies sound. Many of these systems have a built-in circuit that will shut off the instrument in reaction to a loud sound. Or, if a loud sound is amplified, it can be deafening. Always speak in a normal classroom voice.

2. *Don't over e-n-u-n-c-i-a-t-e.* I call this cow mouthing. The hearing impaired child must learn to perceive normal speech visually and aurally. Over-enunciating destroys normal inflection, rhythm, stress, and intonation patterns that carry a great deal of semantic information. Rephrasing a statement may accomplish what enunciating cannot.

3. *Don't let the child get away.* If the child is wearing his own hearing aid, you will have to be close to him if you expect to be heard. Assuming there is no other noise in the room, you should be between 1 and 3 feet from the child's aid. If you move beyond 5 or 6 feet, he will probably not hear much of what you say. If the child has a wireless FM auditory trainer, then you will wear a mike around your neck. Your voice will always be within a foot of the mike, even when you're out of the room. Be careful; many teachers have been embarrassed when they returned to class only to find that they had left the mike on while they were in the teachers lounge. As long as that mike

is on, the child continues to hear—regardless of where you are.

4. *Don't believe a nodding head.* Many hearing impaired children have learned that if they sit quietly and nod their heads, the teacher believes they are following the lesson. (You may have done that yourself while in a graduate course.) Try to check informally to learn if the child is understanding. Asking the child to supply additional examples or to rephrase what is said is a good procedure.

5. *Don't talk down to the child.* Often when we speak with someone who doesn't know our language well, we find ourselves speaking loudly and using nonsentences. Suppose you ask a person, "Where is your home?" and he doesn't respond. After several attempts, you may find yourself shouting, "Where home?" This is not helpful. If you ask a hearing impaired child, "Do you know which of the European countries were involved in colonization?" and he doesn't seem to understand, simplify the question using a complete English sentence: "Which countries established colonies?" Using visual aids often facilitates communication.

6. *Don't be afraid to touch the earmold.* The earmold appears to be a blob of plastic that fits in the ear. It looks strange because of its irregular shape, and it often collects wax. To function properly, it must fit tightly and be clean. Because the child is growing, the earmold may become loose, causing a whistling feedback sound. If it becomes plugged, it prevents sound from entering the ear. The teacher must feel comfortable inspecting and cleaning the mold regularly and should also learn basic care of the entire amplification system.

7. *Don't assume the child is streetwise.* Most of what children know is picked up by being around older children and by eavesdropping on adults. The hearing impaired child does not have access to all of this vast avenue of learning. Be aware that the hearing impaired child might have missed out on a great deal of basic information and skills.

8. *Don't read* The Helen Keller Story. If all hearing impaired children are to be Helen Kellers, then all hearing children must be Albert Einsteins. Be careful about setting unrealistically high goals that only result in frustration.

9. *Don't forget to call the parents.* Behind all successfully mainstreamed deaf children is at least one dedicated and hard-working parent who wants and needs to help with the child's education. Parents can give the teacher much help and information and can reinforce and maintain skills the teacher is developing in school.

10. *Don't be afraid to get help.* The deaf child and his teacher are entitled to support. The teacher should be free to contact specialists, speech therapists, educational psychologists, educational audiologists, linguists, pediatricians, and state education department special education coordinators—at any time, for any reason. If this support is not available, then you need to do some questioning.

Bruce F. Godsave is a special education assistant professor at State University College in Genesee, N.Y.

How to sign for success

I once attended a performance by the brilliant French pantomime Marcel Marceau. At that particular performance, about half of the audience was deaf. During the intermission, the hands of the deaf people flew as they conversed excitedly with each other in sign language. The rest of us chatted about the show. Yet the two groups could not speak to each other. I became aware of the great gulf that separates the hearing impaired from those of us with normal hearing.

My experience that night made me want to learn the silent language of the deaf, and I devoted my next summer to doing so. I found three excellent books to use in my study: *Sign Language Made Simple,* by Edgar Lawrence (Gospel Publications), *A Show of Hands: Say It in Sign Language* by Mary Beth Sullivan and Linda Bourke (Addison-Wesley) and *Sign Language* by Laura Greene and Eva Barash Dicker (Watts). As I proceeded to master the hand gestures of American Sign, a language of the deaf, I began to feel that my sixth graders could learn a great deal from studying signing. Initially, my only idea was that it would help the children become aware of the needs of others. I hoped that sensitivity to the particular problems of the deaf would lead to greater understanding and sympathy for other kinds of differences. Little did I know then how many other purposes it would serve.

Introducing Sign

In American Sign, whole words and concepts are expressed by signs. There is, in addition, a manual alphabet with one hand position for each of the 26 letters. Some deaf people can speak remarkably quickly while spelling out words. I bought a poster of the manual alphabet and hung it in my classroom before school started in September (available from Joyce Media Inc., *Acton News,* P.O. Box 57, Acton, CA 93510). Then I waited to see what would happen.

On the second day of school, I noticed two students standing in front of the poster trying to imitate the hand positions. That was what I was waiting for. I took the opportunity to tell the class that I had been studying sign myself, and that I would be happy to share what I'd learned with them. I said we could start by learning the manual alphabet.

In no time at all, children were wiggling their fingers at each other and at me as they learned the ABCs all over again. When each child felt ready, he demonstrated his mastery of the alphabet to me, and I added his name to a chart on the wall. For some, the task took less than half an hour. For others, the learning came less easily. Helping the children master the manual alphabet gave me a new view of each child's individual qualities as a learner. Much practice made hands ache, but, based on my own experience, I was able to reassure the students that the aches would go away as their hands grew stronger. (An unexpected side effect was that more dexterous fingers came to produce more legible handwriting.)

From letters to words

After the children mastered the alphabet, it was time for step two—the introduction of sign. I began by using the names of our principal and the other teachers on our hall to illustrate the difference between finger spelling and American Sign. Our principal's name is DelBono, which I translated into "the good."

HOW TO SIGN THE ALPHABET

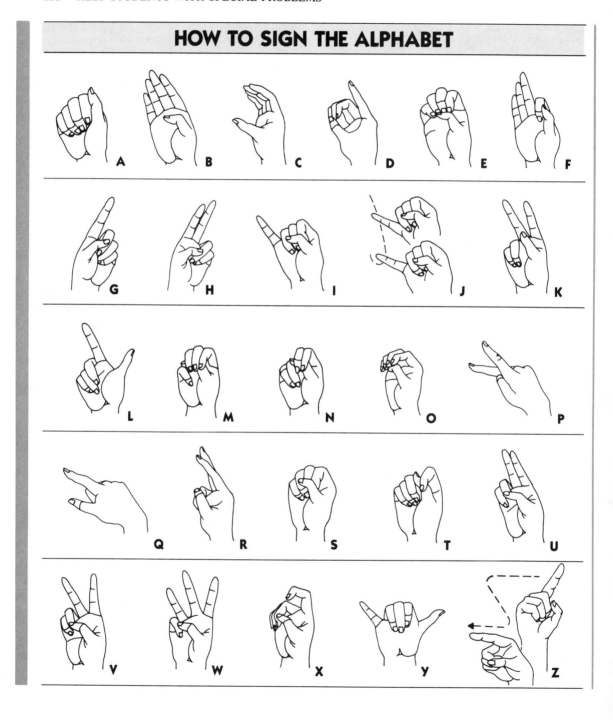

I gave the sign for *the* and *good*. Then, using my fingers, I spelled out *DelBono,* and once again repeated the signed version. The children were delighted and signed "the good" themselves. They wanted to see more. I signed for my name, Silliman ("silly man") and for the names of some of the other teachers. We talked about the difference between sign and the manual alphabet. The students found, of course, that using the signs was quicker and less laborious than spelling out the names.

Beginning simple conversation was the next step in the process. I taught "hello" and "good-bye." We could then greet various teachers by name and, likewise, bid them adieu. I also taught the signs for "teacher," "student" and "principal."

We next learned "How are you?" and "I am fine, thank you." The children really began to feel a sense of accomplishment. As their accomplishments grew, so did their interest. They delighted in discovering that sign is a very expressive language and that the gestures, movements and expressions making up the signs are meaningfully derived. For instance, the sign for "children" is the motion of patting little people on the head; "please" is a circle of the hand around the heart; "dumb" is a tap of the knuckles against the forehead. Secret languages are always tremendously appealing to children, and sign has irresistible charm. The children started greeting me in the morning with "What's our sign for the day?"

I tried to let their interests guide the signs that I taught. They became most adept at conversing about pets, sports, library books, and spiders. We did not forget finger spelling and found many uses for it in the classroom. Our spelling bees were held in silence. When we played spelling baseball, a single was scored by correctly spelling the word orally, but a double was scored by correctly spelling the word manually. Our classroom was often silent, filled with the sound of talking.

I noticed sign showing up in informal situations; for instance, as we were going to the lunchroom one afternoon, an attractive teenager walked by our line. Three of the boys eyed her as she passed and made the sign for "beautiful."

At the Christmas pageant, the class sang and signed "Silent Night." In a school benefit for an injured student, they were proud to sing and sign the song "Day by Day." But the high point of the year came when we attended a performance by the theater company of the Rochester School for the Deaf.

The show combined spoken language, sign and singing. The children thoroughly enjoyed it—and were proud that they understood so much of the signing. The real triumph, though, occurred after the performance, when the actors circulated among the audience. We at last had a chance to use sign language not as an interesting curiosity but as a necessary way of communicating with the actors. We exchanged names and told them where we went to school. They asked us about family and pets and sports, and we joked and laughed together. It was a moment I had first dreamed of in the presence of Marcel Marceau, which was made far more meaningful by its being shared with my eager class.

Deborah Simon Silliman is a sixth grade teacher in Dundee, New York.

How you can help the abused child

Each year, over 2 million American children are abused or neglected, and between 2,000 and 5,000 of these children die. The statistics on sexual abuse are the most disturbing: Experts say that 1 in 4 girls and 1 in 10 boys are sexually molested before they're 18 years old.

Child abuse occurs in all social classes, races, and religions. Worst of all, it feeds on itself. Most abusive parents were abused when they were children. Thus, the "cycle of violence" continues—unless someone breaks it. The question is: Can teachers help?

A personal story

I was abused as a child. Along with my four older brothers and sisters, I was battered, physically and emotionally, by my mother. By the time I began school, I'd been hit, kicked, choked, thrown, and knocked unconscious. I lived in constant terror; I knew my mother could kill me at any moment.

I don't remember my first school day, my first teacher, or my friends that first year. But I do remember loving school. There, I could have fun, make new friends, be creative, and feel safe.

Signals of abuse

Though no one in my family dared to tell anyone about our battered homelife, we must have given our teachers signals. Since those days, I've interviewed many victims of child abuse who told me they gave signals too.

What did I do? I was an overachiever in school. I had to have my teachers' attention as often as possible. I also cowered a lot; if someone else was being scolded, I clung to my desk and shuddered. I had many unreasonable fears. For example, in gym I refused to go over a high bar or hurdles. And I protectively pushed away any object that came near me. (Can you picture me playing volleyball?)

I cried a lot and drew many sad pictures. When asked to draw my family, I drew pictures of cats. I begged my teachers not to make home visits, and I never got into any trouble that would make the school call home.

Unlike me, my sisters were aggressive and got into all kinds of trouble at school. As one of them says, "I knew there was nothing the school could do to me that would even come close to Mom's punishments. I didn't care if I flunked a spelling test. I only worried that Mom might hit me that day."

In all of my school years, no one ever asked me if I'd been beaten or if I had problems at home. This was true for my brothers and sisters also. Once my brother was absent from school for 3 days because my mother had beaten him around the head and face with a metal vacuum-cleaner pipe. He returned to school with a swollen eye and bruised face. When his teacher asked what had happened, he said, "Someone beat me up." No more was asked.

I almost told a teacher once

By the time I reached eighth grade, my mother had pretty much stopped beating me. But I discovered how physical abuse can turn into emotional abuse.

Back then, every day was a nightmare. I spent as much time as possible at school, staying late to avoid going home. I wanted to ask my social studies teacher for help but couldn't find the right words. I finally decided to tell him. My mother must have sensed this, because the night before I was going to talk to him, she told me I couldn't stay after school anymore. She'd convinced my father, who was terminally ill, that I was getting in my teachers' way. She also threatened to cancel my piano lessons and strangle my pet birds. After my father died, she began to lock me in my room.

She drove me to school every morning, just before the bell rang, and she picked me up the moment school ended. My last class was in a room facing the school's driveway. She used to watch me as I picked up my books, said goodbye, and walked out of the room.

One day, my mother was 2 minutes late. When the bell rang, I stood up, faced the window, and waited. I must have looked strange, because my teacher started to ask me if anything was wrong (the words I'd wanted to hear for years). Just then, my mother pulled up. I wanted to blurt out everything to my teacher. Instead, I picked up my books and left the room.

That same year, my grades dropped dramatically. I frequently missed a class, preferring to find a remote place where I could cry until it was time for my next class. Even then, no one asked me what was wrong.

What you can do

Most teachers believe they'd know if someone in their classroom was being battered at home. Take a moment and think about your own students. Can you think of any who've had an odd bruise, an unexplained injury? Have any said peculiar things to you such as, "May I come home with you?" Do you know the signals an abused child sends?

If you think a child may be neglected or abused, start a file on what you notice—bruises, unexplained injuries, hostile parents, anything. Keep this information in a safe place. Later it could help determine whether the state can assist that child.

But don't wait too long to do something with your information. The law requires teachers and other school personnel to report child abuse and neglect. Each state differs in its definitions of these terms, and you are responsible for knowing the laws in your state.

All states stress the importance of reporting "suspected" abuse. So you don't need physical proof of battering; if you have just a "gut" feeling, let someone know. Don't be afraid of being sued or getting into legal trouble. If you report in good faith, the law protects you from civil or criminal liability.

Make sure you know your school's reporting policy. In some schools, teachers must inform the principal, school nurse, or police about abused or neglected children; in others, teachers file reports themselves or go through a reporting committee. If your school doesn't have a policy, ask your principal to set one, and make sure that every teacher knows about it.

As a special education teacher in a city high school, I see many abused children. In fact, over 75 percent of my students with behavioral problems were neglected or abused when they were younger. I can't change what's happened to them. But I can listen to their needs, help them overcome scars from the abuse, and help them find support groups so that they don't abuse their own children.

Rather than tell my students about my own childhood, I invite speakers to my classroom from various abuse agencies, such as Parents United. I use films, slide presentations, puppet shows, and books that are helpful in discussing child abuse with students. I make myself available for conversation; children from abusive

DETECTING COMMON SIGNS AND SYMPTOMS OF CHILD ABUSE OR NEGLECT

Many children who aren't abused or neglected come to school with one or more of these signs and symptoms from time to time. But the child showing many signs and symptoms or an established pattern may have a problem.

PHYSICAL ABUSE
Be alert for a child who:
- has frequent injuries or burns
- doesn't want to tell you how an injury occurred
- explains an injury differently than other members of his family do
- gives a doubtful reason for an injury: "I spilled boiling water all over myself" (burns) or "I fell out of bed" (multiple bruises)
- has serious injuries that are left untreated
- doesn't want you to talk to his parents about an injury
- is afraid of receiving medical help
- acts as if an injury doesn't bother him
- has parents who give an unlikely explanation for an injury or who blame it on another person
- has bald spots (a sign of hair pulling)
- is often sleepy in class
- arrives early to school and leaves late (afraid of going home)
- cheats, steals, and lies
- avoids physical contact with anyone
- wears clothes that cover his arms and legs—even in hot weather
- refuses to undress for gym class.

SEXUAL ABUSE
Be alert for a child who:
- is sexually precocious
- is absent from school frequently
- is extremely moody
- is socially maladjusted, especially with the opposite sex
- shows overly aggressive behavior
- cries easily
- receives unexplained gifts or money
- refuses to participate in physical education or sexual education
- arrives early to school and leaves late (afraid of going home)
- runs away from home often
- complains of genital pain or itching.

EMOTIONAL ABUSE
Be alert for a child who:
- has a poor self-image, saying "I can't" often
- gets overly upset if he makes a mistake
- is afraid of new situations or changes
- says things such as "Can I go home with you?" or "I don't want to go home"
- gets depressed around holiday or school vacation times
- is terrified or nervous if parents are contacted

- is extremely passive *or* aggressive
- laughs when he hurts himself or when he's sad
- is overly affectionate
- has more knowledge about the effects of drugs or alcohol than most children his age.

NEGLECT
Be alert for a child who:
- wears clothes that are unusually dirty, the wrong size, or torn
- has poor hygiene
- has lice
- is always tired
- seems to be underfed and is always hungry
- has untreated medical problems, such as skin infections or vision problems
- is often absent or late
- acts destructively with no signs of remorse
- has nervous habits such as thumb-sucking or rocking
- has poor self-esteem
- doesn't have any friends
- is extremely withdrawn *or* overly aggressive
- has parents who miss appointments and don't follow through on school requests.

homes need to know whom they can talk to and trust. You can do the same things for your students. I've learned that if you teach students about abuse, students who've been abused will approach you.

Talking one-to-one

If you decide to talk to a child you think is being abused, remember that he may feel hurt or afraid. Select a quiet, private place to talk, and help him feel as comfortable as possible. Sit *with* the child, not behind a desk or table. During the discussion, make physical contact; a hug or a hand on the shoulder can be very comforting.

In most states, you must report any information a child tells you concerning abuse. Be honest—carefully explain to the child that you plan to tell someone else who can help. Reassure him that this is the best thing to do. If the police or children's service agency gets involved, stay in touch with the child as much as possible. You may be his only friend.

You may not work in a situation where you can provide personal support to abused children, but you can do other things to help. You can encourage your principal to ask a local child abuse prevention group to organize a workshop for your colleagues. Most school districts have a specialist available to lecture on this issue. You can also appoint yourself "resident expert" on child abuse, keeping a file on useful films, speakers, and articles. You'll be surprised how many of your colleagues will come to you for information. And they'll report suspicions more often if they know someone else on the staff cares.

Remember: These children need our help; let's not let them down.

Rebecca Harrison is a special education teacher at Madison High School in Portland, Ore. She teaches a graduate class in child abuse for the department of special education at Portland State University.

Know what you can do about missing children

For seven years teachers helped Steven to learn his lessons; they called on him to answer questions and to lead the flag salute. Teachers reprimanded him for misbehaving and praised his academic successes. They did these things without knowing that Steven Stayner was a kidnap victim who went home from school to a man who sexually abused him and insisted on being called "Dad."

Teachers had seen Nancy Barros's divorce papers giving her custody of her three children—Afton, Theresa, and Timothy. When told that the youngsters were being sent into hiding because they were in danger of being kidnapped, the teachers provided take-home assignments. And when the children's father came to school, the teachers didn't reveal any information. Unfortunately, several months later, the children's father chose a different place from which to abduct the youngsters. It has now been three years since Nancy Barros last saw her children.

As horrifying as these stories are, they are not unusual and, in fact, are becoming increasingly common. Estimates of the number of children abducted each year vary—for records are incomplete and inconsistent in their criteria for assigning children to this category—but for the last few years most sources have concurred that at least 150,000 children are kidnapped annually. About 50,000 of these kidnapped children, it is believed, are abducted by strangers. Their fate is most often a grim one. Joseph Allen—the former district attorney for Mendocino County, Calif., and the person who prosecuted Steven Stayner's abductor—pointed out that "many thousands (of kidnapped kids) become homicide victims after they have been abused, exploited or mistreated by adults who take advantage of their vulnerability."

The majority of abducted children, however, are taken illegally by a noncustodial parent who is separated or divorced from the parent with whom the child is living. Appalling but true, many of these youngsters suffer greatly—and some die—at the hands of their abducting parents. Spokespersons for agencies involved in locating kidnapped children note that these parents frequently take and abuse their children as a means of retaliating against their former spouses.

Teachers: A victim's best hope for rescue

What does child abduction have to do with teachers? In fact, a great deal. For even though many kidnapped children are hidden away by their captors, or taken out of the country, or—worst—killed, in the vast majority of cases, kidnapped children eventually show up in U.S. schools. Because teachers invariably observe these children, and because their training and experience have taught them to sense when something is wrong, teachers may be young kidnap victims' best hope for rescue.

In addition to helping recover kidnapped children, teachers can take measures that might prevent abductions. A significant number of child kidnappings occur while youngsters are on or near school grounds, and teachers who are aware of custodial difficulties affecting specific children are likely to be more alert for potential abductions. Teachers can also integrate precautionary lessons into their curricula (see "How you can help," opposite).

HOW YOU CAN HELP

Child-search agencies suggest that precautions and responses regarding abduction be presented along with other of life's coping skills as a part of every child's education:

• Explain that it is important to "buddy up" with a friend, even when walking to and from school.

• Caution students to stay away from lonely places.

• Help each child to learn her full name, address, and phone number (including area code) and the name of her parent having legal custody.

• Have children practice locating their hometown and state on a map.

• Make sure children know how to use the phone, including how to dial long distance and how to get operator assistance.

• Talk to students about the fact that they should never accept a ride from a stranger, even if the stranger says that the child's parent is ill or has been in an accident.

Teachers may want to propose that their entire school take some of the abduction-prevention and recovery measures suggested by various action agencies.

• Require that parents—married as well as divorced—complete forms specifying who has the authority to pick up a child at school. In the case of divorced or separated parents, retain a copy of the document dealing with child custody.

• Establish a policy whereby during the school day no student is allowed to leave the school grounds alone; and any adult who wishes to pick up a child must go to the school office and show identification to do so.

• Lock school doors so that they can be opened only from within during school hours.

• Develop a method for confirming student absences with parents soon after the start of the school day.

• Institute a voluntary fingerprinting program. In the typical program, parents retain the only copy of the prints. Child Find endorses such programs but adds that it is more important for schools to concentrate on programs that educate parents and children on how to prevent kidnappings.

In recent years law enforcement agencies and the federal government have begun responding to pressure from victims' families by strengthening measures to aid in recoveries and to discourage abductions. The Missing Children Act of 1982 allowed parents to obtain help from their local FBI office and permitted the descriptions of missing children to be entered into the FBI's National Crime Information Center computer, to which all police departments have access. The Missing Children Act of 1984 established a national center for missing and exploited children.

In the service of children

"Teachers play one of the most important roles in reuniting missing children with their searching parents," said Kirstin Cole Brown, the information director of Child Find, Inc., a national child-search agency. This agency has, since 1981, located and seen safely returned 1,573 children. "Teachers are trained to be alert to behavioral, social, and learning problems," said Brown, and there are some clear tip-offs to lead a teacher to suspect that she may have an abducted child in her class.

"Children who are on the move are frequently one or two years behind in their studies," she said. "Their school records are often incomplete or missing." Brown advises school officials to pay particular attention to children who are registered without birth certificates or whose records list one parent as deceased.

If a child has a difficult time remembering his name, it may be another indication that he is on the run. "A lot of kidnapped children have had their names changed." She also noted that abducted children tend to be withdrawn; they learn that friendships can be risky because they might tell a friend something they have been forbidden to repeat.

An abducted child may also demonstrate an unusual hostility—or contrarily, an extreme devotion—toward the kidnapping parent. The hostility is understandable, but there is a phenomenon known as the "hostage-captor syndrome" in which abducted children feel the need to defend their abductors in spite of the abuse they receive. This psychological reaction is often intensified when abducted children are lied to by their kidnappers—told that their searching parent has died or no longer loves them.

What should the teacher who suspects she has an abducted child in her classroom do?

"We urge teachers who cannot find another solution to a child's difficulties to call Child Find's toll-free number (1-800-426-5678) to see if the child is one we're looking for," said Brown. Teachers might also call their local law enforcement agency.

When a teacher calls Child Find, the agency first takes a physical description of the child and tries to match it with the information it receives from parents who register this missing children. If no match can be made, the agency passes on the information to other search agencies, including the FBI. It also asks that the teacher try to find out the last school the child attended to see if any additional information can be obtained. Child Find is discreet in its inquiries when acting on a teacher's phone call.

If Child Find determines that a reported child has indeed been abducted, it immediately calls the local law enforcement agency. At this point, great care is taken to keep the child and the abductor separated. Generally, while one sheriff's deputy takes the searching parent to the school for a reunion with the child, another deputy goes to pick up the abductor.

Child Find and other child-search organizations assure teachers that their intuitions are excellent, and they advocate a "better safe than sorry" attitude when suspicions are aroused. To aid teachers, all schools should obtain Child Find's annual *Directory of Missing Children*, which contains photos and descriptions of missing youngsters registered with the organization. This directory is available free of charge with a nominal handling charge.

A teacher's experience and sensitivity to children's behavior, and even a directory with pictures and descriptions are not enough, however. Most stolen children are young—some are babies when last seen by their searching parents—and their appearance changes as they get older, confounding the identification process.

In an attempt to reach abducted children directly, Child Find maintains and publicizes an easy to remember toll-free number (1-800-I AM LOST) for the youngsters to call (the same one used by "spotters" of kidnapped children). A poster and bookmark aimed directly at schoolchildren warn, in simple, matter-of-fact terms, about the problem of child abduction and urge children—who are likely to be confused about who they can trust and where to turn for help—to dial the listed number if they are victims.

Asked what he thought about Child Find, Steven Stayner, now back with his parents, replied succinctly: "Child Find makes sense. Kids don't always know about area codes, and they don't always know who to believe. If I'd known about Child Find, things might have been different for me."

Maureen Mackey is a free-lance writer in Beaverton, Oregon.

Know what to do for the diabetic student

Many millions of Americans are insulin-dependent diabetics. From time to time you will surely find a child with this condition in your classroom. Based on what you've heard about diabetics, you probably have many questions and concerns about that child. Will he pass out in the middle of a lesson? Can he participate in all athletic activities? Will he understand what is happening to him if he begins to have an insulin reaction? Will the desserts in the cafeteria prove too much for him to resist?

To deal effectively with a diabetic child, you need to learn as much as you can about the disease, about the way it affects the child, and about the precautions you can take to ensure the child's physical safety.

Begin by talking with the child's parents. Just as each child is different, so too is every diabetic child unique—in the severity of his disease, in his physical needs as a result of the disease, and in the way he handles his problems. Find out his diet, exercise, and insulin requirements. Make plans with the parents for frequent communication.

In talking with the parents, remember neither you nor the parents can be responsible for the child's care of himself. The sooner the child accepts responsibility for controlling the effects of his disease, the better.

Diabetic children are not fragile. You should expect them to participate in all activities. They shouldn't be given special privileges. Even a child in kindergarten must learn to do his own blood or urine tests, give himself injections, and manage his diet.

Understanding the disease

Understanding diabetes is crucial if you are to be effective in helping your diabetic student. Diabetes results from the malfunctioning of glands called the isles of Langerhans, which ordinarily produce insulin, a complex protein the body must have to utilize food. Located in the pancreas, these glands produce the amount of insulin the body needs. However, if the glands manufacture insufficient insulin or none at all, the person becomes diabetic.

No one knows what causes diabetes. Inherited glandular weakness, a virus, emotional stress or shock, and immune disorders have all been suggested as causes. Juvenile diabetes can occur as early as age 6 months and at every age into adulthood. The symptoms are easily recognized—sudden weight loss, lack of energy, frequent urination, excessive thirst, blurred vision, and slight dizziness.

Control of juvenile diabetes means the blood sugar level must be kept as near to normal as possible. In order to control blood sugar, almost all juvenile diabetics must take daily injections of insulin. They must balance diet, exercise, and insulin requirements precisely. A special diet must be carefully planned and followed; exercise should be regular and consistent; and insulin injections should be taken at the same time each day.

Controlling the problem

Although diabetes is a chronic disease with no cure at the present time, controlling the condition is possible by following a carefully prescribed routine. One of the routines the diabetic child must perform is checking the sugar content of his urine or blood before meals. He should come from home prepared to test himself using the simple tape, tablet, or strip produced commercially or a blood-testing kit. Allow him about 5 minutes for performing the test.

Diet is another disease-controlling routine important for the diabetic child. Highly concentrated sweets are not recommended. You should be aware of the child's individual diet restrictions, but he and his parents should have discussed his diet limitations and you should not make diet decisions for him. If the child is determined to eat forbidden food, you won't be able to prevent him. Don't discuss diet in front of others or attempt to shame him into proper behavior. Talk to him and to his parents in private. Remember that his diet restrictions may make him feel isolated from his friends.

You can help him adapt as inconspicuously as possible to his differences. For example, when the class is getting food treats, be sure to have food he can eat. Provide enough sugar-free drinks so that other children can also choose to drink one along with him.

Some diabetic children need mid-morning or afternoon snacks. Discuss with your student the time and place for snacks. He's responsible for providing his own food and should have it with as little attention as possible.

Doctors recommend physical activities as a way of controlling diabetes. If you encourage the child to exercise, be aware that he might need a snack before physical education class or right after, if the exercise is strenuous.

Most diabetic children don't need insulin injections just before lunch, but some children may. Provide the child with a private place and enough time. Don't openly sympathize with him. The shots aren't too painful because the needles are extremely fine and short. Your well-meaning sympathy may be detrimental to the child's acceptance of his situation.

Classroom problems

Even with the most rigorous attention to diet, exercise, sugar testing, injections, and other disease-controlling routines, a child may develop problems requiring your consideration. High or low blood sugar may cause moodiness, fatigue, lethargy, the need for frequent urination, and other symptoms. It's likely that the child's work will suffer during this time. A test taken when he is approaching a reaction or when his blood sugar is high won't reflect his true capabilities because his mind is as lethargic as his body. You may want to excuse him until later.

The need for frequent urination accompanying high sugar won't be a classroom problem if you allow your diabetic child to use the bathroom freely. Of course, he should follow the same bathroom procedure other children are expected to follow.

He may occasionally have problems reading or writing clearly because of blurred vision. High or low blood sugar may be the cause. This is transient and will disappear soon after his normal sugar level returns.

Some children may have brief periods of exhaustion right after an insulin reaction or if the blood sugar level is high. If his exhaustion is post-reaction, let him rest quietly at his desk. The symptoms should disappear in 30 minutes or so. If high blood sugar causes exhaustion, activity may be good. Discuss with the parents and the physician the best course of action to follow here.

Know how to recognize crisis

Even well-controlled juvenile diabetics may face the crisis of an insulin reaction or a diabetic coma. The two conditions are at opposite extremes of the diabetic spectrum.

Because of the serious health threat that reactions and comas pose to the diabetic child, it's essential that the teacher and other school personnel (including substitute teachers) be familiar with the symptoms of each condition and what action to take.

Insulin reactions are the more dangerous. They occur when the blood sugar level drops too low because of too little food, too much insulin, prolonged or rigorous exercise, or a combination. Fortunately, they are usually mild and can be stopped with correct intervention as they are happening. But unconsciousness is a likely result if no action is taken. Reactions usually occur shortly before meals or after strenuous activity. You'll need to be alert during these times.

Symptoms of a coming reaction appear suddenly and require prompt action. Initially, the child may complain of headaches or nausea and may be tired. One moment he may act silly and giddy, the next irritable and angry. He may cry for no apparent reason. His responses may be inappropriate and his thinking confused. As the reaction progresses, the child will become pale, shaky, and sweaty.

The antidote for an insulin reaction is food. Immediately give him something containing sugar: a half cup of some sweet soft drink or sweetened orange juice, jelly beans or sugar cubes, or a small piece of candy. He may need to be coaxed to eat. If he doesn't improve within 15 to 20 minutes after eating, give him more food. If the second feeding isn't effective, call the parents or the child's physician. When the child improves, give him a glass of milk and a piece of fruit or half a sandwich. An insulin reaction is uncomfortable, and he may need a brief rest after recovery. Shortly he should be able to resume normal school activities.

The coma, on the other hand, results from an elevated blood sugar level. A coma may be caused by too much food, too little insulin, too little exercise, or a combination of these factors. Emotional stress and physical illnesses like infections may also elevate the blood sugar and lead to this condition. Comas usually develop over a period of hours or even days. Although they are a dangerous complication of diabetes, they aren't as hazardous as the insulin reaction because there is more time to act. Symptoms that indicate a child is nearing a coma are drowsiness, lethargy, unclear thinking, flushed skin, excessive thirst, frequent urination, loss of appetite and, of course, high urine sugar. When he exhibits these signs, you should notify his parents or his physician.

Educate school staff and your class

A young diabetic may be reluctant to reveal his diabetes because he fears rejection by other students. For the sake of the diabetic and the "normal" students, have a health-science lesson on diabetes. (You may want to include the school nurse, playground supervisors, and other school staff). If he volunteers that he is diabetic, let him answer as many questions as he can. The other children will generally be understanding and encouraging when they see that you are calm and informed about this.

A child with diabetes must live with a unique, sometimes troubling condition. He cannot live a carefree life, but he can learn to cope. You can help him and maintain a productive classroom atmosphere if you accept him as a valuable person and his diabetes as a fact of life.

Sue Baird Blake is a free-lance writer and educational consultant.

Children, divorce, and you

Each year, an increasing number of children become the innocent victims of divorce. Teachers can't lessen the numbers, but they can take steps to decrease the negative impact on children.

Melinda's parents are getting a divorce. David talks to Shelly about visiting his father, stepmother, and stepbrothers. Randy can't even remember his father, who left home when Randy was just two. Jimmy tells about his mother's new boyfriend. Cindy tearfully reveals that her mother and father are going to separate.

An afternoon in divorce court? No, simply personal information about kids in a typical American classroom. Like it or not, the divorce rate in America is on the rise, with no decline in sight.

In the past, a divorce in the family was a failure to be hidden—a negative social stigma for all involved. Children observed that divorce was not acknowledged except in hushed tones and pitied looks from their teachers and other adults. From other children they could expect only ignorance and/or ridicule. It is not surprising that in this environment many children felt guilt and shame and tended to decline socially and academically in school.

The stigma of divorce has begun to lessen due to the increased numbers of families involved, but that is not to say that divorce does not affect children. In fact, divorce may well be one of the most traumatic experiences in a child's life. Yet it need not negatively affect a child's happiness and productivity forever.

What can teachers do to offset the negative effects of divorce on children and to minimize the period of adjustment they must go through? Patience, understanding, and support are key, of course. In addition, teachers might make use of the following guidelines to help create a positive environment for children from divorced families.

What teachers can do

Don't expect failure from children whose parents are divorced. How many times have you heard teachers say, "Oh well, what can you expect from her? She's from a broken home." Teachers should not think that just because children have gone through the experience of a divorce they are doomed to failure. The fact that studies have proved that a teacher's expectations of students critically influences their actual achievement makes this point particularly salient. My own research has shown that there are no significant differences in reading and mathematics achievement, or in self-concept, between children whose parents are separated and those whose parents are married.

Be sensitive to the language you use and avoid familial stereotypes. Beware of using negative-sounding terms such as "broken home" and references to "your mom and dad." Get used to talking about "single-parent homes" and "parents." Be conscious of the traditional stereotype of the family—consisting of a mother, father, and two children—presented in textbooks and teaching materials, and use alternative models in lessons and discussions whenever possible.

When you ask children to make presents for their parents, provide enough materials so that children can make presents for all the adult members of their family. Children who have "two dads" should not have to make the difficult decision of which person will receive their one present.

Be a willing and accepting listener. In a study of 82 children whose parents were divorced, the majority ranked "letting students talk about their feelings" as the most helpful thing the school could do for them. Teachers can let students know they are willing to listen to problems without asking prying questions or trying to offer solutions. They merely need to accept and acknowledge the feelings students express. Examples of accepting responses are: "It sounds as if you're really sad about your dad leaving" or, "I guess you're angry that your mom is gone so much."

Take advantage of social studies units on "The Family" to discuss divorce and single-parent families. When the curriculum calls for studying the family, make certain that the concept of family is not so narrowly drawn that it excludes or devalues the experiences of many of your students. Discuss with students the definitions of what a family is, and invite them to brainstorm different family configurations. Ask children to consider the kinds of events that affect the family: a birth, a death, the leaving home of a brother or sister, a divorce or separation. Ask them what changes these events cause. (*Not Together Anymore,* part of a five-filmstrip set titled *Understanding Changes in the Family,* is available from Guidance Associates and is an excellent discussion starter for elementary grade children.) It's important for students to realize that even though a family member may leave home, it doesn't mean that she or he is no longer a part of the family.

Establish communication with parents. Through conferences, newsletters, parent nights, notes home, and phone calls, let *all* your children's parents know you are interested in working with them for their children's benefit. Encourage parents to tell you when there is a major change in their child's home life: a death in the family, a parental separation, a remarriage. Be sure to schedule conferences at convenient times for parents who work or who are not available during regular school hours—perhaps early in the morning or in the evening, or on an occasional weekend day.

Learn about the custodial arrangements for children of divorced parents. Find out which parent has custody, the visitation patterns, how the parents wish the school to communicate with them, and if both parents wish to attend parent conferences. In cases of joint custody, accept and encourage both parents' desire to remain involved in their child's schoolwork by learning which days the child will be with each parent.

Don't shut out the noncustodial parent. If the noncustodial parent expresses interest in being kept informed of her or his child's school activities—and if there is no legal reason for denying the parent access to information—a teacher should make every effort to keep the parent involved and informed. Give students who request it two copies of special parent announcements and newsletters, and welcome noncustodial parents to conferences and school events. These actions can help children who are separated from a parent feel more secure that the absent parent is still part of their lives.

Janice Hammond-Matthews, school counselor and staff development consultant, is currently principal of Quarton Elementary School in Birmingham, Michigan. She has written articles and conducted counseling and research on the subject of children and divorce.

What you can do about common speech problems

Today's speech clinicians tend to concentrate almost exclusively on children with severe communication handicaps. Few could argue against such a change in the speech clinician's role. The severely handicapped children must be served. But what about those children who lisp, or who pronounce "rabbit" the way cartoon character Elmer Fudd does?

The classroom teacher can do many things that should help children "outgrow" their articulation difficulties more rapidly than if we simply wait for time to pass.

The role of the classroom teacher

Classroom teachers have several distinct advantages over the speech clinician: A teacher is in contact with the child for 4 to 6 hours each weekday and therefore has the opportunity to structure daily speaking activities to meet the needs of the child. If the teacher has some knowledge about how sounds are learned, the teacher is in an ideal position to help kids learn correct articulation habits.

What you need to know

By the time a child is four years old, he should be talking in sentences with a fair degree of fluency. When he's five, the structure of his sentences will be correct for the most part and he'll have enough words in his vocabulary to describe most of his daily wants. His ability to articulate all of the sounds in our language may not occur until he reaches seven or, at the most, eight years of age. Even at eight years we can expect to find some lingering children who occasionally confuse pronouns, treat irregular verbs as regular ones, repeat some syllables or words in a hesitant fashion, and misarticulate *s* and *r* sounds.

Generally, we can expect most children to have mastered the mechanics of communication skills by the time they enter second grade, certainly by the time they are third graders. But roughly 10 percent of schoolchildren will not achieve adequate communication skills. Their faulty speech will have an adverse effect upon their social and academic adjustment in direct relation to the severity of their communication handicap.

Articulation habits usually can be changed—and changed rapidly, *provided certain procedures are followed*. Example: A substantial number of children will be found in the primary grades who misarticulate the *s, r,* and *th* sounds. Whenever I speak to groups of classroom teachers, I ask them to tell me the first instruction they would give to a child who misarticulates one of the three sounds just named. Without fail, the majority of teachers reply that they would ask the child to imitate their own production of the sound. But when I asked 400 speech clinicians this question, only about 13 percent made this suggestion. Eight times out of ten, when you ask a lisping child to imitate your correct production of the *s* sound, you will get *th* in return. What else should you expect from a child who has lisped for 5 years?

Teaching "s"

The speech clinicians I have surveyed almost always recommended telling the child where to put his teeth or tongue in order to make a new sound. The simple request, "Close your

WHAT YOU CAN DO ABOUT COMMON SPEECH PROBLEMS

teeth and say *e*," followed by a second request, "Keep your teeth closed and say *es*" (as in *east*), will almost always result in a correct *s* sound from the child who lisps. After a few more trials saying *es*, the instructor says, "Now keep your teeth closed and say *s*" (the *s* in *sun*, not the alphabet letter pronunciation). After *s* is practiced several times, it is combined with a few vowels such as long *o, e, a,* and *i*. Before the child realizes it, he is saying words like *so, see, say,* and *sigh.* A final consonant is then added, resulting in the words *soap, seat, sail,* and *sight.* Phrases are constructed, followed by sentences containing these words, and finally the child is encouraged to repeat short stories loaded with *s* words. The process is a simple one and has been accomplished, under the supervision of a speech clinician, by third graders acting as tutors for lisping first grade children.

The obvious cue, "close your teeth," appears to be the critical instruction to help children who lisp, and it's a cue teachers could easily employ. But it only works for children who have normal dentition (arrangement of teeth). If teeth are missing, if there is a space between the teeth when they are closed, or if the child has a sizable overbite, then the close-your-teeth cue will not be effective. (It would be best if a speech clinician could quickly check dentition to see if some physical anomaly is causing the lisp.)

Teaching "th"

Teaching a correct *th* sound is almost as straightforward as teaching *s*. The key cue is, "Stick your tongue out and blow." By using a mirror, the child can easily imitate your tongue position. Once in a while a child will bite on his tongue and blow the air laterally from the sides of his mouth. You can remedy the misdirected air stream by holding a feather about 4 inches from the center of the child's mouth and asking him to blow it while following the cue. Or a straw can be placed directly in front of the mid-portion of the mouth. Once the air stream blows through the center portion of the mouth between the top of the tongue and the cutting edges of the front teeth, you can advance to step two. While the child is blowing out air as just described, ask him to quickly open his mouth saying, "Uh." This will result in the syllable *thuh.* Practice it a few times until the child can say it quickly. Add an *m* sound to the end and you have the word *thumb.* The child still may not recognize the word until you hold up your thumb and say, "What's this?" Chances are he'll quickly say, "Fumb." That's your cue to tell him to stick out his tongue and slowly say it like this, "Th----umb," as you prolong the *th* sound. Other words can soon be added—*thing, thick, think,* and *thin.*

Words that end with *th (both, bath)* can be learned easily by prolonging the word and stressing the *th* sound. It may be a little more difficult for him to pronounce words containing the voiced *th* as in *they, them,* or *breathe.*

Teaching "r"

The third sound commonly misarticulated by children in the primary grades is *r.* It is one of the more difficult sounds to evoke from children because you can't see how it's made. But again, tongue position is probably the most important cue you can provide. The most likely reason a child misarticulates *r* is because his tongue rests relatively flat on the bottom of the mouth. The tongue must be in a raised and back position before *r* can be articulated. Actually, the position for *g* and *r* are very similar. The tongue moves very little when the sounds *g* and *r* are produced together *(gr)*.

One effective way to evoke the r sound is to tell the child to lift his tongue tip up and back while saying, "Ah." The "ah" sound should change to "ahr" *(r)* as the tip curls up and backward. Once "ahr" is established, it is easy to produce words like *car, far, bar* and *tar*. Then the child can practice sentences such as: *I see the car; he is far; lift the bar*.

An alternative method for evoking *r* is to tell the child to use his tongue to draw a circle around the roof of his mouth, making the circle swing as far back as he can on the roof of his mouth. He is to vocalize "ah" while doing this. You will find that as the tongue swings backward, the "ah" sound will change to sound more like an *r* sound. That's when you say, "Good." Encourage the production of more sounds of a similar nature and shortly you can dispense with the circular motion while retaining the *r* sound from the backward tongue position.

Evoking the *r* in the initial position can often be accomplished by starting from an "er" sound and adding the vowel "uh." Once "eruh" is produced, move to words like *run, rough,* and *rug*. Other words with different vowels can then be added.

Building articulation skills cannot be done overnight. It may require 5 to 10 minutes of daily practice during several weeks before the child feels comfortable saying sounds in this new way. If the parents provide support at home by helping the child, then you can expect to hear rapid progess. *The Parent's Speech Guide** provides practice materials that can help parents improve their children's speech patterns.

Most speech clinicians would be happy to provide several in-service training workshops for teachers. During these workshops, procedures for detecting and training many communication problems commonly found among young children could be learned.

There are, however, some speech problems that can be more serious than misarticulation. Children with these problems should be referred to a speech clinician, who should be able to work with a teacher in setting up a plan for therapy. Following are a few examples of these problems.

Stuttering—how the teacher can help

The person who discovers the cause of stuttering will indeed become famous. The search for the elusive cause of this speech disorder has spanned 2,000 years, and even today, with all of our accumulated knowledge, we still are not sure what causes stuttering. But we have collected many facts about this unusual communication disorder. We know, for example, that stuttering affects approximately 1 percent of the general population and is found in almost every society, from African bushmen to Asian merchants. The prevalence of stuttering appears to be greatest within societies that stress communication skills and least, if not absent, within societies in which there is little, if any, emphasis placed upon the importance of oral communication.

We also know that there are four boy stutterers for every girl who stutters, and that three fourths of those who stutter are labeled as stutterers before they reach the age of 3½ years. Some stutterers can sing without stuttering, can read aloud with another person with no problem, and become fluent by changing the pitch of the voice or by speaking rhythmically. In some cases, stutterers can become more fluent simply by slowing down.

One theory is that stuttering is triggered by stimuli that evoke fear or anxiety in the mind of the stutterer. These stimuli may consist of certain sounds or words. They may be situational—speaking on the telephone, or to an important person, or to a group of people. Generally, stutterers have the most difficulty when they are requested to answer a specific question or when they wish to make a request. Simple, automatic statements such as "Hi," "How are you," "Let's see now" or "You know" may not present a problem to a stutterer.

Sooner or later, almost every classroom teacher is certain to encounter a student who stutters. The big problem is what to do about the inevitable speaking situations that occur in the classroom. Should the teacher treat the stutterer like everyone else, or should special compensations be made? Should the teacher call upon the stutterer to answer questions in class or should he be gracefully passed over? And most important, what should the teacher do while the child is stuttering?

What you do about stuttering in your classroom depends upon some assumptions you must make about the cause of stuttering. If you see the problem as a learned behavior resulting from past speech conditioning through which the stutterer learned to fear certain speaking situations (a widely held theory), then your course of action would be to reduce the amount of fear the stutterer may have of such speaking situations. The easiest way to accomplish this is to create speaking situations that produce the least possible fear. From a series of observations, you will probably discover that giving a report while standing in front of the class will create the greatest amount of stuttering, but if you go to a stutterer's seat and ask a question that can be answered with a simple yes or no, he will be much less likely to stutter. By purposefully engaging him in unstressful speaking situa-

tions while avoiding anxiety-producing speech situations, it is possible to help build the child's confidence in his ability to speak fluently. Gradually, as he develops confidence in speaking fluently, the child is asked to speak under more stress-producing speech situations, such as giving brief answers while seated at his desk or joining in small group discussions.

During these speaking episodes, the teacher may reward fluency by commenting, "That was a good job of talking" or "You said that very well." Reprimands are unwise.

A different approach, equally defendable, is one that emphasizes personality adjustment and positive self-image rather than fluent speech. Proponents of this view inform children that it is perfectly all right to stutter. It is how you feel about yourself and your speech that is important. Feelings of self-worth and confidence, rather than speech patterns, are targets for change.

Speech clinicians may use widely differing approaches to the treatment of stuttering, depending upon how they were trained and what method they think is best for a specific individual. The teacher should work closely with the speech clinician in devising a treatment model for the stuttering child. Most important, no child should be punished for stuttering!

What about voice disorders?

Voice disorders are found among from 1 to 5 percent of schoolchildren, depending upon one's definition of a voice disorder. The most common voice disorder is one resulting from vocal abuse. Persistent yelling, screaming, and loud talk may result in a noticeably hoarse or low-pitched and breathy voice quality. Some teachers might assume that some children just naturally have hoarse voice qualities and, therefore, never refer these children to the speech clinician or the school nurse for a checkup. But often, prolonged misuse of the voice can cause formation of small growths, called vocal nodules, on the vocal cords.

Early detection, then, is the best protection against vocal nodules. A laryngologist (throat specialist) is qualified to make the diagnosis, but once it's made and treatment is begun (to reduce vocal abuse), the classroom teacher can be of great aid in the treatment program. By pointing out to the child those occasions on which he uses his voice to imitate cement trucks or machine guns, the teacher can help the child become aware of how he is misusing his voice and thus help him reduce these instances of abuse.

Another disorder the teacher may notice is a nasalized quality some children's voices have. Children who were born with inadequate tissue in the soft palate (a valve which keeps the air from escaping through the nasal passages) or who have a cleft in the roof of the mouth will have nasal speech. Sounds that require a buildup of pressure in the oral cavity (such as the plosive sounds of *p, b, k, g, t,* and *k*) will especially be affected. Often, the child will have a visible scar on the upper lip as a result of an early operation to close the cleft lip as well as the roof of the oral cavity. The teacher should, of course, consult with the speech clinician when problems of nasality due to a cleft palate are suspected.

The opposite of nasal speech is a denasal voice quality. In this case, the child sounds as though he has a head cold all the time. The *m, n,* and *ing* sounds that normally are released through the nasal cavity are blocked from entering this cavity due either to enlarged tonsils or adenoids or some other nasal obstruction. The teacher's role is one of referring these children to the speech clinician.

When to suspect a language problem

It is important to distinguish between problems of English language *usage* and the more deeply rooted deficits of language ability. The child who uses double negatives, improper grammar, or who pronounces some words oddly probably does so as a result of learning these speech patterns from his parents or peers. In some areas, local dialects may be considered appropriate within the language community in which they are used. But the child who is unable to use his speech to communicate his needs or is unable to understand the speech of others has a language problem.

Unfortunately, there are no easy solutions to the problems language-deficient children have. Each child's problem is unique and requires special diagnosis to identify exactly the type of training needed to remedy the problem. Language improvement kits used by many classroom teachers were not designed to cope with serious language deficits. Helping children with such deficits to develop adequate language skills frequently requires time and training far beyond what the classroom teacher can provide. The best service the teacher can offer is identification of children who have language problems so that they can be referred to the speech clinician. Once the child is enrolled for language therapy, the teacher will be in a much better position to work with the clinician in helping the child gain language skills.

Donald Mowrer, PhD is a professor in the department of Speech and Hearing Science at Arizona State University and is the author of *The Parent's Speech Guide,* which teaches parents how to recognize and treat misarticulated sounds. This book is available for $6.95 from IDEAS, Box 1494, Tempe, AZ 85281.

How to help the shy child

To be shy is to be afraid of people, especially people who for some reason are emotionally threatening: strangers because of their novelty or uncertainty; authorities who wield power; members of the opposite sex who represent potential intimate encounters.

The consequences of serious shyness can be devastating: it can make it difficult for a person to make friends; it can prevent a person from speaking up for his rights and from expressing opinions; it can encourage self-consciousness; it can interfere with clear thinking and effective communication. And serious shyness frequently is accompanied by feelings of depression, isolation, and loneliness.

Shyness can affect learning

Studies show that nearly 50 percent of elementary students think of themselves as shy. A teacher may not be aware that a student is extremely , painfully shy, because shy children aren't "problems"—they don't make trouble and they don't make noise. But shyness is a problem for some children, especially when it interferes with learning. Scenarios similar to the following one were reported in many of the classrooms I've observed:

"Teach, I need help. I can't figure this out."

"OK, Robert, now what seems to be puzzling you with this math lesson?"

"I don't remember what you said about which of these numbers goes into which."

The teacher helps and Robert completes the rest of the math problems on his own. He then gets to play Space Flight with the other children, who join the game in progress as they finish their mathematics problems.

Warren doesn't finish in time, although his head is buried deep in the math problems. He doesn't get to play in the game and he gets an "unsatisfactory" on his lesson. Double trouble for Warren.

Warren, like many shy children, could neither handle the work on his own nor ask for assistance. Even with the model of Robert in the next seat getting the help so easily, Warren could not bring himself to raise his hand to call for the personal attention he so desperately needed. This inability to ask for help is one of the most serious by-products of shyness. In this case, it affected both Warren's academic performance and the opportunity for social exchange that the Space Flight game provided.

If shyness is such a problem for some of your students that it interferes with their learning, you can take several steps to help:

1. Try to make students feel good about themselves by giving them honest and specific compliments: "I like your sense of humor. I find it an attractive quality." Encourage kids to compliment each other whenever it's appropriate to do so.

2. Use games or activities that break the ice in a nonthreatening way. For example, have kids roar like lions and then chug like the Little Engine That Could. Begin by saying: "We are all lions in a big lion family, and we are having a roaring contest to see who is the loudest roarer. When I say, 'Roar, lion, roar,' let me hear your loudest roar....OK now, lions, roar....You call that a lion's roar? That's a pussy cat. I mean really roar." Now get the children moving in a line around the room by having each put one hand on the shoulder of the child in front of him. You be the Big Engine at first. Start slowly, moving in a circle, chugging and hooting as you go. When you come back to the starting point, go to the back of the train

to become the caboose while the child next in line is the engine. She should chug a little louder and move a little faster. Continue around the tracks replacing engines until everyone has had a turn and the train is really chugging and moving. End with a derailment—all fall down.

3. Excessive self-preoccupation can be set aside by arranging conditions for children to express themselves through another voice, another self. Our research has shown that masks and costumes liberate behavior that is normally inhibited and restrained. If the setting you help to create is one that encourages joyful, playful exuberance, open expressions of feelings and tender sentiments, then anonymity will help make it happen. Provide masks, or have the children make them from paper bags or out of papier-mâché. Have available old clothes to use as costumes for dress-up time, especially for dressing like grownups. Face painting is another way to turn a shy child into whatever he or she would like to be. Don't wait for Halloween to provide an excuse for masks and costumes.

4. Encourage the open sharing not only of feelings but of talents and knowledge as well. You don't have to join the Peace Corps and go to foreign lands before you can share your abilities and specialized knowledge; you can do it here and now, and your children should be encouraged to do it with one another. Any child's gifts then become prizes for all to share and rejoice in. Once a child has accepted this attitude about his or her talents, then "performing" is no longer shyness-inducing. It becomes an act of sharing, of entertaining others, of helping them. It does not mean basking, or suffering, in the spotlight of attention.

5. Create conditions where children learn to use other children as resources, seeking help and giving help to one another. The purpose of the exercise then is to promote cooperation, sharing, and friendship by creating a democratic community of scholar-experts.

Prepare a set of materials that can be divided into as many equal segments as there are children (in groups from two to six). Each child is to receive one piece of the total, which will be put together in the manner of a jigsaw puzzle. If there are several such groups, the same material is distributed to each. The material can, for example, be information about another society. One child gets a paragraph about geography and climate, another about economy, another learns a paragraph about political conditions, while others in the team may get information about child-rearing practices, sports, or other aspects of the culture. Only by combining all the parts does a whole story of the culture emerge. Each child masters his or her paragraph and then teaches it to the others. Obviously, any materials can be used that are dividable; history lessons, stories, art projects, or mechanical-electrical devices will do nicely. In addition, toys and games that require two or more players should be available to encourage cooperative play behavior.

6. Popularity can be taught to shy children who are left out of the social action. They are taught to be pleasant, to cooperate, to initiate games, and to look other children in the eye when they communicate. A research team has shown that third and fourth grade children who were rated low in acceptance by their classmates came to be accepted and chosen as friends after a month of supervised coaching and practice in social skills. You too can achieve similar results if you're willing to be an informed coach.

Philip Zimbardo is a professor of psychology at Stanford University and the author of *Shyness: What It Is, What To Do About It,* Addison-Wesley, 1977 and *The Shy Child,* Doubleday, 1981.

Helping your students deal with a death

One day, after I'd been teaching for several years, the principal peeked into my fourth-grade classroom and motioned me out into the hall. "Jerry Lyndon's father is missing," he told me. While making a routine delivery, Mr. Lyndon had apparently driven his car off the road and down an embankment. The police surmised he had received a blow to his head, had become disoriented, and then had left the car. Mrs. Lyndon took Jerry and her other children home that afternoon as the search progressed.

Later in the day, Mr. Lyndon's body was found. It was my first experience with a death in one of my students' families. I felt terrible for Jerry and his family, but I had no idea what to do. Jerry stayed out of school for a week, and on the second or third day, I sent him a bulging envelope full of sympathy cards from me and his classmates. And that was all I did. I never mentioned Jerry's dad again. When Jerry returned, I simply welcomed him back. And I never even alluded to Mr. Lyndon's death during the parent/teacher conferences with Mrs. Lyndon later that year—or when I had Jerry's younger brother, Chad, in my class the next year.

Fifteen years later

I don't dwell on that incident in my teaching career, but I do regret that I didn't have the skills to handle it effectively. If I'd known what I know now, I could have been more supportive of Jerry, Jerry's family, *and* my other students.

More recently, I had a similar experience. And with the guidance of an outstanding hospice organization in our community, I was able to help a child and her classmates work through a period of grieving and accept the death. In the process, my 11-year-old students learned to reach beyond their own fears and help cushion the pain of a classmate in need.

On a Friday morning in January, I was teaching a math lesson when Mrs. Connors, the school secretary, beckoned me out to the hall. She had a curiously frightened look on her face. As a teacher's aide arrived to watch my class, she told me that the county coroner was in the office waiting to explain some dreadful news. Marsha Garnett's father had been killed in an automobile accident earlier that morning.

Glancing back into the room, I saw Marsha working busily on long division, probably anticipating her weekend sleep-over with her best friend. I wished that moment could be frozen in time. I agonized at the thought of going forward.

I'd known Marsha's dad as a young, energetic, gentle doctor—and a concerned parent. He'd felt strongly about putting down roots for Marsha's sake and regretted that she'd already had to attend a number of schools during his years of medical training. He'd played basketball with his daughter on the school playground after dinner...had treated all her friends to a movie and popcorn after her birthday party...had loved computers, classical music, and Gordon Lightfoot. I wondered how *I* could face the news in the office.

When we arrived, Mrs. Garnett was already there, accompanied by a woman who was introduced as a hospice worker. I hugged Mrs. Garnett and whispered, "I'm so sorry." Mrs. Connors went to get Marsha while the coroner explained some of the details of the accident.

He was death personified for me at that moment.

Next thing I knew, Marsha was in the inner office, and I could hear her mother telling her about her dad. I went to the cloakroom in a daze and got Marsha's belongings for her. I gave her a hug, and they all left.

Facing the kids

When I returned to my classroom, I told the kids I wanted to make an announcement. I stood with my back to them, staring out the window, and I told them what had happened. There was no discussion, not one question, just stunned silence. When the recess bell rang, many of the kids decided to stay in the room. Marsha's best friend, Joanne, and I stared out the window at the other classes romping on the playground...and cried for 15 minutes. Finally, I called Joanne's father at work, and he came to take her home.

I think I cried off and on until noon as I wandered around the classroom. I *did* give a test in reading—why I'll never know. (Three days later, I had to recorrect the tests—I'd mismarked every one of them.) Just before lunch, Mrs. Connors told me that two hospice workers had stopped by the office to suggest I send a note home to parents. And they'd made a few recommendations about what it might include. They'd also left the hospice phone number, saying I could call—any time of day or night—if I needed someone to talk to. I was aware that hospices were established to provide help for the terminally ill, but that's about all I knew. And I didn't think I'd need any help after this day was over.

While the children ate lunch, I wrote a note to send home. It said in part: "We received some very upsetting news this morning. Your child may wish to spend time discussing it

with you this evening." Then I described the accident. "We're going to have to provide a great deal of support for Marsha in the days ahead. In turn, many of the students are going to require your support as they work through their feelings." Later, many of the parents told me they really appreciated that note.

The afternoon was dismal. But somehow we all made it through—despite one child who cried off and on for the entire 2½ hours. (He told me his folks were out of town for the weekend.) I asked each child to make a card for Marsha so they'd have a way to express their concern for her.

Dealing with guilt and learning what to do

Finally it was time to go home. I was anxious to hug my own kids and wait for my husband to come home from work—alive. Despite my concern for Marsha, I was relieved that my immediate family was safe. And I felt guilty about my relief.

Though I had gotten through that day, I began to worry about what I was going to do on Monday. I relived my feelings of inadequacy 15 years earlier. I knew I shouldn't ignore the tragedy and go on with class as if Friday had never happened. But what *should* I do? And how should I approach Marsha when she returned to school? How should the kids treat her? And how could I help them?

I remembered the hospice's offer of help, so on Saturday morning I searched my purse for the number and called it. The receptionist said she'd page a staff person, and Noel Bruch returned my call within the hour. When I expressed my concerns, Noel gave me the support I needed. She said to be open and willing to talk with my students. And she said to face the fact that the worst thing that could have

What to do when someone in—or close to—your class dies

Death challenges the coping skills of children and adolescents and confronts most teachers with a situation for which they're ill prepared. The recent tragedy of the *Challenger* space shuttle is an example on a national scale. The following suggestions may help you respond to such crises and prepare for future times of loss and grief in your classroom.

1. Share the fact of the death with children and parents. Tell the children what's happened, but share only the information that's public knowledge. Explain to younger students that a person dies when his body stops working. Call parents or send notes telling them what's happened and encouraging them to listen to their youngsters' reactions to the death and to talk with them about it. You might want to plan a PTA meeting so parents can learn together how to help children deal with death.

2. Recognize your own feelings. Particular events or anniversaries of losses in our own lives can make it difficult to talk with children about death. It's all right to tell youngsters how hard it is for you to talk about what's happened, and it's all right to cry. If your own grief makes it impossible for you to talk with the children, find someone who can. Stay in the classroom during the discussion, however, so you'll know which youngsters still have questions or concerns.

3. Watch particularly vulnerable children carefully. Identify children who may be "at risk" for later emotional problems as a result of the death—for example, close friends of a child who dies or children whose parents or siblings have illnesses similar to the one that caused the recent death. When someone's parent dies, all children worry about the mortality of their own parents. The death of a classmate raises similar fears, particularly if one has the same symptoms or has done the same things as the child who died. Remind children that most people live to be very, very old.

4. Address the children's fears and fantasies. Children's active imaginations sometimes lead them to think something they've done or not done has caused a death. Give them accurate information about the cause of the death. If a child has in *any* way been responsible for a death (such as challenging a friend to run across the street in front of a car or instigating play with a loaded gun), encourage his parents to seek immediate mental health services for him.

5. Discuss issues specific to the situation. Encourage the children to talk about what happened to their friend or their friend's family. You may need to talk about why troubled adults hurt children, about specific illnesses, about drunk driving, or about suicide. It is perfectly acceptable to say "I don't know" or "What do you think?" or "I'll try to find out more about that for you."

6. Support children as they grieve. Grieving usually involves feelings of both sadness and anger. Recognize and accept both. Let boys, especially, know it is okay to cry. Children grieve differently—and longer—than most adults. They grieve the loss again whenever the person who died would have been present for special occasions. Young grieving children are often boisterous and mischievous, while grieving adolescents can exhibit antisocial behavior—perhaps truancy or stealing.

7. Remember the person who died. Talk with children about their memories of the person who died and about the feelings and needs of those who survive. If a classmate dies, youngsters will want to find a way to commemorate a life that was so tragically short. Encourage students to think about how they'll help a child whose parent, sibling, or other relative has died when he comes back to school.

8. Establish or continue an ongoing death education program. Use "teachable moments" to explore ideas of death and dying and of life and living with your students. Take advantage of opportunities in literature, science, social studies, and other parts of the curriculum to discuss death at times when it is not a personal issue for your students.

Sandra Sutherland Fox, PhD, ACSW, is director of the Good Grief Program (Judge Baker Guidance Center, 295 Longwood Ave., Boston, MA 02115) which helps schools support bereaved children.

happened *had* happened. On Sunday she brought some literature to my home, and I devoured it.

I read a great deal, but what I needed most was the information on grieving. I read that grief is "work" that must be done or the pain will never be resolved. I read also that it's important to express "I'm sorry," "I love you," "Thank you," and "Good-bye." Here was something tangible I might be able to incorporate into classroom discussions.

Dr. Garnett's obituary was in the Sunday paper. He was to be buried on Monday afternoon. On Sunday afternoon, Marsha called and invited me to the funeral. Of course, I accepted her invitation. Then I called my principal. He wasn't sure whether to encourage Marsha's friends to attend the funeral. He worried about how their parents might feel. I called the hospice. Noel suggested that I talk to Marsha's friends' parents and ask what they'd think about having their children attend the funeral as a symbol of support for Marsha.

Discussing our fears

Monday morning before the funeral, the students and I gathered in a circle and discussed our feelings, our fears, and our concerns about Marsha. Then, on Monday afternoon, I took four students to the funeral. Three parents and another student joined us at the funeral parlor.

On Tuesday, as Pat Trafton from the hospice recommended, I and the students who'd gone to the funeral described it and discussed our feelings about it for the rest of the class. Throughout the week, we laid our fears to rest and began to accept the tragedy as part of life.

During that week, I attended a hospice session on helping children deal with grief. I learned how necessary it is for children to express their love for the deceased person in a tangible way. For example, Carol McEvoy,

the presenter, told how two young children were taken on a shopping trip to buy something for their mom after she died. They chose ceramic animals and placed them in her coffin.

To relate the grieving process to nature, Carol gave out twigs, which she said she uses with all bereaved family members. She asks them to put the seemingly dead twig in a jar of water. Each twig will bud at a different time, just as each person will handle grief in his own way at his own rate.

The next morning, I put my twig in a jar on a classroom shelf. I hung a sign on the jar: "This winter twig will bring us hope."

While Marsha was out, we did other things to help us come to grips with the tragedy. The enrichment reading group created a bulletin board in the library based on Doris Buchanan Smith's *A Taste of Blackberries* (Scholastic, 1976), about a child who faces his best friend's death. The display included butterflies, a stained-glass rainbow, a turtle, and two original poems. We posted a dedication to Marsha's dad on the board.

We took up a collection and bought two other books that handle the subject of death sensitively: *Bridge to Terabithia* by Katherine Paterson (Avon, 1977) and *How It Feels When A Parent Dies* by Jill Krementz (Knopf, 1981). In each book, the first-grade teacher wrote a dedication in calligraphy to Marsha's dad. The donors then signed their names in the books, and we gave them to the hospice in Marsha's dad's name.

In my parent newsletter, I encouraged parents and their kids to be open with Marsha and not to deny her father's existence by avoiding talking about him.

Welcoming Marsha back

When Marsha returned, the kids showed her the bulletin board and the twig. She seemed honored that they had been so concerned about her. Then we told her how we'd discussed the funeral and that we expected her to talk about her dad whenever she wanted. I mentioned that some of the kids had said what a good pizza cook he had been at her birthday party. That seemed to set the tone for how we all would act.

Marsha told us about seeing her father at the mortuary, about all the relatives being at her home, and about the fun of being able to be with her best friend during part of the week. The mystery had disappeared. Marsha was still Marsha, and we were relieved.

A sense of hope

A few weeks later, some leaves began to bud on the twig. It really did give us a sense of hope as we talked about nature's cycles. Pat called me from the hospice once in a while just to "keep in touch" and, I suspect, to help me keep things in perspective.

Once, I called Pat in a panic. The track coach was considering dropping Marsha from the team because she was so negative toward him. I didn't want that to happen—track was important to Marsha. Pat suggested that Marsha was possibly resenting the track coach's existence. He was near her dad's age, and her dad had always strongly encouraged her in sports.

Marsha and I talked. The coach and I talked. He was marvelously understanding, and Marsha stayed on the team.

To help her work through her sadness, I encouraged Marsha to write a journal about her dad so her younger sister could learn how wonderful he'd been. Marsha was very artistic, so I also encouraged her to make a puppet of her dad. I was worried that it might be too painful, but instead it seemed to help.

Marsha had her ups and downs. What helped me handle the downs was the support and advice from the hospice personnel. They gave me confidence.

It's been 4 years since Dr. Garnett died. In that time, two of my students have lost grandparents and a young teacher's husband died of cancer. No longer do I ignore death. My students make cards; they discuss feelings; and they offer support. It's a much better way.

Sandy Heffelfinger, a sixth-grade teacher in Helena, Mont., has been teaching for 26 years. She works with local hospices in helping teachers of bereaved students deal with this difficult situation in the classroom.

6
COPE WITH CHANGE

Changing enrollments in recent years have made coping with an assignment to teach a new grade level much more common. How to deal with a new assignment without feeling like a first-year teacher again? How to make a successful start at a new school? Find some practical suggestions in the following articles.

Timely advice for starting a new job

Being a first-year teacher is difficult at best. Even an experienced teacher can be disoriented and nervous when beginning at a new school. When I started my third new job, I arose early on the first day and drove directly to the school—the one I had taught at the year before!

Your job is to teach, but as a new teacher you must also learn how your school works, what people like and dislike, and what is expected of you. For the first few weeks, therefore, it is wise to do your lesson plans ahead of time so that you can set about learning the system—the new terms, the various deadlines, the personalities involved. In short, you need to understand something your education courses probably overlooked: the school as a political and social institution.

Many new teachers do a fine job in the classroom but create unnecessary difficulties for themselves outside it. The following tips, culled from my own experience of 7 years and from that of other teachers wiser than I, may help you keep out of hot water and establish your reputation as a congenial, reliable, competent teacher.

● *Don't believe everything you hear.* When the veterans at your school tell you their ideas about this teacher, that administrator, this counselor, listen, nod, smile—and stay uncommitted. You will be getting plenty of information, free but biased, about which you should politely suspend judgment for the time being.

● *Respond immediately to all memos.* Do not imitate the more experienced teachers who may throw them away or stuff them into a plan book. Fill them out. You will not be praised for doing so, but you will be building your reputation as an efficient worker.

● *Don't forget a duty assignment or miss a meeting because there's too much else on your mind.* People who make decisions about your career could get a wrong impression.

● *Volunteer for small tasks.* If there is typing to do, or if someone needs to be recording secretary for a committee meeting, do it. You will get involved in the life of the school and give others something positive to say about you. But avoid larger tasks, since you will be busy enough teaching and learning about the system.

● *Get to know the front office clerical staff.* Many experienced teachers know that these people virtually run the school. These workers know everything that is going on and can offer a valuable, down-to-earth view of events. Chat with them about the family pictures on their desks or anything else not related to school. This is not to suggest that you be insincere; just don't be so involved with your job that you miss a chance to make a friendly contact. If they are friends with you, these staff members can help by reminding you of memos you have forgotten, warning you of possible problems, and so on.

● *Try to be on friendly terms with at least one administrator.* During my first year of teaching, my zeal about an issue led me afoul of the principal. As I was being criticized at an administrative meeting, an assistant principal whom I had helped with a difficult student spoke up on my behalf. Judgment about me was suspended for the time being. Thus, a friendly professional relationship can make your road smoother.

● *Get to school early and leave late on occasion.* Not only will you get some work done, but you will be showing that you are a hard-working person. (You may well *be* a hard-working person, but it will help if others know it.)

• *Dress to give a proper impression of yourself.* If you see a popular teacher in faded jeans and think you'd like to emulate him, think twice. You can always dress that way next year. For now, look neat, organized, and professional.

• *Stay unaligned with cliques.* If you want to know who belongs to what clique, just notice where people sit during a faculty meeting. Avoid joining a clique during your first year; otherwise, you label or limit yourself unnecessarily. To make your social contacts, drop by other teachers' classrooms during planning periods. Goof off every now and then over coffee. Sit at different tables at lunch. People will get to know you, and you will learn more about the school.

• *Avoid giving the impression that you have difficulty controlling your class.* (Whether you do or not is beside the point.) If you find yourself facing an impossibly wild group of kids, you may consider it your professional duty to send some of the trouble makers to the office. But you may also be giving people the impression that you have poor classroom control, even when the opposite is the case. Find less public ways to handle the problem—phone calls home, detention, one-on-one talks with students—all the tricks of classroom management you learned in your education courses. If you must send a student out, pick a central figure—your class cut-up—and get an administrator involved in the case with you. Show both the student and the principal that you are on top of the situation.

• *Keep your own counsel.* Things I've said in complete confidence to a department head or colleague have later popped up in administrative evaluations. Teachers, counselors, and even administrators have told me private details about others working at the school—details I have not solicited. It was totally unprofessional behavior, but it happened often. If you need to unburden yourself, and you may—first-year teachers can have great emotional and professional ups and downs—pick someone outside of school to discuss your feelings and problems with. Know that what you say to colleagues may come back to haunt you.

You should not take these tips as something more to worry about, nor suggestions that you be suspicious or Machiavellian. I hope, rather, that you can use these ideas to give the people you work with the best possible impression of you. A school's social and political systems can be complicated and intimidating. But if you are friendly, energetic, responsible, and nonaligned, your real job, teaching, will be easier to do.

Bill Prindle teaches English in Montgomery County, Md.

Five ways to survive a change in grade level

John Werner was a great high-school English teacher. But when his position was cut, he had to take a job as a second-grade teacher the next fall. Somehow, his new classroom was never quiet and tidy enough for the principal, and he could never get through all his reading groups in the time allotted. Feeling like a failure, he was ready to quit teaching.

Another teacher, Carol Lee, taught kindergarten creatively for 18 years, then was suddenly forced to transfer. She felt terrified at the prospect of teaching "the big kids" in fourth grade.

Teaching a new grade can make you feel like a first-year teacher all over again. Here are some ways to make it less traumatic.

Whether the jump is drastic or slight, most teachers find that changing grades takes adjustment, stamina, and faith in themselves. Unfortunately, reassigned teachers get little help and may feel the school system doesn't even recognize their problems. Everyone assumes that, like Gertrude Stein's rose, a teacher is a teacher is a teacher—and should be able to teach anything. But this is like expecting a seasoned pediatrician to switch to geriatrics, just because he's a licensed doctor.

If you've been assigned to a new grade, you're probably wondering how you'll adjust and succeed. Most experts recommend carefully planned in-service programs led by teachers who've also changed grade levels. Though these are desirable, they're not always available. Here are five ways you can help yourself.

1
Accept the change

The first step is to accept—really accept—the new assignment and your need to change. The sooner you do this, the sooner you'll make the changes that count. Accept the new assignment as a challenge requiring special effort, and you'll open the door to personal and professional growth.

Even when you acknowledge the need to change, you're still likely to be scared. You're not alone. Competent veterans admit to a real fear of "working with the little ones who need so much direction" or "disciplining students taller than I am." Many teachers with the same fears still make successful transitions.

Finally, be patient with yourself. Don't expect instant adaptation, instant success. You won't be able to perform at your former level of competency right off the bat, but don't feel inadequate or guilty. Your misgivings are quite real, and they take time to be resolved.

2
Learn about your new students

Once you've got a positive attitude, saturate yourself with the materials designed for your new grade level. Compare what you're learning to what you already know, so you can determine the approaches and subjects you'll need to master.

Don't stop with classroom materials. Ask your librarian what kids this age are reading. Find out the puzzles and games they play and the television programs they watch. Read education magazines to learn what other teachers are doing. In short, use all your resources—professional and personal—to find out about your new students.

This is also the time to talk with teachers who are familiar with your new grade level. You already have practical experience with children at one stage; try to find out the normal behavior of your new group of students. Teachers will tell you, for example, that second graders wiggle in their chairs a lot (and sometimes fall out of them); sixth graders don't. Third graders love tattling; eighth graders abhor it.

3
Be open to peer advice

Don't let insecurity about your new position prevent you from asking other staff members for help. Admit that the waters are unfamiliar and listen to advice on the currents. People respect honest concern and tend to tolerate minor failures. Many teachers are flattered when asked for advice, and this positive attitude may pay off later.

Find yourself an informal mentor, someone you can rely on for advice. (If you can't find your own mentor, ask the principal to assign one.) If you're lucky, that person will also feel protective toward you. If you're in a new school, ask your mentor about things everyone else takes for granted—fire drill rules, lunchroom procedures, detention policies, and so on. No matter how complete a teacher handbook may be, critical items are always missing.

Of course, some teachers may not be supportive. When John Werner went from high school to second grade, he was the constant target of snide remarks from a teacher who'd

never left the first grade. You might just find that you'll have to tolerate unreasonable colleagues—and steer clear of them as much as possible.

4
Get to know the principal

The principal is an important element in a successful transition. Donald Oliver, a veteran personnel director, says, "A new teacher should arrive early the first day and meet with the principal as soon as possible to determine his expectations." If you win over your principal in the beginning, you'll have his support when you need it.

Unfortunately, like teachers, principals aren't always supportive. If that's the case, the last thing you want is to antagonize him unknowingly. Ask other teachers what the principal's likes and dislikes are, and go along with them as best you can.

5
Adapt your teaching style

Any sixth-grade teacher, however new and inexperienced, can feel comfortable saying, "Class, please head your papers with today's date, then turn to page 19 and answer the questions silently." A second-grade teacher can't. When I was reassigned to the second grade, I presented my first lesson, gave the students an assignment, and began to prepare for the next lesson. When I looked up, I saw that not one child had even lifted a pencil. A small boy in the front row informed me that I hadn't told the class to begin.

GUIDELINES FOR CHANGING GRADE LEVELS

• As soon as you've made the commitment to change grade levels, check out the classroom that will be your new home. Find out whether you'll be heir to all those beautiful games and puzzles that currently line its shelves—or whether they're the personal property of the present teacher. If the cupboards will be bare when you move in, you will need to make arrangements for obtaining necessary supplies.

• Familiarize yourself with texts and other instructional materials well before September arrives. If you don't, you'll be running fast to stay in place all year. Anticipate the difficulties that might occur in the chapter about regrouping in subtraction. Experiment with the formation of cursive letters so that you will be able to aid students making the transition from printing to writing.

• Expect to be a bit more anxious than usual before the first day of school. If you're too confident and self-assured, you're probably overlooking the real significance of a grade-level change: the opportunity to begin anew, to make the familiar strange.

• Be willing to ask for help. Just because you taught the eighth grade for five years, you shouldn't feel that it's beneath your dignity to ask another teacher about the best kind of supplementary materials to accompany the sixth-grade basal. Most teachers are happy to share the wisdom they've gained from experience.

• Obtaining needed assistance is professionally creditable; blindly adhering to grade-level traditions is not. Don't be afraid to think for yourself and to abide by your own judgment. Just because the first-grade teachers have always taken their classes to recess right after lunch does not mean you have to follow suit. Maybe your kids are more in need of a break later in the day. Stick with your decisions; no one should resent you for them.

• You'll probably want to adapt some of your favorite fifth-grade projects to your new third-grade curriculum. However, don't pass up the chance to invent new strategies especially for this age level: a different approach to discipline? a new seating plan? Be bold and experiment.

• Be patient with yourself. Your initial attempts at new disciplinary techniques may be a disaster. But suitable alternatives eventually will present themselves. Remember all the mistakes you made your first year of teaching? You attributed them to youth and inexperience. The latter, at least, has become a factor again.

• Finally, maintain a sense of humor. This may be critical when you discover in mid-November that the real reason your predecessor abandoned this classroom was because its radiators malfunction. You're going to have to teach your kids to print—with their mittens on.

Nancy Naumann Boyles is a teacher in North Haven, Conn., and an adjunct instructor at Southern Connecticut State University.

New primary teachers may find it hard to accept the responsibility for teaching basic socialization processes. All the little mechanisms upper-grade teachers take for granted were instilled by the careful persistence of an earlier teacher who is now *you.* Consistent routine, for example, may border on dull sameness, but it takes on new significance in a primary classroom. If you line up the students one way Monday and another way Tuesday, on Wednesday no one will know where to stand.

Going from lower to higher grades has its pitfalls too. An old maxim says if you can teach first grade you can teach any grade. If you can organize and orchestrate a year's worth of activities and make readers out of children who can't tie their shoes, you can run any classroom. Why, then, are primary teachers afraid to move up?

The answer: Discipline. Primary teachers really run their own show; their mere adulthood allows them a control that meets relatively little resistance. Older children bring their own opinions and determination to the classroom. They may have longer attention spans, but keeping their attention is more difficult.

If you've been reassigned to an upper elementary grade, be prepared for constant, deliberate challenges to your authority. Older students don't cry; they retaliate. They won't automatically look up to you as a surrogate parent; you must earn their respect.

Older students are also more tuned in to their peers, so every scene is played "center stage." You must be constantly on guard, careful not to escalate bad situations. Normal preadolescent high jinks can turn into chaos if you misinterpret them or overreact.

On the brighter side, you may find older students easier to discipline because you can reason with them. If you're fair and consistent, they'll catch on. Another plus is that older children can be more exhilarating to teach because they understand and respond to a lot more.

A successful transition

If you have to switch grade levels, how well you succeed probably has more to do with your attitude than with the needs of a different level. No one says it'll be easy, but teachers who change grade levels *do* survive. Some just bide their time, hoping to go back to the previous level; a few are so unhappy they leave the profession. But many teachers grow to love their new grade level. If you approach reassignment in the right spirit, the change can enrich your career.

Janice J. Mercurio, a veteran of grade-level changes, is now librarian at Central High School in Providence, R.I.

PREVENT &
OVERCOME

STRESS

7
PREVENT AND OVERCOME STRESS

Teaching, though it can offer incomparable professional satisfactions, is also, almost by definition, a stressful job. The pressures, problems, and chronic irritations that accompany responsibility for educating young students can add up to stress that becomes overwhelming and destructive. How to cope? Read on for some coping strategies that really work.

What is teaching doing to you?

Every occupation has its hazards. Whether the dangers are avoided, handled, or permitted to damage and destroy depends largely on the attitude of the individual—and whether that individual is even aware of danger.

Teaching, like every other job or profession, entails a certain amount of irritation, frustration, boredom, encounters with difficult personalities, fatigue, and what amounts to everyday "dusting." If that assertion inspires you to shrug and say, "So what! Doesn't everybody?"—don't. Because all these things cause small wounds, so small that they almost pass unnoticed, but they bleed somewhere, and they scar. You should not ignore them because over the years they add up, often tragically. Happily, something *can* be done about them. But before moving to remedies, let's identify these stresses as they apply to the teacher, especially the elementary school teacher, who runs the greatest risks in the entire profession.

The catalyst that transforms small stresses into a force of tremendous proportions is also the reason for the profession's existence: children. Children, even one at a time, can be exhausting. Two children, because of their interaction with each other, multiply the pressures manifoldly. Thirty in one room become a battering ram. They are filling all the space around them with enormous bursts of energy, energy that the teachers must control and channel. To do that the teacher alone must put forth an amount of energy virtually equal to that produced by the children. Since they do not all fire at the same time, but with different rhythms, children keep a teacher under constant bombardment. There can be no slack-

ening, no letting down, no rest.

True, teachers of higher grades and other persons who deal with the public also face pressures, but at no time is the human so alive, so filled with outward-directed energy, so in need to home in on some positive influence as the child in the first 12 years of life. The elementary school teacher cannot escape being the target.

To understand what this means, the teacher needs to know how the body reacts to stress. Your body is not essentially different from the ones inhabited by your ancestors eons ago. Nature equipped those ancestors either to fight for whatever was needed to ensure survival or to flee if the odds were against them. Before they could take either action, their systems went on emergency alert. Blood pressure rose and hearts beat faster as they pumped blood to lungs and extremities. Adrenaline shot into blood streams, muscles tensed, breathing quickened, and digestion shut down. They were *ready*. This is called "the fight or flight reaction."

At least it allowed them to survive long enough to ensure that you, who are so like them, would be around today. You react to stress much as they did. The next time you are barely missed by a speeding car, have a run-in with the landlord, or see a child fall off the slide, notice how your heart beats faster, your muscles tighten, your palms sweat, and you feel that belt of adrenaline tie your stomach in a knot. But there the similarity ends.

When your ancestor found his neighbor uncooperative, he threw him in a thicket, a response to frustration you'd never get away with. Your ancestor ran long and hard to catch his dinner. You sit behind a wheel in heavy traffic to get home to yours. He fought or he ran. He used up his adrenaline. His readied heart, lungs, and muscles put out physical effort. When the emergency was past, he felt spent and could make the most of his rest.

You, on the other hand, are in a bind. Your fighting is limited to "a few choice words," and you know that "only cowards run away." You must stand or sit and take it, whatever "it" turns out to be. Any physical response to the distressing stimulus is blocked. Your muscles remain tense and may well precipitate a backache or headache. The adrenaline keeps coursing round and round, making you jittery and sick. There is no real work for your pounding heart, your heightened blood pressure, and no way to unlock the emergency clamp on your digestive system. Your ancestor's survival kit won't work for you in today's world.

Now let's put three problems together: the small but constantly occurring stresses that come with the job, the close proximity of 30 explosive personalities, and your body's reaction to stress. It's only Tuesday, they've turned the heat up to 80 degrees (heat is a stress), and it's been raining for a week. The children are restless, feet scrape, pencils drop, and nobody is listening. Everybody wants to "leave the room" at the same time, and you'd like to say, "Oh, put your hands down and pay attention." But you recall vividly the time you did just that and the puddle that resulted. So you let two go. You *know* they just wanted out. For that matter, you do too. The rain, falling steadily on the windows, reminds you that there will be no playground time, no chance for fidgety youngsters to run off pent energies, no change of scene. You are tired of sitting and they are tired of sitting (inaction is also a stress).

In desperation you show a movie and then wonder whatever gave you the idea that it would interest your third graders. It doesn't, and the pressure mounts. You scramble mentally for *something* that will capture their attention, but there is too much against you and you feel control slipping. There is a very strong urge to shout, "Shut up!" You don't. The clock has stopped and you wish desperately for a fire drill, even in the downpour. When the endless morning finally does end, you realize with dismay that it is your day for lunchroom duty. You feel a knot in your stomach and decide against eating.

Back in the classroom, they are noisier and jumpier than ever, these children who should have been out in rain or sun, sleet or snow, releasing pressure through action. So far they have sat in a noisy bus (stress), sat in an overheated classroom (stress), sat in a din-filled lunchroom (stress). There has been no physical outlet for any of them, nor for you. The afternoon is a teacher's nightmare. Nor is that the end. Tuesday the faculty meets, and after two long, boring hours, the only decision reached was that the window shades should be pulled all the way up at the close of each day.

You drive home in the rain with 30 spelling papers to correct. A quick glance at the one on top tells you that at least one child didn't learn *anything*. Your back aches, your left shoulder is tight and beginning to hurt near your neck, your stomach still feels crampy, or maybe you are hungry. When you finally crawl into bed, you take two aspirin and pray that what you now feel will not be Timmy Brown's cold by morning.

Was that day just unpleasant or was it hazardous? It was hazardous and this is why. Everyone selects his or her own target for tension, and once determined, that area is set for life. Some tighten their shoulders when under any form of pressure, even that of concentrating. In time the shoulders become stiff and may develop a thickness that is sometimes called "fibrosis." Others tighten their upper arms,

Continued, page 170

EXERCISES TO HELP YOUR BODY OVERCOME STRESS

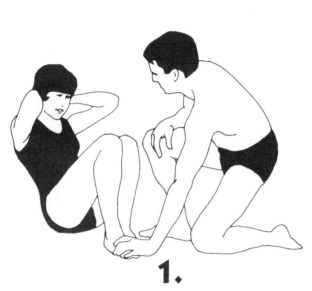

1.

2.

Regular exercise keeps your body in condition to deal effectively with stress. Do these exercises daily before setting out for school. For even better and faster results, do them again before bedtime.

BENT KNEE SIT-UPS
Purpose: **To strengthen and flatten abdominals. To prevent backache due to muscle deficiency.**
Sit with bent knees, feet held down or under a heavy chair. Place hands behind head. Drop head forward and roll upper body *slowly* down to rest on floor. Roll *slowly* up to sitting position. Start with five and work up to ten.

If you cannot do even one sit-up, start in the sitting position and roll slowly down. Do not try to roll up, but get up any way you can and repeat the roll *down*. Do five until you can do one roll *up*. Increase roll *downs* to ten. You will soon be able to do the five roll *ups* as suggested.

WAIST TWIST... STRAIGHT
Purpose: **To increase flexibility of torso, to relieve tension in back muscles, and to slim waist and midriff.**
Stand with feet apart, elbows bent at shoulder level. Twist right and left, letting the elbows lead in pulling upper body around. Try to keep hips still. Start with 10 and work up to 50.

(This is a good classroom exercise. Check to see that hips are rigid.)

3.

WAIST TWIST... BENT
Purpose: **To work upper back, the seat of much tension. To increase chest flexibility and slim upper back.**
Feet apart, elbows bent at shoulder level. Lean forward from hips until upper body is parallel with floor. Repeat same twisting action as before. Start with 10 and work up to 50. This can be alternated with exercise 2—10 and 10.

(If you use this in class suggest that there is a nasty gnome standing in front of each child and then say, "Hit him in the head." You may get no kudos from Freud, but the children will love it.)

4.

HALF KNEE BEND AND HEEL STRETCH
Purpose: **To strengthen quads and stretch heel cords, both tension areas.**
Stand with feet and knees together. Bend knees as far as possible without lifting heels from floor. *Keep seat tucked under.* At farthest stretch do ten bounces. Return to straight leg stand and repeat. Do three. Children who will one day ski will be grateful.

5.

TOE RISES WITH BOUNCE
Purpose: **To strengthen legs and feet and relieve tension in both areas.**
Feet together. Tighten legs and seat muscles and pull abdominals taut. (That does not mean pull shoulders up.) Tip body foward so heels *just* clear the floor. Do ten bounces in this position. Return to floor.

Rise slowly to full stretch taking eight counts to reach the top and eight for return to floor. Do two.

Rise to full height to four counts and return in four. Do four.

Rise to full height to two counts and return in two. Do eight.

Rise to one count and down in one. Do eight. Shake feet to relax. If you are subject to foot cramps at night, this may help to prevent them.

EXERCISES TO HELP YOUR BODY OVERCOME STRESS *(continued)*

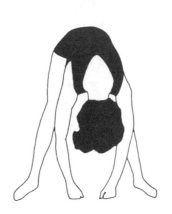

6.

SWIM
Purpose: **To relax tension in arms, shoulders, and upper back. You and the children could prevent many shoulder, arm, and upper-back problems and even some headaches by doing this exercise at the change of each subject.**

Stand with feet well apart, bend forward from the hips and, using an overarm crawl stroke, "swim" forward for eight counts, to the left for eight, right for eight, and finish with eight forward. Combine this with exercise 3 several times a day. Don't wait till you feel shoulders tightening.

7.

FLEXIBILITY BOUNCE
Purpose: **To improve the flexibility of both the back and hamstring muscles. This is a good exercise for anyone living under stress without sufficient physical outlet.**

Stand with feet well apart, hands clasped behind back. Bend forward from the hips *but keep the head up.* Bounce the upper body downward ten times. You will feel it in the backs of the legs.

Drop arms and head downwards; let them hang completely relaxed. Bounce downward ten times. Do not push; let gravity do the work. Check for bent knees.

Do the above exercise often, especially after sitting for long periods. It goes very well with multiplication tables, spelling, and other repetitive work.

8.

DEEP KNEE BENDS
Purpose: **To strengthen knee joints and quads. To slim thighs.**

(Whatever you do not use, you lose. It would be criminal to cause stiff knees through lack of use. Weak knees and contact sports, not knee bends, cause knee injuries.)

Stand with feet and knees together. On count of one, rise to toes and extend arms for balance. On two, bend knees fully, on three, rise to toes. On four, lower to heels and drop arms. Work up to ten.

If you cannot do this exercise with ease, hold onto a table, desk, or doorknob. Make a practice of doing five whenever you wash your hands. By tying an exercise to a habit, you are assured of a constant workout.

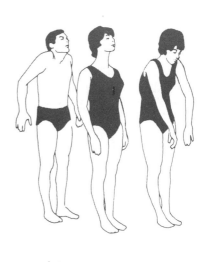

9.

KNEE TO NOSE... KICK
Purpose: **To relieve tension in the lower back and to slim seats and thighs. To strengthen abdominals.**
Down on hands and knees. Bring the right knee as close to the nose as possible. Then kick that leg back and upward as high as possible. Repeat four times. Do the same with the left leg. Gradually work up to eight.

This can also be done in the classroom holding onto the desk or seat of the chair.

10.

RUNNING IN PLACE
Purpose: **To improve the action of heart, lungs, and circulation. To build endurance, relieve tension, use pent-up energies, and relax.**
Run in place for 16 counts.
Run with toes turned in for 8 counts.
Plain run again for 16.
Run with toes turned out for 8.
Plain run for 16.
Apart-together jump for 8.
Run again for 16.
Scissors jump for 8.
Run for 16.
Side-to-side jump for 8.
Plain run for 16.

Do not start with all of that, but with a little at a time. It may take a few minutes for your class to quiet down after so much effort, but when they do, you will have *all* their attention.

★

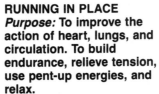

BONUS FOR SHOULDER TENSION
Purpose: **To prevent muscles in target areas from tightening and causing sitffness and pain in shoulders, neck, arms, and head muscles.**
Pull shoulders up to ears. Hold three counts.
Press shoulders down to make a long neck three counts.
Press shoulders forward to make a round back. Hold for three.
Press shoulders back and lift chest. Hold for three.

Do two sets of shoulder shrugs often during the day. *It will be too late if you wait for pain to tell you to start.*

thighs, or back muscles. Constant tensing leads to pain and stiffness, headaches and backaches.

Sitting under tension and without sufficient physical outlet can cause yet another problem: inflexibility. Women seem to choose shoulders and thighs as targets; men prefer the backs of the legs (hamstrings) and lower back. It is the rare man in our society who can put his feet together, keep his knees straight, and lean over far enough to touch the floor with his fingertips. The inability to perform so simple and basic a movement is not due to build, but to shortened back and hamstring muscles. It is also an indication that the individual has too few physical outlets for the emotional stresses under which he lives. It might not be important if it did not lead so often to backache.

Weak abdominal muscles are to be found in both men and women, and that condition also contributes largely to backache. Studies have shown that only 20 percent of America's backaches have pathological causes. The rest are caused by muscle deficiency, insufficient physical outlets, and stress.

One cannot avoid stress, nor would that be advisable. Everyone is faced with job stress, noise, heat, cold, inaction, living with others, crowds, speed, worry, and much, much more. One *can* work on body needs not normally met in the century in which we live. One *can* provide physical outlets. By so doing you can protect your body from the backfires resulting from stress in a closed circuit.

It is important to know that the sooner you can do something *physical* after a tension-producing situation, the better. You dare not wait until a Saturday golf game. If things have been very tense—if, for example, there's been a most unpleasant run-in with the principal—go to the faculty restroom and do exercises Nos. 2, 3, and 6. You *will* feel better and at least your body will not suffer.

There's another consideration, which is that your class needs exercise even more than you do. When feet start to scrape and pencils drop, recognize those signs as calls for help. Stop everything, push the chairs back (if yours are fastened down, use the aisles between the desks) and do three exercises *with* the children.

Studies show that children taking math tests after exercise do far better than when given the same test after sitting for an hour in a classroom. Exercise relaxes children and improves their circulation, which means more blood to brains, which in turn means they can absorb more of your teaching. By the same token, you too will find your job easier. Your circulation, after all, is no different from theirs, just a bit older.

Two minutes of exercise done whenever the stress signals clang will guarantee you a brighter, more alert class, a better figure for yourself (on school time), a lessening of distress in your target area, and no more of those dismal Tuesdays.

Easy exercises for the school day

There are a few more tricks you can use in school that are so valuable to you and to children that the results must be seen to be believed.

1. Stairs are a wonderful exercise. You can burn up more calories going up and down them than any other way open to you. Have your class follow you as you go up with toes pointed in. *Good for muscles in the thighs and in the lower legs. Helps slim thighs and improves the arches in feet.*

2. Lead them down again with feet turned out. Be sure to tuck your seat under. *Very good for flabby inner thighs.*

3. Have them (you too) hop up every third

step with both feet, but every step on the way down. *Strengthens weak legs and feet.* You will soon see that America's children have very weak legs and feet indeed.

4. Take long steps going up, touching only every other step, and as they improve, every third. *This is excellent for everyone's leg and back flexibility as well as strength.*

5. When you have to stand for any length of time, do three deep knee bends. (If you have heard the rumor that knee bends are bad, forget it. Knees were designed to bend, and if you don't use a part of your body, you lose its use.) The children would like nothing better than a ritual of three knee bends after standing at the board. *They will be stronger; your thighs will be better looking.*

6. When you must stand in the hall or on lunchroom duty, tighten your feet, then lower legs, then thighs, seat and abdominal muscles. Go right up your body as though encasing yourself in plaster. Hold the contraction for a count of three; then let every muscle relax. Somewhere in that chain was the muscle or muscles you use as targets in your lower body. By overtightening and then relaxing everything, you have forced them to let go. Repeat this series throughout your day.

7. When seated in meetings or at movies, or even at the table, tighten abdominal and seat muscles, hold for five seconds and then relax. That 2-hour meeting about the shades could have been made to pay off handsomely in abdominal and gluteal tone if only you had known.

To wind up on a paradoxical but cheering note, if you are over 40, you can be put in shape in 8 weeks. For today's average teenager, it takes 2 years. The reason for this is that your body is essentially built between birth and 6 years and polished between 6 and 12. The children in your class have already passed their best building years, and they spent too many of them slouched before television sets. Take a good look at their postures, their awkward movements, and their overflow jerkiness. The closer they draw to 12 without rigorous physical training, the smaller their chances for even an adequate body. So while you may need repair, they need emergency aid because of what modern-day living did to them before they ever got to your classroom. Their main hope for help is you.

Remember, the mind and the body are one. How you use the body affects the mind and emotions. Give your own and the children's bodies a chance to work *for* rather than against you. It could change all 31 lives in the classroom.

Bonnie Prudden is one of America's foremost authorities on physical fitness. Her most recent books on this subject include *How To Keep Your Child Fit From Birth To Six*, Ballantine Books, New York, 1986; *Bonnie Prudden's After Fifty Fitness Guide*, Villard Books, New York, 1986; and *Myotherapy: Complete Guide to Pain-Free Living*, Ballantine Books, New York, 1985.

13 rules for getting through the day

Some time ago, another teacher asked me, "How do you get through the day?" I couldn't quite tell whether that was a request for help or a challenge to prove that I didn't give up around lunchtime and go home. But I was getting through most days, so I had some suggestions for her. They may help you too.

Rule #1: Never approach your mailbox until after lunch. One memo from central office can turn a blithe spirit into a leaden blob with about as much sparkle as boiled cabbage.

Rule #2: Be ready for anything, but don't worry about it when it comes. In every classroom, calm is always followed by commotion. A teacher invented the phrase *calm before the storm,* you know. She was describing third graders, not weather patterns. But don't let this worry you. Commotion is followed not always by collapse, but often by contentment.

Rule #3: Don't sweat the little things. There are lots of things in the universe besides apostrophes.

Rule #4: Think big. Life is too short to stuff a mushroom or to correct a workbook page. Shoot for more than workbook skills, even if you have to pass up toys that can light up, dance a jig, or whistle "Home on the Range."

Rule #5: Avoid unproductive competition. It's demoralizing, destructive, and just plain tiresome. Refuse all lures to enter the unofficial, but nonetheless powerful, Bulletin-Board-of-the-Month contest. Put the kids in charge of your bulletin boards and use your creative energies elsewhere.

Rule #6: Don't eat school food products. Life is also too short to take this risk. School pizza and that Silly Putty passing as mashed potatoes were invented by a federal hot lunch committee. They decided that ketchup counts as a vegetable and that teachers should be punished for not getting up early enough to pack their own lunches.

Rule #7: Never praise a meal or respond to an administrative edict for 24 hours. In either case, your stomach needs time to adjust.

Rule #8: Don't plan too far ahead. Just as a pitcher figures out his second pitch after he's thrown the first one, so, too, in the classroom. Build tomorrow on what happens today, not on what you planned for yesterday.

Rule #9: Manage your trash flow. After you've taught 5 years, you've accumulated more reproducibles, resource books, and bulletin board ideas than anyone can keep track of. For every new one you take in, make sure you throw out two old ones.

Rule #10: After every faculty meeting, read a detective story. It provides an antidote to many irritations.

Rule #11: Don't get down on yourself. If you've gained 10 pounds, remember that's only 4½ kilograms.

Rule #12: Stand up for what you believe in. Morality and rightness of purpose count. Cultivate your prejudices. Pick your battles carefully. When something matters to you and the kids, dig in your heels and follow Winston Churchill's advice: Never give in, never, never, never, never.

Rule #13: Take all advice with a grain of salt. Everybody's been to school, so everybody knows the way it's supposed to be. Wherever you are, 16 free-lance experts on education are nearby, eager and anxious to offer advice every 4½ seconds. In the end, trust yourself.

Susan Ohanian, an editor of *Learning,* is a former teacher and the author of many articles about education.

How to cope with the bad days

Have you had a day recently when nothing went right? Bad days happen to everyone, but not everyone knows how to handle them. Read on for more techniques that can help you turn a bad day around.

It's only 10 in the morning when third-grade teacher Valerie Winslow realizes she has a headache, a disruptive class, the symptoms of a bad mood, and recess duty! She needs a few minutes alone to collect herself, but she can't leave the room. The more she tries to control her irritation, the more tense and irritated she feels, and the less she's able to carry out her lesson plans. Valerie Winslow isn't a bad teacher; she's having a bad day.

We need to talk about bad days, the ones we don't hear about in teacher training. We know they happen—now how can we keep them from taking over our classroom?

What makes a bad day?

"Sometimes you can just sense one coming," says one teacher.

"Days before holidays are the worst," comments another.

We tend to describe the bad day, rather than define it. We speak of feelings: feeling the hollowness of lessons that fail, the frustration of students gone astray, the loss of control as unplanned events crop up.

A bad day can be a minor irritation or a major catastrophe. It can change how we see and respond to what's around us. It can cause guilt and repression that steal our energy and self-esteem.

We're not the only ones affected. If we're having a bad day, chances are the students are having one too. Sometimes there's a common cause, such as schedule changes, the weather, frequent interruptions, unforeseen problems. Other times, the kids pick it up from us. Or they bring the bad day into class all by themselves.

What can we do about bad days? Plenty. We can find out how to keep them from happening, control them when they do happen, even turn some into memorable learning experiences.

Look to yourself

To analyze your chances of having a bad day, look first to yourself. Haim Ginott, when he was a young teacher, wrote, "I have come to a frightening conclusion. I am the decisive element in the classroom.... In all situations it is my response that decides whether a crisis will be escalated or de-escalated" *(Teacher and Child)*. You need to know what *your* responses are likely to be, and this calls for an honest appraisal each day of how you really feel. It calls for tending to yourself before you tend to your students. Here are some tips to help you:

Do some reflecting. Each morning before the students arrive, spend a few minutes reflecting on how you feel—physically, intellectually, and emotionally. See how these feelings relate to the day's lesson plan. For example, if your allergies are making you feel stuffy and tired, and your plan for the day happens to be low-key and sedate, you can start the day with confidence, even though you don't feel "up to par."

Be flexible. If your reflection shows that you're out of sync for today's lesson plan, *change it*. Lesson plans aren't carved in granite, nor are they judged for neatness. Any idea can be presented a number of ways. So change your plan; you might even be able to use new information you didn't have when you first wrote it. (If you can't change your plan, build small breaks into the day to reward yourself and your students for hanging in there.)

Throughout the day, periodically check your personal needs. If necessary, give yourself a few minutes to regroup; you'll easily recover the time because you'll be teaching more effectively.

Take a 10-minute vacation. You can give yourself a break without leaving the classroom by taking a 10-minute "vacation." Post a sign that says where you've gone and when you'll be back. Use the time to improve your plans for the rest of the day. If students speak to you (they're bound to check your sincerity), point to your sign and continue your vacation. When the time's up, take down the sign and ask how things were while you were gone.

You might be surprised at your students' reactions to this technique. The first time I "returned" from 10 minutes in Hawaii, my class greeted me with a barrage of questions about what I saw and did there. To my delight, the bad day was turning out to be fun. We had a short, impromptu lesson on Hawaiian culture and geography, complete with a rendition of the hula. Afterward, we were all more inclined to tackle the work at hand.

That experience taught me an important lesson. By taking care of my own needs, I broke the cycle of an already bad day and was rewarded by enthusiastic questions. Taking that breather had actually encouraged learning.

Hold a class meeting. In a positive, non-threatening way, share your feelings with the class. See this as an opportunity to build problem-solving skills in an actual and concrete situation. Even if your students are young, ask for their suggestions in dealing with your prob-

lem—you may be surprised at their enlightening alternatives. Also, you'll have changed a bad day into a shared experience in which your students learn about values and relationships, and you learn about your students on a personal level.

Look to your students

As you know, you can learn a lot about a child's feelings just by how he enters the classroom. Use this knowledge to avoid a bad day by helping the student let go of bad feelings in a safe and fun way. Some ideas:

Sit with the panda. A teacher recently told me about a stuffed panda that sits in the back of her primary classroom, sporting a smile from ear to ear. When a child enters the classroom looking grouchy or sad, the teacher simply tells him to spend some time with the panda until he feels a little better. What a clever way to deal with an unexplained bad mood!

Start over again. The panda might not work with older students, so try this. If a child comes in looking like he "got up on the wrong side of the bed," tell him so in just those words. Make that statement a signal for him to reverse his regular routine and begin the day again. For example, it might mean that he goes out the door, then comes back in—only facing backward. Or that he leaves his chair from one side, walks around the room, and returns to it from the other side. This small acknowledgment, coupled with the silly consequence, can break the ice and get a student's mind off his bad mood.

Get some exercise. If you think a problem is brewing with a number of your students, break the tension with a little exercise. Pick something that gets them laughing, such as pretending they're monkeys as they walk around the room. More "sophisticated" students may prefer batting a balloon around the room, or a few minutes of jumping jacks. You might even use the exercise to introduce the next lesson.

Write it down. A journal can be just the thing for a class that has lots of bad days. When something goes wrong, tell those involved to take out their journals and write about it. That way, they'll be learning to express their feelings clearly as they vent their anger and aggression safely.

This works especially well when two children are disrupting the class by arguing. Have them write one paragraph about the problem itself and one paragraph about their personal reaction to it. Then they should put their journals aside until a time when they can meet privately with you. At the meeting, give them a few minutes to look over what they wrote. Then have them discuss it calmly and try to come up with their own solution.

This technique benefits everyone. You don't have the stress of functioning like a police officer. And the students have a "cooling off" time, plus the opportunity to describe the dispute, express their feelings, and solve their problem.

Look to your surroundings

Check the classroom atmosphere for its subliminal effects on your day. Problems with weather, temperature, and overcrowding are usually beyond your control. But noise and disruptions aren't—and together they may be the greatest single stress factor you face. Raising your voice only adds to the din and probably makes you more angry. Instead, try these techniques for lowering your classroom's decibel level.

Give nonverbal signals. A nonverbal signal can quiet a classroom simply by drawing attention away from the noise. Many teachers turn off the lights as a way of signaling students. The action can mean something specific, such as "return to your seat" or "put your heads down on your desks." It also tells the students that they can still avoid a confrontation with you if they quiet down. (I know one teacher whose nonverbal signal is a windup bird. When her class is getting disruptive, she sets the bird in motion across her desk and simply watches it. The children know this means they should take steps to stop the disruption.)

For primary and intermediate grades, try a game called "Freeze." When the time comes for the class to settle down, ring a small bell as a signal for the children to freeze exactly as they are. At that point, quietly direct them to return to their seats, or take out their books, or do whatever you've planned. Ring the bell a second time for them to proceed as directed. The beauty of this technique is that it provides a safe and easy transition from a tense situation to the lesson at hand.

For older children, try a variation of the names-on-the-board technique. When there's disruptive behavior, write a simple sentence such as "We can be rude at times when we don't really mean to be." If the behavior continues, keep writing; describe the situation, then list your options for regaining an attentive atmosphere. Your writing alerts the students to the problem without putting them on the defensive; it might even alleviate the situation without further discussion or action.)

Hold a class discussion. When a problem has lasted several days and you can't seem to resolve it, call a class discussion. If possible, hold the discussion some place other than your classroom so you won't have the "home court advantage" or be so obviously "the boss." That way, the students can talk while you remain an unparticipating observer.

Here's a technique that works wonders in this kind of discussion: Require that everyone speak in the third person and about a hypothetical class. This removes any feeling of personal criticism and makes the discussion less subjective.

Look toward tomorrow

When you've had a bad day, probably the last thing you want to think about is tomorrow. But tomorrow brings the chance to start anew. Make sure your students know that, so they'll go home looking forward to a better tomorrow. Discuss with them ways you can all make tomorrow better. If necessary, use a tape recorder to preserve any promises or new rules you've agreed will help your effort. Finally, be sure you say a personal good-bye to each child so they all know you're not angry with any of them. Amazingly, these end-of-the-day actions can make a bad day seem not so bad.

Elizabeth Strauss, formerly a primary grades teacher, is a free-lance writer in Chicago, Ill.

Stress-reducing techniques for teachers

"The worst health problem teachers have to contend with is stress," says Robert Sylvester, a professor of education at the University of Oregon.

The list of symptoms and disorders related to stress stretches from cardiovascular diseases to warts. Some of the better-known stress-related maladies include depression, ulcers, cancer, diabetes, allergies, headaches, infectious diseases, hyperthyroidism, high blood pressure, arthritis, colitis, premenstrual tension, insomnia, thrombophlebitis, gout, and impotence. Some of the consequences of stress among teachers are alcoholism; obesity; tobacco, caffeine, and drug addiction; accidents; divorce; and even suicide.

Studies show that stress makes teachers sick. In a nationwide survey of 7,000 teachers, 33 percent reported that most of their sick leave was taken because of illnesses related to stress or tension in the school.

What causes this stress? A study of Chicago teachers pointed to four major areas of stress-inducing concerns: (1) student discipline and violence; (2) problems with school administration, including overcrowded classes, implementation of school board goals, and involuntary transfers; (3) job performance; and (4) pedagogical functions, such as lesson plans and teacher-parent conferences. More recent threats to teachers' well-being involve declining enrollments and job security. Many teachers feel locked into their positions, doubting there would be a job for them to fill should they find themselves on the street.

Still other stress-causing factors, which pervade both the teaching and the business world alike, include job challenge, working conditions, relationships with co-workers, promotional opportunities, and financial rewards.

Adding up all these potential sources of stress, one might question why anyone would want to go into teaching to begin with. Which brings us to still another area of dissatisfaction for teachers. Many enter the field with high aspirations of changing the world, of becoming "the catalyst for just one great mind." Unfortunately, all too often in the classroom, daily distractions such as discipline, time pressures, and bureaucratic paper-shuffling invade. The result is disillusionment, which, compounded with the accumulation of stressful situations, can lead to battle fatigue, teacher burnout, and eventually ill health.

What are teachers to do? Build barricades in their classrooms and refuse to come out or let students in? Resign? Check into hospitals for an extended rest? Nothing quite so drastic is necessary. Listed below are nine techniques for reducing stress. Some require direct action; others call for a readjustment in teachers' thinking. All of them aim to alleviate the kinds of stress inherent in teaching.

A simple breathing exercise

Here's an easy exercise that can help relieve stress and induce relaxation in a quiet minute between classes. Sit up straight at your desk, feet on the floor, and inhale deeply through your nose. As you breathe in, count to five, hold your breath for an additional five, then completely exhale, making a "haaaaa" sound as you do. Repeat the procedure nine times. With each exhalation, also expel all thoughts and worries. As your breathing returns to normal, you should find yourself feeling more comfortable and relaxed.

Positive self-indulgence

If you find yourself ready to throw up your hands and surrender your roll book for good at the end of a particularly trying day, don't despair. And don't punish yourself. Instead, pamper yourself. Treat yourself to a hot bath, a good meal, or a movie. Enjoy a well-earned "mental health break."

Relaxation and meditation

Meditation has been practiced for thousands of years to help bring about a sense of peace, enlightenment, and spiritual growth. A simplified version of meditation is the "relaxation response," which can be used in any quiet room.

You'll need about 15 minutes to try to relax every part of your body. Begin by concentrating on relaxing your toes and work right up to your scalp. Linger on each part of the body until it is thoroughly free of tension. As each part of your body becomes relaxed, be aware of the breath coming out through your nose. As you release your breath, say the word "one." Remain quiet for a minute or two after you've finished. Try to imagine your day going as you'd like it to.

A healthful diet

"Your nutrition can determine how you look, act, and feel; whether you are grouchy or cheerful, homely or beautiful, physiologically and even psychologically young or old; whether you think clearly or are confused, enjoy your work or make it a drudgery, increase your earning power or stay in an economic rut" (from *Let's Eat Right To Keep Fit* by Adelle Davis).

Eating well combats stress; eating poorly can actually add to it. Coffee, tea, cola, and chocolate are well-known stress-causing agents. Some other stress-inducing foods are more surprising: salt, meat tenderizer, milk products, citrus fruits, wheat, hot dogs, and peanut butter, to name just a few.

During especially stressful times, high levels of certain vitamins, such as vitamin C and B-complex, are needed to maintain properly functioning nervous systems. One way to ensure that you're getting enough vitamins is to eat well-balanced meals with many natural foods. Or check with a nutritionist about taking vitamin supplements.

Physical exercise

Exercise is an ideal way to unwind after a hard day of teaching. Try to establish a schedule of 15 minutes daily, and then work in two to three half-hour sessions of vigorous exercise (tennis, running, swimming) per week. One of the greatest advantages of exercise is the total feeling of relaxation that follows.

Time management

One of the greatest pressures on teachers is time. There seems never to be enough of it. But learning to budget time is both possible and essential.

Don't wait until the last possible minute to leave the faculty lounge for your classroom. Try sleeping a half hour less to avoid the early-morning race against the clock. Getting to school a little bit earlier instead of rushing in as the tardy bell rings can go a long way toward starting your day off right.

Stress-management workshops

There isn't one teacher who hasn't experienced job-related stress, even though some teachers with problems see theirs as unique.

School districts across the nation are recognizing teacher burnout as a major symptom of teachers' inability to cope with stress. Many are responding by organizing in-service workshops on the management of stress. If you feel you and your colleagues could benefit from such a workshop, suggest it at the next faculty meeting. You may find you're not alone in wanting to learn to deal with stress.

Heat and cold

After a day of coping in the classroom, a warm bath or a hot tub, or even a cold shower, can be very effective in alleviating stress and helping you to relax.

A sense of proportion

When you have a bad day in the classroom, instead of taking it home with you and letting it disrupt the rest of your day, learn to examine the day and keep it in proportion. Avoid dwelling on the problem and enlarging it. Don't let anger and self-pity take hold. Instead, spring to action: exercise or practice the relaxation response. Forget your tough day—everybody has them.

Kathleen E. Gann teaches high-school English in Burbank, Calif., and is a free-lance writer.

Index

A

Abducted children, 134-136
Abused child, 130-133
Acceptance, as teaching skill, 5-7
Acceptant response, to student behavior, 5-7
Adrenaline release, during stress, 164-165
Affirmation, children's need for, 87
American Sign, as language of the deaf, 127-129
Animal metaphors, as validation strategy, 86-87
Appraisal, of present position, 2-11
Art area, in classroom, 65-66
Articulation habits, changing of, 142
Autonomy, in classroom
    setting limits for, 96
    students', 94, 96
    teacher's, 95, 96, 97

B

Bad days, coping with, 173-175
Behavior problem, excuse making as, 58-60
Blind student, orientation of, 120-121
"Brag book" photo album, 92
Breathing exercise, to reduce stress, 176-177

C

Change, coping with, 155-161
Child abduction, 134-136
Child abuse
    reporting suspected, 131
    signs of, 130, 132
Child-centered schools, student strategies in, 54-57
Child Find, Inc., 135, 136
Child-search agencies, 135, 136
Classroom, as microsociety, 75
Classroom discussion, 12-14
    benefits of, 14, 19
    essentials of, 12-13
    inhibition of, by teacher's questions, 19-20
    teacher domination of, 13
    techniques and arrangements, 13-14
Classroom meeting
    types of, 77-81
    as vehicle for initiating change, 77, 81
Classroom strategies, 29-71
Classroom style, 1-27
Class time, using for testing, as teaching sin, 16-17
Communication
    with foreign student, 116-118
    with deaf student, 122-129
Competition, unproductive, avoidance of, 172
Computers
    creativity and, 100
    individualization and, 99
    motivation and, 99-100
    personal growth and, 100-101
Consequences, as punishment, 96
Conversation, as teaching sin, 15
Creativity, computers and, 100
Curriculum, strict adherence to, 23-24

D

Deaf student, mainstreaming of, 122-126
Death, helping students to deal with, 149-153
Decision-making classroom meeting, 80-81
Denasal voice quality, 146
Desk, as physical barrier, 7
Diabetes, 137-138
Diabetic coma, 139
Diabetic student, 137-139
Diet, healthful, as stress reducer, 178
Directions, students' ability to follow, 47-51
    games to improve, 49-51
    writing assignments to improve, 47, 49
Disruptiveness
    as student strategy, 56-57
    techniques to control, 175
Distancing, emotional, between teacher and students, 7
Divorce, impact on children, 140
    teacher's action to offset, 140-141
Do-mores, as homework, 62
Dr. No student strategy, 57

E

Effective praise, as motivator, 98
Emotional abuse, signs of, 132
English language usage problem, 146
Enrichment activities, as homework, 62
Evaluation
    of instructional materials, 112-113
    of others, 5-7
    of self, 2-11
Excuses
    common forms of, 58
    coping with, 58-60
Exercise(s)
    breathing, 176-177
    as coping mechanism, 174-175
    for strengthening and flexibility, 168-171
    stress-relief, for school day, 166-167
    to alleviate tension, 168-171
Eye contact, with students, 32

F

Fight or flight reaction, 164
Fine-motor skills, development of, 26